SHAK

AND

THE ARDEN SHAKESPEARE

THE ARDEN CRITICAL COMPANIONS

Shakespeare and Renaissance Europe
ed. Andrew Hadfield and Paul Hammond
Shakespeare and Renaissance Politics   *Andrew Hadfield*
Shakespeare and the Victorians   *Adrian Poole*
Shakespeare and Comedy   *Robert Maslen*
Shakespeare and Music   *David Lindley*

Forthcoming
Shakespeare and Elizabethan Popular Culture
ed. Stuart Gillespie and Neil Rhodes
Shakespeare and Language   *Jonathan Hope*
Shakespeare and the Law   *Andrew Zurcher*
Shakespeare and Religion   *Alison Shell*
Shakespeare and his Acting Company   *Scott McMillan*

Further titles are in preparation

THE ARDEN CRITICAL COMPANIONS

SHAKESPEARE AND COMEDY

R.W. MASLEN

The Arden website is at
http://www.ardenshakespeare.com

This edition of *Shakespeare and Comedy*
first published 2005 by the Arden Shakespeare

© 2006 Thomson Learning
Arden Shakespeare is an imprint of Thomson Learning

Thomson Learning
High Holborn House
50–51 Bedford Row
London WC1R 4LR

Typeset by Photoprint Typesetters, Torquay, Devon

Printed in Croatia by Zrinski d.d.

British Library Cataloguing in Publication Data
A catalogue record for this book is available from the British Library

Library of Congress Cataloguing in Publication Data
A catalogue record has been requested

ISBN 1-90427-144-8 (pbk)
13-digit ISBN 978-1-90427-144-4 (pbk)

NPN 9 8 7 6 5 4 3 2 1

ISBN 1-90427-167-7 (hbk)
13-digit ISBN 978-1-90427-167-3 (hbk)

NPN 9 8 7 6 5 4 3 2 1

CONTENTS

TEXTUAL NOTE

All references to Shakespeare are to *The Arden Shakespeare Complete Works*, ed. Richard Proudfoot, Ann Thompson and David Scott Kastan, revised edition (London, 2001). In working on the plays I also made extensive use of *The Norton Shakespeare*, ed. Stephen Greenblatt, Walter Cohen, Jean E. Howard and Katharine Eisaman Maus (New York and London, 1997). Titles of early modern books have been modernized, and in quotations 'i' for 'j', 'u' for 'v'and 'v' for 'u' have been amended in accordance with modern practice and all abbreviations expanded.

ACKNOWLEDGEMENTS

This book was completed with the aid of a generous grant from the Arts and Humanities Research Board and of a semester's leave given me by the University of Glasgow. A version of the Afterword was given as a paper in the English Department at the University of Strathclyde in March 2005; I am very grateful for the helpful discussion that followed. Part of Chapter Four appeared as an essay, 'Twelfth Night, Gender, and Renaissance Comedy', in *Early Modern English Drama: A Critical Companion*, ed. Patrick Cheney, Andrew Hadfield and Garrett Sullivan (Oxford: Oxford University Press, 2005).

My delight in the early modern period springs directly from my experiences with Shakespeare and comedy, especially as an actor. I owe a profound debt of thanks, then, to those who gave me the chance to act in his plays: Hal Milner-Gulland, Nick Milner-Gulland, John Field and Andy Paget. Thanks, too, to the teachers who made me think about them – Rory Stuart, Richard Jacobs, and Peter Conrad – and about the period in general – Anne Barton and Helen Cooper. I still can't believe my good fortune in having sat at the feet of these extraordinary people. Thanks to the ebullient and witty Michael Dobson, alongside whom I first taught Shakespeare; to my colleagues and friends at the University of Glasgow, especially John Coyle, Mike Gonzalez, Paddy Lyons, Donald MacKenzie and Willy Maley; and to Alison Thorne of the University of Strathclyde, whose learned conversation and encouragement enlivened me at crucial moments. Thanks to Andrew Hadfield for the nice things he has said about my writing through the years, and to him and Paul Hammond for the work they have put in as editors of the Arden Critical Companions series. Special thanks to Bob Cummings for guiding me through so many scholarly labyrinths and lending me so many books (I think I've given most of them back); to my mother, Elizabeth Maslen, for getting me started on Shakespeare early – her ideas about him are now indistinguishable in my mind from my own; and to my father-in-law Kenneth Palmer, who has had a greater impact on my intellectual development than he could possibly imagine. I am proud to be contributing to the Arden tradition to which Ken made a so much more distinguished contribution with his edition of *Troilus and Cressida*.

Finally, thanks and apologies to my two daughters: Bethany, who missed out on so many cycle rides and adventurous outings while I was putting this book together, and Grace, who was born while it was being written and can now talk to me on the phone while I'm at work. And thanks, above all, to my wife Kirsty. I first really noticed her when I was acting Falstaff at fifteen and she was an eleven-year-old Francis, so our fate seems to have been entwined with Shakespeare and comedy from the first. She kept me laughing while I wrote, and gives me hope that the future too will be full of laughter.

This book is for Kirsty, Bethany and Grace; and for the late Philip Hobsbaum, colleague, teacher and friend.

LIST OF ILLUSTRATIONS

INTRODUCTION

SHAKESPEARE'S COMIC TIMING

For Shakespeare and his fellow Elizabethans, comedy was a matter of timing. Sixteenth-century accounts of its past history and current practice are anxiously evasive, fenced in with warnings, provisos and qualifications concerning the appropriate time and place for the comic. Comedy in the theatre was represented as subject to periodic interruption, as comic playwrights and performers repeatedly overstepped the limits set by the authorities in ancient Athens, Rome, or Elizabethan London, tumbling into and out of controversy with each succeeding generation. Accounts, too, of the comic mode outside the theatre – of jokes, pranks, witticisms, pratfalls, and the countless unclassifiable means of inciting people to laughter – insist on its vulnerability to the problem of bad timing, and the impossibility of formulating clear rules to determine the appropriate moment for mirth.

This question of comic timing went well beyond the theatrical. It obtrudes itself into sixteenth-century discussions of manners, of rhetoric, of history and of national and international politics. Real as well as imagined danger surrounds it: the same punch-line, the same gesture that could send a company into paroxysms of laughter one minute might be a death sentence the next. Indeed, in the sixteenth century death and laughter went hand in hand, in political, historical and religious texts as well as in plays, ballads and stories. Shakespeare's Yorick, the professional court clown in *Hamlet* who finds himself after death still intervening unexpectedly in state affairs from the narrow circuit of the graveyard, could stand for perceptions of the comic throughout the Tudor and Stuart periods. So could Sir John Falstaff in *Henry IV Part 1*, who cheats death at the Battle of Shrewsbury by pretending to die in combat, then staging a comic resurrection; or Pompey Bum in *Measure for Measure*, who swaps a career as a punning pimp for that of a humorous hangman. Frightening as well as funny, subversive as well as subservient, rooted in the past but capable of uprooting the present, Elizabethan humour bursts out unexpectedly at moments of crisis to startle people into wholesale reassessments of their positions – or to punish them for failing to be capable of such reassessments.

In this book I shall argue that Shakespeare was fascinated by the precariously contingent status of the comic moment. From the beginning to the end of his career he returned repeatedly to a topic that encapsulates the problem of comic timing: that of the joke that goes too far, the jest out of time and out of measure, as he might have put it. From *The Comedy of Errors* to *The Merchant of Venice*, from *All's Well that Ends Well* to *The Winter's Tale* and *The Tempest* the topic surfaces again and again in new shapes and situations throughout his comedies. But it is by no means restricted to these. His tragedies, too, show an obsession with the comic performance that gets out of hand, from the crazed laughter that is the only apt response to the monstrous trickery of Aaron in *Titus Andronicus* to Cleopatra's final, fatal practical joke on her Roman lover in *Antony and Cleopatra*; from the horrible pranks played on Othello by Iago to the still more horrible pranks played by the gods on the whole of humanity in *King Lear*. And in some of Shakespeare's histories the theme acquires something of the status of an organizing principle. *Henry V*, for instance, from one rather shocking perspective, can be read as an English monarch's appallingly witty retort to a bad French joke (a few tennis balls sent to Henry by the Dauphin to remind him of his misspent youth). My aim here, among other things, is to trace Shakespeare's changing attitudes to the joke that goes too far – or threatens to do so – in ten of his comedies and one token tragedy: from what may be the first comedy he wrote, *The Two Gentlemen of Verona*, to his first Jacobean excursion into the comic, *Measure for Measure*. But I shall be writing about the comedies in the conviction that they are separated from the tragedies and histories only by the narrowest margins of time and space – that each of them harbours the potential to change its genre at a moment's notice – and that this potential is what gives each play its power. I hope, in fact, to show that the delicate problem of comic timing is fundamental to the way Shakespeare thinks about the stage and the world, and that the way he examines it has a good deal to tell us about the links between theatrical, political and social action, both then and now.

Our views on which of Shakespeare's plays should be counted 'comic' are partly based on the organization of the first more or less complete edition of Shakespeare's works (1623), a book now known as the First Folio. The edition was compiled by two actors and former colleagues of Shakespeare, John Heminges and Henry Condell, who divided his dramatic productions into comedies, histories and tragedies, a taxonomy which most succeeding editors have replicated ever since. But as Samuel Johnson pointed out in 1765, these early actor-editors 'seem not to have distinguished the three kinds by any very exact or definite ideas'.[1] The plays, Johnson argued,

> are not in the rigorous or critical sense either tragedies or com-
> edies, but compositions of a distinct kind; exhibiting the real state
> of sublunary nature, which partakes of good and evil, joy and
> sorrow, mingled with endless variety of proportion and innumer-
> able modes of combination; and expressing the course of the
> world, in which the loss of one is the gain of another; in which,
> at the same time, the reveller is hasting to his wine, and the
> mourner burying his friend; in which the malignity of one is
> sometimes defeated by the frolic of another; and many mischiefs
> and many benefits are done and hindered without design.[2]

The last few phrases neatly summarize the plot of *Hamlet*, which Johnson goes on to defend against the charges of contemporary critics – notably Voltaire – that it is diminished in stature by its failure to meet the critical criteria that would make it a 'true' tragedy. Johnson recognized in *Hamlet* a self-conscious generic playfulness that is char-acteristic not only of Shakespeare but of English drama as a whole during his lifetime.[3] The categories into which Shakespeare's works are traditionally sorted were imposed on them by Heminges and Condell after his death; but the individual editions in which many of them were published during his lifetime show the same inability or reluctance to distinguish between the three dramatic kinds 'by any very exact or definite ideas' that Johnson noticed in the plays themselves. Some histories are described as tragedies, some tragedies and comedies as histories, while many plays are given no generic labelling at all, as if to signal the printers' bafflement as to their precise generic placement – or their writer's unwillingness to be circumscribed by theatrical tradition.[4] And since the printing of the First Folio the comedies in particular have been subdivided into many further categories – 'romantic comedies', 'festive comedies', 'problem plays', 'romances' – whose contents vary widely depending on the tastes and ideological positions espoused by commentators.[5] I shall argue in this book that the problem of labelling the comedies springs, in part, from the plays' active participation in a heated contemporary debate over the function of the comic; a debate in which Shakespeare was intensely interested and about which he was very well informed.

All of Shakespeare's plays participate in this debate, and a reasonably full account of Shakespeare and comedy would need to include an analysis of every play he wrote: the dreadful laughter of the sado-masochistic men and women who populate *King Lear*; the camp comedy of *Coriolanus*, with its over-the-top investigation of one of Shakespeare's favourite topics, the murderous link between masculinity and violence; the wrestling-match between potential comic and tragic endings in *The Tempest*. Within the constraints of a short book this is clearly impossible – especially since my point about Shakespeare's interest in comic timing depends on close analysis of his texts. For reasons of space alone, then, I have chosen to terminate my discussion with the end of Elizabeth's reign, before Shakespeare had written some of his greatest 'comedies' – let alone most of the great tragedies I have already mentioned. But I do this from no conviction that his attitude to theatrical laughter underwent a radical shift in the reign of James I. It might be more accurate to say that Shakespeare's art was *always* undergoing radical shifts, so that each play constitutes a genre by itself, rewriting the terms of the fragile contract between actors and audience in its opening lines, and rewriting them again half-way through – or even in the epilogue.[6] By finishing my account in 1603 I have given myself a chance to trace some of these shifts in detail; and my Afterword suggests how the first of Shakespeare's Jacobean comedies, *Measure for Measure*, predicts his continued preoccupation with yet more daring forms of comic experiment in the years after James's accession.

This introduction seeks to sketch the parameters of the Elizabethan debate about the uses of the comic. In it, as throughout the book, I shall for the most part use the term 'comedy' to refer to a dramatic genre and 'comic' to mean what makes people laugh or smile; but I shall refrain from defining the words more rigorously than this, since one of the points I wish to stress is that the comic was regarded in Shakespeare's time as fundamentally indefinable, and comedy as a highly slippery theatrical phenomenon. My purpose is to show how far Shakespearean comedy was a product of its cultural climate, and to provide vital reference points for the discussion that follows. I hope too to evoke the mood in which that discussion ought to be conducted: a mood where the comic can be serious, unsettling, even horrifying, without losing an iota of its ebullience, wit or (occasionally) charm. Needless to say, I have a good deal less confidence in my own ability to evoke that mood than in the fact that Shakespeare breathed it in along with the pungent air of Elizabethan London.

THE TROUBLED HISTORY OF COMEDY

For the Elizabethans the history of comedy in the theatre was inseparable from that of class conflict. Comedy was the dramatic form that dealt with commoners – all those below the level of the aristocracy – 'never medling with any Princes matters nor such high personages, but commonly of marchants, souldiers, artificers, good honest housholders, and also of unthrifty youthes, yong damsels, old nurses, bawds, brokers, ruffians and parasites', as the courtier-critic George Puttenham put it in 1589.[7] The genre concerned itself, in fact, with the social stratum occupied by the actors themselves, giving it a voice and placing it at the centre of the action at a time when it had few opportunities to articulate its concerns at the highest level of political life.

No wonder, then, that the Elizabethans saw comedy as having been subject to the suspicion of rulers from ancient times to the present. Tragedy made tyrants weep and change their ways: Sir Philip Sidney tells the story of the murderous dictator Alexander Pheraeus, whose willingness to 'make matters for tragedies' did not prevent him from weeping at a tragedy on stage.[8] Comedy, on the other hand, made tyrants uncomfortable and roused them to rage. The often-reprinted collection of historical poems *A Mirror for Magistrates* (1559) includes the tale of the poet Collingborne, who was put to death for writing a comic lampoon about that most notorious of English tyrants, Richard III.[9] Tragedy dealt with times that were safely past, granted neatness and closure by being incorporated into the narrative of history: Puttenham explains that the ancient tragedians reprehended the vices of princes 'after their deathes when the posteritie stood no more in dread of them'.[10] Comedy, by contrast, dealt with the dangerous present, whose inhabitants have an awkward propensity for taking umbrage and seeking revenge. For this reason, Puttenham tells us, the ancient comic playwrights 'were enforced for feare of quarell and blame to disguise their players with strange apparell, and by colouring their faces and carying hatts and capps of diverse fashions to make them selves lesse knowen'.[11] It seemed inevitable, then, that censorship should have hounded comedy from generation to generation, first struggling in vain to prescribe limits to its licence, then giving up in despair and banning it from the stage as an offence against law and order. Only comedy's extraordinary flexibility – its capacity to reinvent itself repeatedly in response to new developments – had enabled it to survive its own indiscretions through so many centuries of vilification and belittlement.[12]

The notion of comedy as a uniquely flexible medium, adapting itself with chameleon promptness to every innovation, was authorized for the Elizabethans by the Roman poet Horace, whose *Art of Poetry* (*De arte poetica*) was the single most important source for theoretical thinking about poetry and drama in the early modern period. The *Art* is filled with the sense that imaginative writing changes with the changing times, from its diction to its metre and form. Poetry mimics, in fact, the mutations of the natural world: the transformations that accompany the seasons, the alterations in a man's body and mind that come with advancing years. But Horace also implies that comedy in particular has changed as a result of pressure from outraged governments, whether in ancient Greece or in Italy. In each of its new incarnations comedy begins with grand promises to restrain its ebullience within permitted bounds, but ends by demonstrating its resistance to any form of containment, kicking over the traces and running riot for a time before being crushed beneath the weight of authoritarian retribution.

The first dramatic genre, Horace tells us in the *Art*, was tragedy, into which the tragedians were soon obliged to introduce a comic element as a means of holding their spectators' wandering attention: 'rough rude satyrs naked', exchanging acerbic quips and obscenities in the satyr-plays that followed tragic performances.[13] The satyrs and their plays still hold the stage in Roman times, says Horace, but he hedges in their dispensation to 'turn all earnest into jest' with careful caveats: their mockery should offend neither the gods nor 'men of birth' in the contemporary audience.[14] These earliest excursions into comedy as an adjunct to tragedy were succeeded by the ribald 'Old Comedy' of Aristophanes and his contemporaries, which was at first highly regarded in Athens. But later, he goes on, the 'liberty' of the comedians:

> Fell into fault so far, as now they saw
> Her licence fit to be restrained by law:
> Which law received, the chorus held his peace,
> His power of foully hurting made to cease.[15]

As the Elizabethans knew, the scurrilous 'Old Comedy' was replaced by the reformed 'New Comedy' of which Menander was the chief exponent; but Horace does not dwell on this development. From beginning to end his *Art* is concerned first and foremost with the many ways poets can come unstuck, whether by 'daring all' or simply by going mad from imaginative excess.[16]

In *Epistles* 2.1 Horace traces the same movement in the history of Roman comedy as he did in the Greek. In Italy the genre began as an exchange of abusive verses between farmers at harvest festivals, but it quickly degenerated into a cruel and indiscriminate taunting which 'stalked amid the homes of honest folk, fearless in its threatening':

Stung to the quick were they who were bitten by a tooth that drew blood; even those untouched felt concern for the common cause, and at last a law was carried with a penalty, forbidding the portrayal of any in abusive strain. Men changed their tune, and terror of the cudgel led them back to goodly and gracious forms of speech.[17]

Thereafter Italian comic-satiric verse was reformed from its savage state by the importation of more mannerly literature from Greece, including the comedies of Menander. 'Good taste banished the offensive poison', Horace tells us in one breath, but in the next he adds that relics of the old rustic versification live on in the present day, vestigial reminders of the crude rural origins of the Roman theatre – and that the comedy of his time is more concerned to satisfy its auditors' lust for spectacle than to improve their minds.[18] For Horace, then, comedy's flexibility makes it volatile, with a tendency to mutate into forms that bring its authors and actors into danger or disgrace. But it is also vital enough, and slippery enough, to survive every kind of authoritarian assault. Each period that witnesses the death of comedy is followed by a miraculous rebirth, when comedy returns to the public stage reinvigorated by its own repression.

This point was taken up by the sixth-century grammarian Aelius Donatus, whose essays on drama and comedy were printed at the beginning of many sixteenth-century editions of Terence.[19] In Donatus's version of theatrical history the satyr play emerged from early comedy rather than tragedy. 'As the poets came to use their pens with greater license and began to pillory good men right and left just for the fun of it', he writes, 'they were silenced by a law forbidding anyone from writing a poem slandering another person'.[20] Satyr plays were invented as a means of getting round this law, since in them poets 'attacked the vices of citizens without mentioning specific names'. But the satyr plays too fell foul of the authorities, accused of 'disgracing the upper class by their manner of writing', and were themselves replaced first by the non-dramatic satire of Lucilius and later by the New Comedy of Menander and Terence.[21] For Donatus, then, as for Horace, comedy went through at least three reincarnations in its history as a result of authoritarian intervention; and this version of its past, dogged with social and political scandal, prosecuted by the powerful, and assuming new shapes to evade censorship, is the one that found its way into the English histories of poetry that Shakespeare could have known when he started to write.

For the literary historian William Webbe, for instance, author of *A Discourse of English Poetry* (1586), the history of comedy provides a vivid illustration of poetry's perennial tendency to lose its balance. From earliest times, he argues, poets have taken pleasure in their unique ability to 'drawe mens mindes into admiration of theyr inventions', choosing to privilege one of the dual functions of their art, that of 'delighting the readers or hearers wyth pleasure', over the other, that of providing them with 'profitte or commoditye'.[22] The early comedy writers had not been working for long before they lapsed into this kind of self-indulgence, finding themselves expelled from Athens as a penalty for 'scoffing too broade at mens manners, and the privie revengements which the Poets used against their ill wyllers'.[23] Later the comic genre was reformed by the exponents of New Comedy; but in recent years the theatre has been in trouble once again: 'The profitte or discommoditie which aryseth by the use of these Comedies and Tragedies, which is most, hath beene long in controversie, and is sore urged among us at these dayes'.[24] Webbe is referring to the extraordinary outburst of anti-theatrical polemics and pro-theatrical responses that followed the opening of the first substantial purpose-built theatre in London, the Theatre (1576).[25] And once again comedy was at the core of the dispute, both as its most provocative topic and as its vehicle.

COMEDY UNDER ATTACK

This is nowhere more obvious than in the work of the wittiest and fiercest of theatre's critics, Stephen Gosson.[26] Gosson wrote for the stage before turning against it, and as one of his respondents pointed out, he exploits all the imaginative resources of the theatre in his efforts to put it down. His first and most famous polemic was *The School of Abuse* (1579), which rightly describes itself as 'a pleasaunt invective' against 'Poets, Pipers, Plaiers, Jesters, and such like Caterpillers of a Common-welth'.[27] It is (among other things) an entertaining and stylistically inventive call for the 'reformation' of the forms of corruption perpetrated by contemporary men of the theatre, and it seems to have been taken by Gosson's contemporaries as an invitation to a 'flyting': a literary battle of wits designed as much to display the rhetorical skills of the disputants as to promote the cause they espoused. A number of people took up Gosson's challenge, among them another university-educated writer, Thomas Lodge, and the players themselves, who first staged Gosson's own plays in order to embarrass him, then mounted several dramatized defences of the theatre: among them a lost comedy called *The Play of Plays*, an interpolated scene in a play by Robert Wilson, and a jig (that is, a satirical song-and-dance act) performed by the famous clown Richard Tarlton.[28] But Gosson's position on plays seems to have hardened under this assault, and his second major pamphlet, *Plays Confuted in Five Actions* (1582), not only takes an uncompromising line on drama – plays 'are not to be suffred in a Christian common weale' (150) – but directs its fire specifically at comedy.

This may partly be due to the fact that comedies were the players' chosen medium for responses to *The School of Abuse*. But right from the start Gosson's attacks on the theatre were always transforming themselves into specific attacks on comic theatre, and in *The School of Abuse* he more or less admits that this constitutes his primary target. 'Now if any man aske me', he writes, 'why my selfe have penned Comedyes in time paste, and inveigh so egerly against them here, let him knowe that . . . I have sinned, and am sorry for my fault: hee runnes farre that never turnes, better late then never' (97). Comedy, with its propensity for privileging entertainment over instruction and its inexhaustible fund of bawdy jokes and erotic situations, offers the perfect illustration of the central tenet of Gosson's attack: that the theatre is useless, an over-sophisticated luxury item fundamentally at odds with the English tradition of plainness and honesty; and that its uselessness makes it dangerous. Gosson stresses the point by referring to his past involvement with the theatre as a prime example of economic mismanagement – a waste of time. 'I gave my selfe to that exercise in hope to thrive', he tells us, 'but I . . . loste bothe my time and my travel [i.e. labour], when I had doone' (97). For many Elizabethans, work that has no economic or social function is idleness, idleness is a breeding-ground for psychological and sexual depravity, and depravity is the basis for insurrection. Hence Gosson's startling capacity in his pamphlets to trace a direct path between laughter and the collapse of English society; a capacity which his contemporaries shared to an astonishing extent.

To describe something as a waste of time implies that it fails to fit into the social, economic, and historical structures by which a dominant culture defines itself. Comedy is in fact for Gosson fundamentally anti-historical, never learning from past mistakes (unlike Gosson himself) and therefore condemned to repeat its vices forever in a perpetual cycle of corruption. *The School of Abuse* dedicates itself, among other things, to refuting the notion that Elizabethan comedy has a distinguished ancestry, or that its history bears witness to its determination to leave its faults behind. 'Here I doubt not', he writes at one point, 'but some Archplayer or other that hath read a litle, or stumbled by chance upon Plautus comedies', will resort to the hackneyed defence that their work resembles the reformed New Comedy, as opposed to the ribald Old Comedy that was banned from Athens (87). They will argue, in other words, that the faults of the comic mode belong to the past, and that modern players and playwrights have since cleaned up their act. 'Nowe are the abuses of the worlde revealed', they will say:

> every man in a play may see his owne faultes, and learne by this glasse, to amende his maners . . . Deformities are checked in jeast, and mated in earnest. The sweetenesse of musicke, and pleasure of sportes, temper the bitternesse of rebukes, and mittigate the tartenesse of every taunt. (88)

Gosson's answer is to cite the goings-on in the modern theatre audience as proof of comedy's hidden agenda, damning evidence that the genre still acts as a bluff host to the kinds of scurrility it has always encouraged. 'In our assemblies at plays in London', he writes,

> you shall see suche heaving, and shooving, suche ytching and shouldring, too sitte by women . . . Such ticking, such toying, such smiling, such winking, and such manning them home, when the sportes are ended, that it is a right Comedie, to marke [their] behaviour. (92)

As prostitutes hawk their wares among theatrical spectators made eager and knowing by the performance on stage, the players' claim to have 'purged their Comedyes of wanton speaches' loses all credibility (94). How can the stage be said to have been purged when the sophisticated dialogue of the New Comedy produces the same effect on its spectators as the obscenities of the Old?

In the last part of *Plays Confuted* Gosson describes the effect on a gathered crowd of a play performed in ancient Greece by a man, a woman and a boy, whose erotic enactment of the tale of Bacchus and Ariadne spreads lust like wildfire through the mesmerized spectators (193–4). Gosson cites their performance as evidence against the theatre as if it had taken place only yesterday. For him, comedy has no history, because it is always and everywhere the same. It has never been reformed: it simply varies the techniques by which it depraves the minds of its spectators. And it is the sheer subtlety of these techniques that Gosson finds most objectionable. The players claim that the stage is the ultimate educational tool, exploiting a mixture of jest and earnest, sweetness and bitterness, sports and rebukes as a way of teaching people about 'the abuses of the worlde' (88). But for Gosson these instructive methods are damaging by reason of their sheer complexity. Their fusion of disparate elements destroys the capacity of the audience to distinguish right from wrong; their stimulation of the senses, and of sexual desire in particular, robs their spectators of the power to reason. Far from enlightening the young, the modern theatre seeks to confuse them by the overwhelming richness of the goods it has on offer: 'straunge consortes of melody, to tickle the eare; costly apparel, to flatter the sight; effeminate gesture, to ravish the sence; and wanton speache, to whet desire too inordinate lust' (89). 'There is more in them then we perceive', Gosson adds, 'the Devill standes at our elbowe when we see not, speaks, when we heare him not, strikes when wee feele not, and woundeth sore when he raseth no skinne, nor rentes the fleshe' (94). The players' claim to have reformed the stage is simply one more in the succession of masks which they are called upon to adopt professionally, and which both imitate and help to engender the peculiar vices of the present age.

This theme of players as felons disguised in elaborate masks was taken up by Gosson's successor William Rankins, whose anti-theatrical pamphlet *A Mirror of Monsters* (1587) represents the Elizabethan theatre allegorically as a profane marriage between the deadly sins Fastus (Pride) and Luxuria (Lechery). To celebrate this marriage of sensuality to insubordination – a grotesque perversion of the traditional comic ending – an infernal deity (Pluto or Beelzebub) arranges a masque performed by hounds from Hell. Each hell-hound stands for a particular vice associated with players, and each adopts an appropriate mask representing some virtue to conceal their true identity; thus Idleness disguises himself as Honest Recreation, Flattery as Courtesy, Blasphemy as Godly Learning, and so on. Rankins may have got his idea for the demonic masque from a hint in *The School of Abuse*. 'Pul off the visard that Poets maske in', Gosson writes, 'and you shall disclose their reproch, bewray their vanitie, loth their wantonnesse, lament their follie, and perceive their sharpe sayings to be placed as ... chaste Matrons apparel on common Curtesans' (77). But both writers were drawing on the theatrical tradition of the Vice, the dominant comic figure of the early Elizabethan stage, a kind of allegorical devil-clown whose trademark technique for inveigling more or less innocent souls into his power was to improvise a succession of disguises, with or without the help of actual masks.[29] Tyrants and their apologists have always liked to keep things simple, claiming for themselves a unique capacity to sort experience into good and evil, legal and illegal, black and white, yet claiming too that these distinctions are permanent and universal ones. Gosson's *School of Abuse*, which advocates tyranny in the form of censorship, is an attack on complexity and change. As an example of the ideal life it cites the ancient Britons, who lived on peas, dressed in skins and led an unchanging, simple life dedicated to the pursuit of the military virtues (90–1). The newfangled Elizabethan comedy, by contrast, pays homage to the complex and the changeful through its preoccupation with the rapid and ingenious shifting of speech, clothes and action that are necessary for any successful career based on disguise. As such it represents everything that is degenerate and foreign, and threatens to undermine the national defences of contemporary England.

The political implications of Gosson's attack on comedy are most fully worked out in *Plays Confuted in Five Actions*. Where *The School of Abuse* took plays to be the seeds from which great evils could potentially spring, *Plays Confuted* represents the structure of English culture as already under sustained assault by the beguiling narratives of comedy, and brings to the fore the class conflict that is a central component of classical histories of the genre. To make its case his pamphlet imitates the five-act structure of a comedy by Terence, weaving into each act or quasi-legal 'action' evidence of the deleterious effects of the theatre on its spectators and the community at large.[30] And this time Gosson's premise is that the subtleties of drama, especially those of comedy, secretly operate to undermine all distinctions between the social classes, and that this makes playing and play-going the artistic equivalent of popular rebellion.

Gosson builds up towards this devastating conclusion with meticulous logic. In the first of the pamphlet's five 'actions' Gosson represents plays as an infection spread by the Devil designed to break down the moral health of the English nation. They are the second wave of an assault on English morals, the first of which was the importation of 'wanton Italian bookes, which being translated into english, have poysned the olde maners of our Country with foreine delights' (153).[31] Because not all Englishmen are literate, the Devil followed up this first assault on the nation's identity by presenting 'Comedies cut by the same paterne, which drag such a monstrous taile after them, as is able to sweep whole Cities into his lap' (153). The second action of the pamphlet dismisses the theatre's pretensions to edify its audience by attacking the social status of players and the audiences for whom they perform. How can plays reform the 'corruption of manners' (163), as the players claim, when they are performed and attended by 'the worste sorte of people ... which in respecte of there ignorance, of there ficklenes, and of there furie, are not to bee admitted in place of judgement' (164)? Any 'rebuking of manners' that goes on in this context is 'nether lawfull nor convenient, but to be held for a kinde of libelling, and defaming'(164) – hence the laws made against libellous stage performances in ancient Rome. Then in the third action Gosson assaults the players' practice of unsettling the social hierarchy by cross-dressing. In plays boys put on the garments of women, 'contrarie to the expresse rule of the worde of God' (175), while craftsmen don the robes of the aristocracy, and both these acts of transvestism prove plays to be constructed from damaging lies.

The fourth action charts the debilitating effect of comedy on the brain, showing how its stimulation of excessive delight or pleasure robs the mind of its capacity to think. Excessive laughter, Gosson maintains, 'like a kinde of drunkennes, maketh us stagger, very unfit, either to speake; or to walke as we shoulde in our vocation' (186); in other words, it makes its victims unfit for useful employment. Like drunkenness it is addictive, making us yearn for more of the same: 'in Comedies . . . the longer we gaze, the more we crave, yea so forcible they are, that afterwards being but thought upon, they make us seeke for the like an other time' (186). Comedies represent, in fact, 'rebellion raysed against reason' and against the 'lawes of God' (187).

Clearly, there is no great distance to be travelled between a rebellion against the laws of God and an insurrection against the state; and Gosson argues just this in the fifth and final action. Here he summarizes the combined effects on English society of the processes traced in the first four actions: above all the tendency of drama to arouse anarchic sexual passions and to deprave the labouring classes. By frequenting theatres, players and their audiences are rendered unable to fulfil their duty to work, and this does irreparable damage to the state. Gosson explains this by means of a familiar metaphor: 'A common weale is likened to the body, whose heade is the prince', he writes:

> if any part be idle, by participation the damage redoundeth to the whole, if any refuse to doe their duetie, though they be base, as the guttes, the gall, the bladder, howe daungerous it is both to the bodie, and to the heade, everie man is able to conjecture. (195)

The abuse of the private body in the theatre leads inexorably to the infection of the entire body politic. Players, in fact, resemble the rebellious organs in the fable of Menenius Agrippa (retold in Philip Sidney's *Apology for Poetry* and in Shakespeare's *Coriolanus*),[32] whose efforts to destroy the upper-class belly are calculated to destroy themselves as well as their enemy. *Plays Confuted* ends, then, not as a tragedy

– its subject is too petty for this, since tragedy concerns itself with princes and great men – but as a kind of anti-comedy, which demonstrates how the comic can have the most appalling of social and political consequences, bringing down kingdoms and condemning their inhabitants to eternal damnation, all through the most innocuous and pleasurable of performances.

IN DEFENCE OF THE COMIC

The defendants of the theatre replied to Gosson's slurs by giving a daring new slant to the history of comedy. Thomas Lodge's *Defence of Poetry* (1579), written in response to *The School of Abuse*, may have been commissioned by the players themselves, and was withdrawn from circulation by the Elizabethan censors.[33] This is a fate that it prophesies for itself in its own pages. Lodge's chief concern in his defence is with the theatre's historical relationship with the censors, a relationship that has broken down in recent years, leaving the theatre and its defendants vulnerable to exactly the sort of authoritarian intervention to which his own text succumbed. The *Defence* opens with a confident justification of poetry in general, refuting Gosson's general attack on imaginative writing. But when Lodge turns to the defence of the stage, and of comedy in particular, he expresses a sense of having strayed into dangerous territory. 'I must now search my wits', he declares, 'I see this shall passe throughe many severe sensors handling; I must advise me what I write, and write that I would wysh' (79). And the reason for his anxiety soon becomes apparent. Like Horace and Donatus he sees the history of the theatre as having been interrupted by successive waves of persecution; but for Lodge this persecution is the reaction of the indignant ruling classes to the exposure of its own corruption, a reaction that in his own lifetime has become excessive. Theatre is being barred from its old function of engaging in lively dialogue with the authorities, Lodge contends, and this has dire implications both for the acting profession and for the society that seeks to suppress it.

The history of the theatre which Lodge tells to illustrate this contention begins conventionally enough, but ends by making high claims for comedy's role in the community. Tragedies and comedies, he says, were first invented 'to no other purpose but to yeelde prayse unto God for a happy harvest' (80). Tragedy gave rise to satire, or staged performances of 'the lives of Satyers', invented by playwrights 'so that they might wiselye, under the abuse of that name, discover the follies of many theyr folish fellow citesens' (81); and the crude early comedies, too, 'were mervelous profitable to the reclamynge of abuse' (81). Lodge's repeated use of the term 'abuse' in this part of his argument implies that playwrights have always done the job that Gosson took on in *The School of Abuse* – that of harrying wrong-doers and uncovering social scandals. 'These therefore', he concludes – that is, the old comedians and satirists – 'these wer they that kept men in awe, these restrayned the unbridled cominaltie' (81). So far this is innocuous enough – he is implying that comedy deals only with commoners (the 'cominaltie') and leaves the affairs of the ruling classes to the more decorous tragic genre. But as Lodge goes on, it becomes clear that he is extending comedy's remit to include criticism of governors as well as their subjects, and that for him one of the chief functions of the comic is to articulate legitimate resistance to the abuse of power. The old Greek and Roman comedy writers, he claims, such as Menander and Terence, became adept at attacking corruption at all social levels without antagonizing the authorities:

> A poet's wit can correct, yet not offend. Philemon will mitigate the corrections of sinne by reproving them covertly in shadowes. Menander dare not offend the Senate openly, yet wants he not a parasite to touch them prively. Terence ... dare not openly tell the Rich of theyr covetousnesse and severity towards their children, but he can controle them under the person of Durus Demeas ... Wil you learne to knowe a parasite? Looke upon his Davus. Wyl you seke the abuse of courtly flatterers? Behold Gnato. And if we had some Satericall Poetes nowe a dayes to penn our commedies, that might be admitted of zeale to discypher the abuses of the worlde in the person of notorious offenders, I knowe we should wisely ryd our assemblyes of many of your brotherhod. (182)

The notion that comedy corrects the vices of its audience by holding them up to ridicule is widespread in Renaissance criticism; but that it should chastize the sins of the senate and the court extends its range well beyond the limits set by Donatus, who insisted that 'in comedy the fortunes of men are middle-class'.[34] Under these circumstances Lodge's use of the word 'control' – meaning 'rebuke' – hints at the ambition of ancient comedians to rein in the excesses of the ruling classes, who themselves had struggled so long and so ineffectually to restrain the excesses of comedy.

But Elizabethan England, Lodge adds, has become too hostile to comedy to enable any latter-day Terence to perform the same invaluable service. Whereas Gosson argues for a ban on the genre, Lodge argues that England needs a more audacious brand of the comic than it currently countenances. 'Would God', he writes,

> our realme could light uppon a Lucilius [the founder of Roman satire]; then should the wicked bee poynted out from the good ... But as these sharpe corrections were disanulde in Rome when they grewe to more licenciousnes, so I fear me if we shold practise it in our dayes the same intertainmente would followe. (81–2)

This last sentence contains a highly suggestive ambiguity. It is by no means clear whether Lodge is saying that comedies and their 'sharpe corrections' were banned from Rome when the comedies or the Romans themselves 'grew to more licenciousnes'; but it seems clear from the words that come next, 'I fear me if we shold practise it in our dayes the same intertainmente would followe', that the latter is the intended meaning: why should the banning of comedy be regretted if it was the comedy that was licentious? And he confirms this reading shortly afterwards. 'Surely we want not a Roscius', he writes (Roscius being the greatest of Roman comic actors),

> nether ar ther great scarsity of Terence's profession, but yet our men dare not nowe a dayes presume so much as the old Poets might, and therfore they apply ther writing to the peoples vain;

wheras, if in the beginning they had ruled, we should now adaies
have found smal spectacles of folly. (83)

The decline of comedy, Lodge implies, is the fault of 'severe sensors'
like Gosson, who have left playwrights no choice but to cultivate popu-
larity instead of the 'sharpe corrections' of satire. Gosson is therefore
indirectly responsible for the sorry state both of the English stage and of
English society, having inhibited the former from reforming the latter. 'If
our poets will nowe become severe', Lodge goes on, 'and for prophane
things write of vertue, you I hope shoulde see a reformed state in those
thinges' (83). He has already implied that such an outcome is unlikely,
given the hostile forces ranged against the poets. Nevertheless, Lodge
spent much of his literary career trying to bring it about. Until 1600 or
so, his published work consisted largely of 'sharpe corrections': satires
in prose, verse and dramatic form aimed at reforming the state of
England, though from a Catholic rather than a Protestant viewpoint.[35]
After 1600 Lodge gave up writing anything but translations, and committed himself to healing society's physical ills in his capacity as a
respected physician; but he may have seen his medical career as serving
much the same ends as his career as an imaginative writer.

What stands out from the pamphlets of Lodge and Gosson is their
shared conviction that theatrical comedy makes things happen: that it
delights and seduces every social class and affects them in ways that
directly affect the well-being of society at large. Lodge and Gosson
agree, too, that this comic efficacy is the reason why the genre has been
subject to persecution throughout its history. For Lodge, comedies
expose and expunge corruption from the highest ranks to the most
humble, and their periodic banning from the stage is a token of their
success. For Gosson, on the other hand, comedies are capable of bringing about the collapse of the social order itself and the invasion of
England by demonic foreign powers, and their banning is necessary in
the interests of national security. The positions of the two men, in fact,
are more or less identical. The difference is that Lodge is willing to
appropriate the power of the comic for what he sees as good ends, while
Gosson wants it extirpated altogether, erased from English history like
the rebels it resembles.

FIGURE 1   Isaac Oliver (*c.* 1560–1617), 'An Allegorical Scene', *c.* 1590–5.
The painting contrasts virtuous and vicious love in terms that recall the
sixteenth-century debate over representations of desire in the theatre.

LAUGHTER, RHETORIC, LEARNING

The history of comedy as Gosson and Lodge discuss it is that of theatrical comedy, licensed by law and policed by the state authorities. But
the comic mode beyond the stage generated just as much anxiety as
comedy confined within the limits of a designated performance area;
and as with dramatic comedy, the roots of this anxiety lay in the classical heritage that underpinned the early modern educational system.
The rhetoricians whose work lay at the heart of that system stressed the
power of laughter as a weapon in public speaking; but like the historians of drama, they also stressed its resistance to regulation and its
tendency to spill over into anarchic excess.[36] Cicero, for instance, stated
in *De oratore* that comic techniques cannot be taught, since people are
either naturally funny or not funny at all; that humour refuses to be
theorized or reduced to a set of rules; and that those who try to analyse
laughter only make themselves laughable.[37] All the same, *De oratore*
went on to classify the types of humour that might appropriately be
used by Roman lawyers and politicians, and Cicero's classifications –
like everything he wrote – became immensely influential among early

modern teachers. Yet the sense that the comic resists analysis continued
to haunt Renaissance rhetoricians, raising awkward questions about
the art of rhetoric itself (is it an art at all? can it be taught?) just as
theatrical comedy epitomized Renaissance anxieties about the nature of
theatre.

Anxieties about laughter were fuelled by the account of witty rhetoric in Quintilian's *Institutio oratoria*. Quintilian delights in wit, and
specifically in Cicero's deployment of wit in his speeches; yet he points
out that some have accused the great orator of having had an excessive
fondness for jokes – of being willing, in fact, to sacrifice almost anything
for the sake of a giggle.[38] Disapproval of the Ciceronian sense of
humour springs, he suggests, from a distrust of laughter itself, with its
irrepressible spontaneity and its contempt for authority and reason.
Laughter is libellous and opportunistic, manifesting itself most effectively at the most unexpected moments.[39] The power to incite it is not
restricted to educated men, but is as readily available to the peasant as
to the lawyer. And nobody has any real idea how it works, physiologi-
cally or psychologically speaking. This powerful political tool, able to
turn the tide of opinion in a law-court or the city streets, capable of
saving its exponents from seemingly certain death, can in the end be
neither defined nor analysed, and its operations can only be demon-
strated by putting it into practice. Accordingly, Quintilian's discussion
degenerates into a series of illustrative anecdotes that threaten to transform his treatise into 'a common jest-book' – an ironic outcome, since
he began by complaining about the impropriety of the three books
of jests attributed to Cicero.[40] He strives to contain these anecdotes by
sorting them into categories – *urbanitas, venustus, salsus, facetus* and so
on – refining on Cicero's classification of the types of humour. But these
efforts at containment are doomed to failure before they begin, since he
has already told us that any attempt to give a comprehensive overview
of laughter 'would be an interminable task and a waste of labour'.[41]
The orderly framework of a classical education dissolves at laughter's
touch like the dignity of the schoolmaster who falls victim to a schoolboy prank.

So too does the framework of the social hierarchy. The works of
Cicero and Quintilian address the needs of the Roman ruling classes,

instructing them in the linguistic skills required by patricians preparing to take up the reins of government. Their sections on laughter are filled with recommendations for distinguishing the aristocratic quipster from the lower-class buffoon, the chief of which is that the aristocrat takes care to show what Shakespeare's Malvolio calls 'respect of place, persons, [and] time'.[42] As Cicero puts it, 'regard ought to be paid to personages, topics and occasions, so that the jest should not detract from dignity' either of the nobly-born orator or of his patrician auditors.[43] In other words, such an orator must be scrupulously careful to restrain his sense of humour within the bounds of decorum or decency; and this notion became a commonplace of every early modern discussion of laughter. But the two greatest Roman rhetoricians also confess that there are no rules to determine just where these bounds lie, and in doing so they are effectively confessing that there are no hard and fast rules to determine the difference between one social class and another.

Despite its imprecision, Cicero's phrase prescribing the appropriate moment for humour – that 'regard ought to be paid to personages, topics and occasions' – is endlessly repeated in early modern manuals on language and good manners. The Italian writer Baldassare Castiglione, for instance, introduces an extended discussion of laughter into his influential treatise *The Book of the Courtier* (1528), and centres the discussion on the problem of finding the right moment for mirth in an aristocratic context. A gifted mimic at court, says one of the speakers, must 'have great respect to the place, to the time and to the persons with whom hee talketh, and not like a common jeaster passe his boundes'.[44] Amusing comparisons, too, must be made with due respect for 'the place, the time, the persons'.[45] But Castiglione also implies that his frequent repetitions of Cicero's phrase are rendered necessary by the widespread *disregard* for good manners and good timing among the laughter-loving nobles of his day. Too many of these nobles, he complains,

> in too much babling passe sometime their boundes . . . because they have no respect to the condition of the person they commune withal, to the place where they bee, to the time, [or] to the great gravitie and modesty which they ought to have in themselves.[46]

For Castiglione, in fact, laughter encapsulates the subjection of even the highest human ideals to the vagaries of time that is a dominant theme of his book. His text is a heroic effort to paint a picture of the perfect courtier against the backdrop of political turmoil in early modern Italy, and constantly acknowledges the transience and imprecision of the picture it is painting. Its definition of man (derived from Aristotle) as 'a living creature that can laughe' identifies laughter as the compensatory resource of those who, under pressure from history, have abandoned the other common definition of a man, that he is a creature endowed with reason.[47] 'Whatsoever therfore causeth laughter', says Castiglione's spokesman, 'the same maketh the mind jocunde and giveth pleasure, nor suffereth a man in that instant to mind the troublesome griefes that our life is full off'.[48] This makes humour sound like a temporary escape from history, and confirms the view of classical theorists that the comic should only concern itself with trivial things: as Cicero puts it, 'neither outstanding wickedness . . . nor outstanding wretchedness is assailed by ridicule'.[49] *The Book of the Courtier* is laughter-filled, even at its most serious, but one is left with the impression that its humour is powerless, both against the atrocities committed in the name of modern politics and against the relentless march of time; a fleeting diversion from matters of moment.

But in the later sixteenth century laughter became inextricably entangled with matters of very great moment, through its association with the political and religious upheavals of the Reformation. Two great humanists who got caught up in the Reformation ensured that laughter played a prominent role in later accounts of religious troubles and resistance to tyranny. One was Desiderius Erasmus, the founder of educational systems throughout Northern Europe, and the most influential of latter-day writers on the art of eloquence. Erasmus was deeply critical of corruption in church and state, and his controversial fiction *The Praise of Folly* (1514) gave his successors a hugely influential model for satire, holding up the absurdities of the ruling classes to ridicule and mocking them for treating wise but humble men – like Christ's disciples – as inconsequential fools. The other was the man to whom *The Praise of Folly* was addressed, Sir Thomas More, who was executed for his refusal to accede to the demands of a tyrant, but who went laughing to his execution. More died for Catholicism, but his use of laughter as an instrument of resistance to state oppression was admired and emulated by Protestants and Catholics alike throughout the sixteenth century. Both these thinkers were perceived as having a strong rapport with the common man: More famously wrote a serio-comic book, *Utopia* (1516), about an egalitarian state, and Erasmus celebrated the wisdom of ordinary people in his great collection of popular proverbs, the *Adagia* (1500–33), as well as in *The Praise of Folly*. And what endeared both men to popular tradition, providing the driving force behind the many books, anecdotes and plays in which More, in particular, was fondly remembered, was their wit: an instinct for spontaneous comic improvisation that had little to do with erudition – or with prudence.

LAUGHTER AND IMPROVISATION

Cicero and Quintilian distinguish two kinds of verbal joke: the sort that is told as a continuous narrative and the sort that relies for its effect on speed and spontaneity – the 'quick answer', as it is often called in the sixteenth century.[50] As the English rhetorician Thomas Wilson puts it, 'Some can pretely by a word spoken, take occasion to be right mery. Other can jest at large, and tel a round tale pleasantly, though thei have none occasion at that tyme geven'.[51] Of the two forms of humour, the 'quick answer' was by far the more highly prized in early modern Europe. 'But assuredly', Wilson goes on, 'that mirth is more worth, whiche is moved by a word newly spoken ... For asmuche as bothe it cometh unlooked for, and also declares a quickenesse of witte, worthy commendacion'. The French physician Laurent Joubert, whose *Treatise on Laughter* constitutes the earliest effort to diagnose the physiological causes and effects of laughter, agreed with Wilson: for him the best kind of verbal humour is 'the ability to render tit for tat, and for a taunt, to come back with a clever reply'.[52] And English readers in general seem to have shared the taste of these learned men for rapid-fire witticisms and spontaneous repartee, if we may judge by the humorous books they most enjoyed.

John Lyly's *Euphues: The Anatomy of Wit* (1578) was perhaps the most popular work of Elizabethan fiction.[53] 'Wit' in the title means something like 'native intelligence', and Lyly displays it in his book both in an elaborately patterned prose style and in the ability of his protagonist to improvise spontaneously, brilliantly and elegantly on any given subject. Euphues is a cultural chameleon, capable of changing himself like the mythical god Proteus into any shape his circumstances demand. 'If I be in Crete', he says, 'I can lye, if in Greece I can shift, if in Italy I can court it ... I can carous with Alexander, abstaine with Romulus, eate with the Epicure, fast with the Stoyck, sleepe with Endimion, watch with Chrisippus'.[54] This gift for improvisation means that he has no stable system of values: as soon as temptation arises he succumbs to it, betraying his best friend by seducing his fiancée – once again with the aid of his dazzling skills in repartee and extemporary rhetoric. Yet his moral duplicity did not prevent Elizabethan readers from seeking to emulate his verbal quirks, and for more than a decade after the publication of Lyly's book English prose style was dominated by the alliterative balanced clauses of the style known as 'euphuism', punctuated by references to exotic animals, plants and minerals and laced with elaborate puns. It was a style perfectly adapted to the needs of clever young men and women, and its potential to be exploited for dubious purposes – to make the most flawed statements look plausible, the most superficial learning look profound, the most glibly spontaneous remarks sound premeditated – was part of what made it attractive.

Euphues is a young man of flashy erudition, who studied in Athens before prematurely breaking off his studies to visit the fleshpots of Italy. But Lyly shares the opinion of the classical rhetoricians that verbal wit is a resource as freely available to the uneducated as to the learned: and the women in his novels repeatedly put down the men in extemporaneous exchanges, without the benefit of an Athenian training. The wit of women presides over his second novel, *Euphues and his England* (1580), much as the undeniably learned Elizabeth I presided over the nation it celebrates, and it is a witty woman who provokes the book's most eloquent paean to the seductiveness of improvisation:

It is wit that allureth, when every word shall have his weight,
when nothing shall proceed, but it shall either savour of a sharpe
conceipt, or a secret conclusion. And this is the greatest thing, to
conceive readely and aunswere aptly, to understand whatsoever
is spoken, and to reply as though they understoode nothing.[55]

Lyly's delight in stylish repartee represents a levelling influence in the
comedies he went on to write for Elizabeth's court during the 1580s,
where humbly born women, servants, tradesmen and even labourers,
night watchmen and apprentices hold their own in dazzling verbal
duels with monarchs and noblemen. The fame brought to Lyly by
Euphues gave him a voice in the highest household in the land, and his
plays are full of a sense of their own temerity in holding the royal ear, of
the precariousness of royal favour, and of wit as the fragile tool of the
middle and lower classes for keeping that ear and that favour fixed upon
them – a tool capable at any moment of twisting in its users' hands and
inflicting irreparable damage on their persons and prospects.

Lyly's conception of wit owes something to the collections of comic
anecdotes now known as 'jest-books' that were widely read by all
classes throughout the sixteenth and seventeenth centuries. Like
Euphues, these cheerful miscellanies dedicate themselves to celebrating
the skills of agile improvisers; their narratives aim to reconstruct the
unexpected circumstances that lead to the sudden quip or sharp retort,
a purpose enshrined in the title of one collection, *Merry Tales, Witty
Questions and Quick Answers* (*c.* 1532).[56] *Euphues* is a representative
example of what might be called the Elizabethan literature of truancy:
it concerns itself with how the rhetorical skills acquired in the class-
room take on a new life outside the schoolhouse walls, adapting themselves to situations very different from those anticipated by
conventional teachers of the arts of language. But the jest-books have a
rather different relationship with the pedagogic system. For the most
part the wit of their protagonists explicitly opposes itself to the ornate
rhetoric recommended by early modern teachers to their students. They
are written in mostly unadorned, colloquial prose, and their denouements give equal weight to physical and verbal humour. If Euphues is
the master of improvised imitations of his teachers' precepts, the jest-

book protagonist makes all precepts look foolish as he twists logic and syntax in his efforts to deliver a good punch-line – or a good hard punch.

For the classical rhetoricians, impromptu wit was the type of humour that epitomized laughter's resistance to pedagogic regulation. As Cicero puts it, 'what room is there for Art in raillery ... wherein the shaft of wit has to be sped and hit the mark with no palpable pause for thought?'[57] Quintilian concludes from this that 'even mere country bumpkins are capable of producing effective witticisms';[58] and Thomas Wilson waxes eloquent on the improvisational skills of the 'varlet or common jester' who 'is able to matche with the best' – that is, with the most highly educated:

> It appereth that thei, whiche wittely can be pleasant, and when time serveth, can geve a mery answere, or use a nippyng taunte, shalbee able to abashe a righte worthy man, and make hym at his wittes ende, through the sodein quip and unloked frumpe geven. I have knowen some so hit of the thumbes, that thei could not tell in the world whether it were beste to fighte, chide, or to go their waie.[59]

The rhetoricians' acknowledgement that the ability to seize opportunities is more important than learning in this kind of humour is borne out by the abundance of jest-book anecdotes that ascribe the most devastating of 'sodein quips' to the disadvantaged and the disenfranchised. Labourers, beggars, boys and village idiots are the heroes of these narratives, and women of all classes are their heroines.[60] As Kiernan Ryan has reminded us, the verb that describes the quick answer – to extemporize – means 'to speak out of time, which connotes talking out of turn, in contempt of sequence and decorum'.[61] The quick answer, like theatrical comedy, violates the social hierarchy by giving a voice to the otherwise voiceless. It disrupts the working day by interrupting spells of productive labour with spontaneous hilarity. It perverts the orderly sequence of the calendar, which divides up the year into brief periods of festival and long periods of graft, holy days and work days, none of which are respected by the glib-tongued clown.[62] And it dismantles the framework of learning that sustains the social hierarchy by exposing its redundancy, its comparative helplessness in the face of unpleasant surprises.

The most universal manifestation of learning in the sixteenth century was the *sententia* or sentence: the pithy saying that conveys some timeless truth, drawing on the great encyclopaedia of all learning into which early modern thinkers imagined their studies to tap. Collections of such eternally useful sentences, purportedly derived from the works of the great philosophers, sold well in the sixteenth century.[63] They served as cribs for show-offs like Euphues who wished to look learned without working too hard for it, or as armouries to be ransacked by ambitious public speakers keen to garnish their oratory, or as pearls of wisdom to be mulled over by readers with a contemplative cast of mind. The quick answer is the opposite of the sentence: it foregrounds the present moment rather than eternity, seeks an instant reaction rather than mature appreciation, deflates pretensions rather than elevating the soul, and caters for the body rather than the spirit. The books that celebrate the quick answer often have little formal structure, but bundle together pranks, witticisms and pratfalls in loose handfuls, available to be raided at random by all and sundry. They wittily invert the grandiose claims of the sentence collections with which they compete, exposing the underlying motives for reading such collections – self-advancement and personal pleasure, rather than some altruistic desire to advance the sum of human knowledge. The one serious claim they make for themselves is that they are an antidote for that most debilitating of diseases, melancholy: physicians like Laurent Joubert maintained that a laugh could put a sick patient on the road to recovery more effectively than any pill or purge.[64] Yet as Joubert himself recognized, if a joke can cure a patient better than a pill, the skills of the trained physician are rendered risible. Jest-books and the quick answers they contain exist in cheerful rivalry with sixteenth-century educators, threatening to unmask them as a bunch of pretentious and unnecessary upstarts.

This is not to say that the jest-books did not acknowledge the quick answers of learned men. On the contrary, the so-called 'biographical jest-books' – story-collections centred round the exploits of a single comic figure – often take scholars as their protagonists.[65] There is no surviving jest-book about the exploits of Thomas More; but there is one about his near contemporary, the poet-priest John Skelton, and another about the Oxford scholar Scoggin, who was beaten up by Sir John Falstaff when he was a boy.[66] And in each of these books the scholar in question dedicates his pranks to deflating the pretensions of his superiors. Skelton is celebrated as the scourge of arrogant friars, bishops and cardinals, and Scoggin's career progresses from Oxford academic to court jester or fool, employed at the courts of kings for the purpose of cutting them down to size, often at the risk of life or livelihood.[67] In each case, too, the learned protagonist operates on a level playing-field with the unlearned. Scoggin's comrades in comedy, who sometimes outwit him, are two of his students – the boy Jack and the fool Will – and Will's success in becoming first a deacon, then a priest, makes a mockery of the church hierarchy, proving (among other things) the parodic *sententiae* that 'money is better than learning' and that 'hee is a starke foole that can make no excuse for himselfe that is culpable'.[68] Skelton is outwitted many times by a wily miller named John, in a series of episodes that Gabriel Harvey found the funniest in any English jest-book.[69] Between them, Skelton and Scoggin demonstrate the extent to which learning fails to prepare the learned for the exigencies of earning a living. For this, native wit (or native folly combined with good luck) is the only key. And in demonstrating the shortcomings of knowledge they make the records of their adventures as indispensable to the young as the earnest books recommended by serious schoolmasters.

To be killed for one's jests is the ultimate in poor comic timing; but to be nearly killed for them and to rescue oneself at the last minute by sheer force of wit is the ultimate in comic skill. Elizabethan jest-books are always treading a fine line between these two very different outcomes, separated from one another by no more than an instant. All the biographical jest-books deal with protagonists who are dead at the time of writing. Perhaps this protects these risqué story-collections against censorship or accusations of libel, fates that can kill off the careers of comic writers as surely as execution; but the effect is to cast them in a strangely sombre light. The jest-books pay tribute to a deftness, a slipperiness, a mental agility that has been abruptly terminated, fixed in the past despite the best efforts of its possessor. The achievement of Skelton and Scoggin consists in successfully negotiating the deadly world of Tudor politics with the help of laughter; but theatrical personalities, too, were the subject of posthumous jest-book biographies, and these too testify to the foolhardy skill of their protagonists in dallying with death. The playwright George Peele, whose exploits are remembered in *Merry Conceited Jests of George Peele* (1607), is less concerned with death than with finding tricky ways to stay alive in spite of his acute penury; but the fact that his adventures are recorded posthumously suggests that he finally failed to keep body and soul together, for all his wit.

The celebrated clown and comic actor Richard Tarlton, whose impromptu witticisms are commemorated in *Tarlton's Jests* (1608), shares Scoggin's flare for provoking the victims of his jokes to potentially lethal fury. Famed for his 'wondrous plentifull pleasant extemporall wit',[70] in these anecdotes Tarlton engages in a constant merry war with his public, whether inventing spontaneous responses to quips, jibes and even apples flung at him by theatre audiences, or engaging in duels of wit with passers-by in the streets of London and the provinces. From time to time this wordplay turns to swordplay – not surprisingly, since Tarlton was a Master of Fence. In one story the professional swordsman Little Davy is hired by a prostitute to fight Tarlton for insulting her (Tarlton breaks his nose); in another an enraged gentleman swears 'to fight with him at next meeting';[71] in a third the clown provokes a rapier-wielding 'gallant' into assaulting him in the street. Once Tarlton saves his life with a well-timed jest when attacked by a madman at an inn; but more often the clown's aggressive jokes put him in serious danger, from which he is rescued by the crowds of admirers that gather wherever he shows his face. For the compiler of *Tarlton's Jests*, Tarlton's lively wit manifests itself by its willingness to be deadly.

As well as an actor, Tarlton was a professional fool, who did his clowning at inns and the royal court as well as on the stage, like a fore-runner of Shakespeare's itinerant jesters Touchstone and Feste, whose 'foolery . . . shines everywhere', like the sun.[72] *Tarlton's Jests* pays tribute to the clown's mobility by dividing itself into three parts, detailing his 'court-witty jests', his 'sound city jests', and his 'country pretty jests'. Another book of comic stories, *Tarlton's News out of Purgatory* (1590), suggests that he continued to make himself at home even in the hostile

Tarltons Jeſts.

Drawne into theſe three parts.

> 1   *His Court-witty Ieſts.*
> 2   *His ſound City Ieſts.*
> 3   *His Countrey pretty Ieſts.*

Full of delight, Wit, and honeſt Mirth.

LONDON,
Printed by *I. H.* for *Andrew Crook*, and are to be ſold
in *Pauls* Church-yard, at the ſigne of
the *Beare.*   1628.

FIGURE 2   Richard Tarlton playing the pipe and tabor, from *Tarlton's Jests*
(1638 edition; first published before 1600).

environment of the Infernal Regions. Here the great clown's extemporary skills enable his ghost to triumph over one of the burning issues of
sixteenth-century theology, revising contemporary views of Hell to suit
his own requirements. The anonymous author of the book meets

Tarlton's ghost outside a theatre, and is seized at once by a religious scruple: he suspects the ghost of being some sort of devil, since every Protestant knows that the souls of the departed can't return to the earth before the Last Judgement, 'for either are they plast in heaven ... or else they are in hell'.[73] Tarlton is wholly untroubled by this assertion, in defence of which so many Protestant martyrs perished. Instead he willingly lends his support to the 'popes and holy bishops of Rome' who argue for the existence of a third place in the afterlife, Purgatory – thus reducing this key Catholic concept to the status of a fool's fantasy – and claims to have gone there after his death in search of the batch of amusing tales that follow.[74] Although the author 'could not but smile at the madde merrye doctrine of my freend Richard', there is something faintly disturbing about this easy dismissal of 'the sacred principles' of Calvinism in the interests of telling a few funny stories.[75] In his lifetime Tarlton may often have taken the part of the devilish Vice in the theatre, as a contemporary rhyme suggests ('Now Tarleton's dead, the consort lacks a vice'),[76] and his most celebrated work was the 'most deadly, but most lively playe' *The Seven Deadly Sins* (1585), a show dedicated to staging the full range of damnable offences against God's law.[77] *Tarlton's News out of Purgatory* unsettlingly suggests that the clown remains as much at ease with the damned, and with damnable doctrines, after death as he was when alive on stage. For some Elizabethans, Tarlton's death was not so very far removed from the death of that more famously self-destructive clown, Doctor Faustus.

The scent of sulphur and brimstone that clings to the ghost of Tarlton is a legacy both of his twin roles as fool and Vice, and of the demonizing of the theatre on the part of the anti-theatrical lobby. William Rankins's imagining of the Elizabethan theatre as an infernal masque of vices disguised as virtues recalls Tarlton's play on the Seven Deadly Sins; and Gosson's condemnation of comedy as devilish clearly had direct relevance to the most celebrated of Elizabethan comic actors. It comes as no surprise, then, when in Henry Chettle's pamphlet *Kind-Heart's Dream* (1593) Tarlton's ghost takes up the cudgels in defence of his former profession against its opponents. For Chettle's dead clown, the chief enemies of the theatre are money-grabbing brothel-keepers and the con-artists of the London underworld, who complain that players:

open our crosse-biting, our conny-catching, our traines, our traps, our gins, our snares, our subtilties: for no sooner have we a tricke of deceipt, but they make it common, singing Jigs, and making jeasts of us, that everie boy can point out our houses as they passe by.[78]

The cultivation of extemporary wit, the ghost implies, is a necessary means of keeping up with the irrepressible inventiveness of the urban criminal mind; but he adds that players, unlike criminals, are keenly aware of the need to watch the timing of their improvisations. 'Mirth in seasonable time taken', he piously proclaims,

is not forbidden by the austerest Sapients. But indeede there is a time of mirth, and a time of mourning. Which time having been by the Magistrats wisely observed, as well for the suppressing of Playes, as other pleasures: so likewise a time may come, when honest recreation shall have his former libertie.[79]

The problem is that the Elizabethan sense of comic timing relies on the violation of such chronological restraints, as all the great Elizabethan clowns knew very well. They knew, too, that it was easy enough to slip from petty violations of city regulations to very much more serious violations of the moral or divine order. When anti-theatrical polemicists compared the players to devils, they were merely applying to them in earnest a role that the comic players had embraced in jest. For the Elizabethans, jest is always turning to earnest and earnest to jest; timing is crucial for comedy, but time itself is out of the comedian's control; and this is what gives an uneasy edge to so many of the comic roles in early modern drama.

UNSTABLE MIXTURES

Like all Elizabethan playwrights, Shakespeare was thoroughly familiar with the anxieties old and new concerning comedy and the comic. Every text I have referred to in this introduction is one he could have known, and in many cases scholars have proved that he did know them. He would have learned about the turbulent history of comedy from his study of Horace, Donatus and Terence at school; and there, too, he would have discovered the rhetoric of laughter, which refuses to respect the boundaries of class. No playwright who began to write at the end of the 1580s could have ignored the case made against the theatre by Stephen Gosson and his imitators, or the various ways this case was being answered by the players and their defenders. Shakespeare knew and admired the novels and plays of John Lyly; and he was well acquainted with jest-books, decent and indecent, tame and out-rageous, from *A Hundred Merry Tales* to *Scoggin's Jests*.[80] He knew Dick Tarlton's reputation, and perhaps the man himself; and his many allusions to that devilish clown the Vice indicate that he was steeped in the English theatrical tradition in which the Vice was dominant. He contributed a significant passage to a play about the wit of Sir Thomas More and the death to which it brought him.[81] He had immersed himself, in fact, in the cultures of print and performance of the six-teenth century, and raided an astonishing variety of disparate texts and traditions, both native and continental, for material to be transmuted into his plays.[82]

We can assume, then, that Shakespeare thought long and hard about the nature of comedy. The intrusion of laughter into what are now known as his tragedies and histories is carefully calculated and pays thoughtful homage to a well-established practice of mixing genres on the sixteenth-century stage. And the seriousness of his comedies, their edgy flirtation with the stuff of tragedy, the sense of precarious-ness that pervades even their warmest moments – as if time is always monstrously straining against the efforts of wits and clowns to suspend it – is an inevitable product of the controversy that surrounded the genre in his own particular historic moment. Shakespeare's comedies do not really constitute a privileged space where the 'normal' rules do not apply, any more than the imaginative goods purveyed by the Elizabethan theatre could exist independently of the regulations that governed public performances in early modern London.[83] They sprang from his time, and official time – days, months and years enclosed by fences of numbers and names that have been sanctioned by the authorities and imposed on their subjects for the convenience of government – exerts its pressure on them, both explicitly and implicitly, from beginning to end. But there is also a sense in which these plays exert a counter-pressure on the apparatuses of control with which they are circumscribed. They were performed, complained the city authorities, at inappropriate times of the day and week; audiences were profoundly affected by them – or so their critics and defenders believed; and their performers moved with as much ease between different echelons of society as they did through the streets of the city itself, despite all the efforts of the urban authorities to restrict their movements. Elizabethan comedy interpenetrated the places dedicated to serious activities, just as it infused the serious theatrical genres from which it was theoretically debarred.

My contention in this book is that Shakespeare's comedies make drama out of the anti-comic crisis in early modern England. The 1570s and 1580s brought that crisis to a head, and these decades exerted a powerful pull on Shakespeare's imagination throughout his career. *Measure for Measure*, a Jacobean comedy, draws on Whetstone's tragicomic *Promos and Cassandra* (1578), whose preface defends the stage against its detractors; while one of the last plays he wrote, *The Winter's Tale*, is based on a novel of the 1580s by Robert Greene, *Pandosto: the Triumph of Time*, which ends with the decision of its protagonist to 'close up the comedy with a tragical stratagem' by committing suicide, instead of participating in the happy ending enjoyed by his friends and family.[84] In the two or three decades that preceded the start of Shakespeare's professional relationship with the stage, comedy's potential to become tragic – and conversely, tragedy's proximity to laughter – became a dominant theme of the English theatre. Richard Edwards addressed it in the first self-professed English tragicomedy, *Damon and Pythias* (1564–5), whose happy ending depends on a race against the clock; Marlowe made it the motif of his hysterical horror-shows *The Jew of Malta* and *Doctor Faustus*, whose protagonists play their ambitious pranks in defiance of a fast-approaching deadline. And for Shakespeare, the possibility of generic reversal remained the driving force of his drama: it is as evident in *The Tempest* as it is in *The Two Gentlemen of Verona*.[85] The possibility is lent urgency by his consciousness of the solid and extensive grounds on which his contemporaries constructed their hostility to comedy, and by his sense that only time divides the comic from the tragic, the horological equivalent of the mobile wall that divides the lovers in Peter Quince's production of *Pyramus and Thisbe*.

The book is divided into four long chapters, each focusing on an aspect of Shakespeare's comic theatre. In each chapter I have chosen to examine two or more plays one after the other, roughly in chronological order,[86] so that readers interested in a particular play will find most of what I have to say about it conveniently located in one place. The chronology of the chapters, on the other hand, as opposed to the plays within each chapter, is a little haphazard. A book that celebrates the eccentricities of Shakespeare's comic timing should not be too respectful of sequence and order. And the themes of the chapters, too, overlap with one another. The first chapter deals (among other things) with the centrality of violence to Shakespeare's early comic efforts; but violence is inevitably central to my discussions of many later plays. The second chapter concentrates on Shakespeare's comic language, but the other three chapters are just as preoccupied with language as this one. If the third takes love as its subject, this could hardly prevent love from occupying centre stage elsewhere; and the body, which presides over the fourth chapter, figures largely in its precursors. Each chapter breaches its own boundaries, slipping in and out of the thematic straitjacket imposed by its heading; and once again this seems appropriate in a book about the comic resistance to – and playful obsession with – many varieties of bondage.

As I said earlier, the bulk of my discussion of Shakespeare and comedy deals with the reign of Elizabeth I, although the Afterword considers the first of his Jacobean comedies, *Measure for Measure*, as a manifesto for his treatment of the genre in the reign of Elizabeth's successor. I do not stop where I do from any conviction that his Jacobean plays show a decisive break from what came earlier. Quite the reverse; as you read, I hope it will become clear that I see all his plays as in constant dialogue with what came before and what comes after. But a book has to end somewhere. Knowing when to stop is as difficult for a writer as for a clown, and a conclusion mistimed can be disastrous. What if *The Winter's Tale* had ended at the close of the third act, with Hermione dead and Perdita lost forever? But then again, as Yorick, Tarlton and *The Winter's Tale* all show us, few endings are absolute ones. There will always be more to say about Shakespeare and comedy – even after the longest and most comprehensive of treatises has drawn to a close, and the book has been shut and stowed away on a dusty shelf, to the accompaniment of gently mocking laughter.

Chapter One

COMIC MANIFESTOS

UNCIVIL WARS IN *THE TWO GENTLEMEN OF VERONA*

Mid-Elizabethan England was a paradise for clowns; there has never been a richer range of comic forms for them to play in. From faithful imitations of Roman New Comedy, bustling with twins, military braggarts and clever servants, to interludes full of moral and political allegories, presided over by a demonic Vice;[1] from Ovidian fantasies thronged with gods and transformations to rambling romances where knights do battle with monsters, magicians and each other;[2] from history plays stocked with aggressive comic heroes to apocalyptic social satires, in which commoners threaten to root corruption out of the state at every social level[3] – the Elizabethan public could indulge their appetite for comedy with a thousand varieties of comic plot, a thousand variations on the comic happy ending. And clowns were their heroes. The most celebrated players of the 1580s were clowns: Richard Tarlton and Robert Wilson. All performances, including tragedies, ended in jigs or song-and-dance numbers performed by one or more of the company comedians;[4] and even the greatest tragic actor of the following decade, Edward Alleyn – who played Tamburlaine and Faustus – was compared on one occasion to the greatest Roman *comic* actor, Roscius.[5] Any discussion of Shakespeare and comedy must begin with the acknowledgement that he inherited a theatrical tradition that was dominated, in all its hybrid kinds and monstrous metamorphoses, by laughter.[6]

The ideas about comedy presented in my introduction circulated through every permutation of Elizabethan comic practice. Attacks have been launched on theatrical laughter since before the days of Plato, and comedy has always found itself shaped by those attacks;[7] but the polemics of Gosson and his imitators offered an abundance of controversial new material, ideally suited for adaptation, transmutation and distortion on the Elizabethan stage. From the 1570s onwards, playwrights seemed to take a perverse pleasure in dramatizing Gosson's fears about the deleterious effects of comedy.[8] Shakespeare composed his early works at a time when comedy was at its most embattled and aggressive as well as at its most popular; and I shall be arguing in this chapter that aggression plays a key role in his first experiments with the comic. I shall also be arguing that each of his early plays constitutes a preliminary manifesto, a declaration of intent with regard to the theatre – and especially to comedy and laughter. In composing such manifestos he was working in a long-established English tradition, stretching from the interludes of John Redford in the 1530s to the plays of Nicholas Udall in the 1550s, Richard Edwards in the 1560s and George Gascoigne and George Whetstone in the 1570s.[9] For generations English comedy had been self-reflexive, prone to lapse into anxious meditations on its own practices. It is hardly surprising, then, if Shakespeare's first excursions into the comic mode seem to be marked, like those of his precursors, by an eagerness to establish his engagement with the old and new controversies that surrounded his chosen medium.

It is also hardly surprising if from the beginning he wrote tragicomedies rather than 'pure' comedies as Donatus defined them.[10] For Donatus comedies are plays about the middle and lower classes, in which nothing very dangerous or shocking ever happens and every problem finds an ultimate solution. *The Two Gentlemen of Verona* and *The Comedy of Errors* display their comic credentials in their stress on wordplay, disguise, confusion, a happy ending; but dukes head their cast lists, terror and grief are included in their spectrum of emotions, and rape, death and even damnation are never entirely dismissed from the range of possible outcomes for the events they set in motion. They inhabit a world that is recognizably related to that of Shakespeare's early histories: a world where civil war is always breaking out between the sexes, between generations, between relatives and friends, and between one dramatic genre and another, as the comic and the tragic compete with one another for ascendancy over each successive situation. Even the breeziest of his early works, *The Taming of the Shrew*, has this element of civil war in its composition, together with an ever-present threat of violence that seems to spring directly from its engagement with Gossonian anti-theatrical paranoia. In his first experiments with comedy Shakespeare represents it as forever on the verge of violating its own comic status, reproducing in Elizabethan times the ungovernable waywardness of its long history.[11]

The Two Gentlemen of Verona, for instance, is very nearly a tragedy of love, the ebullient forebear of *Romeo and Juliet*. The links between the two plays are many.[12] The main characters in both hail from the same Italian city; one of the heroines of *Two Gentlemen* has a name that recalls Romeo's sweetheart; while the other is promised, like Juliet, to a man she does not love, and goes to dangerous lengths to escape the unwanted marriage. Like Juliet, Silvia's first port of call in her flight is the cell of a friar, where she arranges to meet a friend before running away from home. Meanwhile the man she loves is condemned, like Romeo, to an exile he thinks worse than death. But these similarities of plot are not, perhaps, so striking as certain *thematic* similarities between the two plays. In both, a general failure of communication among the characters is marked by the frequency with which letters are misread or go astray. And in both there is a sharp division between the social spaces occupied by men and by women: a division that manifests itself at crucial moments in sudden outbreaks of male violence, periodic reminders of the unnerving proximity of comic civility to tragic barbarism.

The Two Gentlemen of Verona is, in fact, the first of many Shakespearean plays to confront the gulf between the genders in early modern Europe: a gulf that is central to the controversy over comedy, since Gosson claimed that comedy could close it – to the detriment of its auditors, as he thought. The gulf is established in the opening scene, which pits the feminine private sphere of love against the masculine sphere of public action. Two male friends, Valentine and Proteus, commit themselves to two contrasting ways of life: Valentine sets off to serve the Duke of Milan in court and in combat, while Proteus loiters 'sluggardis'd at home', cultivating the 'shapeless idleness' imposed on him by his infatuation with Julia (1.1.7–8). Despite this physical parting of the ways, the men are in perfect agreement as to which of them has made the better choice. Valentine regards Proteus's 'fond desire' for Julia as an utter waste of time (1.1.52), and Proteus concurs whole-heartedly with his friend's opinion. 'Thou, Julia', he soliloquizes,

> thou hast metamorphos'd me,
> Made me neglect my studies, lose my time,
> War with good counsel, set the world at nought;
> Made wit with musing weak, heart sick with thought.
>
> (1.1.66–9)

Gosson and his colleagues would have nodded in sardonic agreement. Women feminize men, and this feminizing process is precisely the topic of, and rendered attractive by, comedies like the one we are watching.

But Proteus's name should alert us to the fact that he needs no woman's help either to 'metamorphose' him or to make him sexually suspect. It is the name of a horny classical sea-god who could alter shape at will and had (in some texts) a boundless appetite for rape;[13] so it is only to be expected that the verbal shapeshifting of Shakespeare's Proteus should lead him inexorably from indolence to sexual assault. The young man first manifests his metamorphic abilities when his father sends him after Valentine to serve the Duke of Milan. Proteus promptly falls in love for a second time – this time with Silvia, daughter to the Duke and Valentine's fiancée. Once again Proteus knows that he is wrong to give rein to his passion; and once again he persuades him-self to do it, this time through a spectacular feat of sophistry, whereby he demonstrates to his own satisfaction that this sudden shift in loyal-ties is really a supreme display of loyalty. After all, he argues, he has remained true both to love and to friendship; he has simply changed the *objects* of his affections in both cases. Where first he loved Julia, he now loves a more 'precious' object, Silvia; and where at first his friendship was committed to Valentine, it is now devoted wholly to himself ('I to myself am dearer than a friend') – as well as to Silvia, who is a 'sweeter friend' than Valentine (2.6.23–30). In the course of this chain of false reasoning, Proteus converts Valentine from his best friend to his enemy

(2.6.29), and Julia from his lover to nothing at all (2.6.27–8). Which makes it easy, at a later stage, for the young man to pull off yet another treacherous volte-face, when he decides that Silvia's father the Duke is now his best friend, and that this justifies him in his efforts to make Silvia forget Valentine, of whom the Duke does not approve.[14] Proteus may be modelled on the notorious hero of John Lyly's first novel, *Euphues*; but not even Euphues could have executed so many immoral manoeuvres in such a narrow space.[15]

The secret of Proteus's success in the art of self-persuasion lies in his mastery of the pun: his capacity to make a single word – such as 'friend' or 'faith' – take on any sense he chooses. It is a skill that finds its most disturbing manifestation in the final scene, after he has saved Silvia from a would-be rapist. At once he sets about wooing her for himself; and when she begs him to stop he tries in his turn to rape her, switching from friend to enemy, from rescuer to ravisher in an instant:

> Nay, if the gentle spirit of moving words
> Can no way change you to a milder form,
> I'll woo you like a soldier, at arm's end,
> And love you 'gainst the nature of love: force ye.
>
> (5.4.55–8)

Here Proteus's slipperiness might convince an enemy of the theatre that he has been feminized by love – that his masculine constancy has been supplanted by female mutability as a result of his surrender to a womanly emotion. But in fact the speech identifies the *refusal* to change as the chief characteristic of women, while the ability to love 'against the nature of love' – that is, to reverse the sense of a word on a whim – is specifically masculine, something that shows Proteus to be 'like a soldier'. And the speech also implies that men are constitutionally incapable of hearing objections to their own 'moving words'. Silvia's near-rape is the natural culmination of the male attitude to women's language in this play, an attitude summed up by the glibbest of couplets: 'Take no repulse, whatever she doth say, / For "Get you gone" she doth not mean "Away!" ' (3.1.100–1). Men are not only capable of inverting the significance of their own utterances, but also those of the women they court; and in inverting the meaning of women's words they effectively erase them. Under these conditions, rape or betrayal might be the outcome of any sentence uttered by either sex, no matter how bland. In this play the comic mode is as dangerous as the anti-theatrical lobbyists said it was, and the two near-rapes that take place in its final scene are a measure of its capacity to work a deadly metamorphosis.

One would expect Proteus's contempt for women to be counterbalanced by the other male lover in the play, who has the promising name of Valentine; but as it turns out, his attitude is not much better. At first dismissive of love, Valentine undergoes the customary conversion at the beginning of Act 2 ('you are metamorphosed with a mistress', says his servant Speed (2.1.29–30)), and for the rest of the play he is the most conventional of lovers – a Romeo stuck in the Rosaline phase, as it were, speaking as though he had swallowed an instruction manual for Elizabethan suitors. Unlike Romeo, however, he seems a good deal more interested in putting down his male rivals than in courting his mistress. He derides her suitor Thurio for his dullness (2.4.14ff.), and praises Silvia so extravagantly at the expense of Julia that he arouses envy and desire in Julia's lover Proteus. At the same time, despite his praise for Silvia, Valentine is capable of parroting the worst excesses of early modern misogyny. When Silvia's father asks his advice on how best to court a woman nowadays, Valentine's advice – delivered once again in the manner of an instruction manual – displays a contempt for women quite as offensive as his friend's. It is he, not Proteus, who tells the Duke to 'Take no repulse, whatever she doth say', and the rest of the speech is equally objectionable:

> A woman sometime scorns what best contents her . . .
> If she do chide, 'tis not to have you gone,
> For why, the fools are mad, if left alone . . .
> Flatter, and praise, commend, extol their graces;
> Though ne'er so black, say they have angels' faces;
> That man that hath a tongue, I say is no man,
> If with his tongue he cannot win a woman.
>
> (3.1.93–105)

In the final couplet, women are reduced to just another test of a man's mettle, one of several means by which he can competitively assert his

FIGURE 3   Crispin van der Broeck, (1524–c. 1590), 'Two Young Men'.
They exchange an apple as casually as the two gentlemen of Verona propose to
exchange a woman, Silvia.

dominance over his fellow males. This is Valentine's priority just as it is
that of Proteus, and leads inexorably to the most controversial moment
in the play, when he gives Silvia away to mark the restitution of the
bond of friendship between the two gentlemen of the play's title.

Valentine's interest in asserting his own manhood emerges yet again
shortly before this moment. Driven into exile after his plan to elope with
the Duke's daughter has been discovered, Valentine wanders into a
forest, where he meets a gang of outlaws who have been banished like
himself. His fellow exiles are so impressed by his appearance ('he is a
proper man', they tell each other (4.1.10)) and violent past (he informs
them, quite untruthfully, that he was banished for killing a man 'man-
fully, in fight' (4.1.28)) that they make him their leader. Valentine's ability to lie his way into favour with the outlaws – turning them from
enemies into friends – links him once more to Proteus. So it is not
altogether unexpected when in the final scene, after Proteus has con-
fessed all his various acts of treason to Valentine and asked forgiveness
for them, Valentine immediately forgives him, transforming his enemy

back into his friend again. All the same, when Valentine goes on to seal their new alliance by offering him Silvia – the woman Proteus has just tried to rape, and who has been unwaveringly true to Valentine – an Elizabethan audience might well have been just as shocked as any modern theatre-goer. There could be no cruder or more humiliating demonstration than this of the low status of women in the two men's minds; they are goods to be bartered, possessions to be acquired, gifts to be exchanged in order to strengthen bonds with other men, and nothing more. And if we needed further proof of their status as commodities among Italian males, it comes when Silvia is given away for a second time in the very same scene. Her father the Duke of Milan arrives in the company of her fiancé Thurio, whose claim to Silvia the Duke supports. But Thurio is so terrified by Valentine's threats against him that he disclaims all interest in her, and the Duke is so disgusted by this display of unmanliness that he cancels Thurio's engagement to his daughter and gives her to Valentine instead (5.4.119ff.). This second unceremonious handing over of Silvia is only less shocking than the first because Valentine happens to be the man she loves. But we are clearly in a world where friendship with men is the thing men prize most highly (although they are often prepared to change the object of their friendship), and where men's relationships with women are so casual as to be laughable.

What, then, of the women in the play, whose lovers hardly seem able to keep them in mind from one scene to the next? From a Gossonian point of view, they seem fully to justify the men's misogyny. Sex-obsessed, contemptuous of authority, and exerting an enfeebling influence over anyone who becomes entangled with them, they embody all the theatre-haters' objections to comedy. One heroine, Julia, indulges in cross-dressing, as if to illustrate women's capacity to dissolve the barriers between the sexes; the other, Silvia, flees her father's house, thus illustrating the fundamental unruliness of her gender. But there is one thing in this comedy that sets women on a vastly higher moral plane than their male admirers. Men change their inward allegiances while proclaiming their constancy to a gullible outside world; women change their outward appearance while remaining inwardly constant. Men preserve the outward form of words while altering the meaning of words at will; women will make any outward changes necessary in order to preserve their inward faith and integrity. The play, then, mounts a stalwart defence of women at men's expense; and in doing so it mounts a defence of the comic mode to which women were allied by Elizabethan culture.

Of the two heroines, it is Julia who makes the distinction between the genders most apparent. Throughout the play she is fully conscious that her actions will be condemned by a world hostile to women, a world with so narrow a view of women's virtue that it allows them no chance for the active pursuit of desire. When we first meet Julia, she is looking for a way to read a letter from her lover Proteus without incurring the suspicion of sexual 'lightness' (1.2.41ff.).[16] Half-way through the scene she comments in a kind of laughing despair on the absurd lengths to which she has been driven by the need to seem conventionally chaste ('How angerly I taught my brow to frown, / When inward joy enforc'd my heart to smile' (1.2.62–3)). Finally, having torn the letter to shreds to reinforce her protestations of chastity, she gratifies her desire for Proteus by pressing fragments of the letter together in a simulated sexual act:

> Lo, here in one line is his name twice writ:
> 'Poor forlorn Proteus', 'passionate Proteus'.
> 'To the sweet Julia': that I'll tear away.
> And yet I will not, sith so prettily
> He couples it to his complaining names.
> Thus will I fold them, one upon another:
> Now kiss, embrace, contend, do what you will.
>
> (1.2.124–30)

Elizabethan misogynists and anti-dramatists alike would have pounced on this moment as proof of the forbidden passions aroused by women and the theatre. The miniature drama Julia stages with the help of the fragments of Proteus's letter is quite as erotic as the anti-theatrical lobby would have expected. But Julia is fully and touchingly aware of the way her actions will be judged. She knows that she is in a no-win situation, loving in truth but deprived by her culture of the means to show her love without resorting to fictions – especially dramatic fictions. And this dilemma is still more touchingly caught in the scene where she dons a boy's disguise in order to follow Proteus to Milan.

The scene begins with Julia declaring her intention to follow Proteus despite all advice to the contrary. She compares herself to a stream that wends its way 'With willing sport to the wild ocean' (2.7.32); and her simile articulates three things at once: joyful anticipation of her reunion with her lover; contempt for the way her journey will be seen by her enemies (who will dismiss it as nothing more than irresponsible 'sport'); and a subconscious knowledge of her lover's character ('wild ocean' invokes the predatory sea-god Proteus from whom the young man takes his name and nature). Clearly, Julia's decision to change her clothes is not unmixed with anxiety; yet she sees no better means of satisfying her desire. 'tell me, wench', she asks her friend Lucetta, 'how will the world repute me / For undertaking so unstaid a journey? / I fear me it will make me scandalis'd' (2.7.59–61). 'If you think so', Lucetta replies, 'then stay at home'; and when Julia refuses to stay, her friend concludes:

> Then never dream on infamy, but go.
> If Proteus like your journey, when you come,
> No matter who's displeas'd, when you are gone.
>
> (2.7.64–6)

For Lucetta, the motive behind Julia's disguise is what matters; if the 'world' chooses to see it as scandalous, this has nothing to do with Julia. She wishes only to show her commitment to her lover; and if she can only do this by breaking the Elizabethan dress code, her good ends must justify the compromising means by which she attains them.

Shakespeare seems to be suggesting, in fact, that disguise of the sort encouraged by the theatre can be a means of investing things with their proper value. The world is inclined to dismiss Julia's desire for her young man as fleeting, immodest, worthless; she believes it to be permanent and precious; and her playing of a boy expresses this belief. Later, when in boy's disguise she comes across Proteus singing a love-sonnet to Silvia, she gives her opinion of his performance: 'I would always have one play but one thing' (4.2.69). And later still, when Proteus sends her – still disguised as a boy – to woo Silvia on his behalf, she develops this preliminary statement into what is effectively a full-blown theory of the theatre. At one point during the scene, Silvia asks the supposed boy whether he knows Julia, the fiancée whom Proteus has abandoned. This prompts the inevitable answer: 'Almost as well as I do know myself' (4.4.140); and when Silvia asks, 'How tall was she?' the boy replies that she is about his height (4.4.154–5). He knows this, he says, because he once borrowed her gown to act the part of a woman in a play:

> Madam, 'twas Ariadne, passioning
> For Theseus' perjury, and unjust flight;
> Which I so lively acted with my tears,
> That my poor mistress, moved therewithal,
> Wept bitterly; and would I might be dead,
> If I in thought felt not her very sorrow
>
> (4.4.164–9)

Like the earlier comparison of Julia to a stream seeking the ocean, this passage works on many levels. The performance described never took place; its description, then, is itself a performance. Yet the situation in this imaginary play – a woman's abandonment by her lover – reflects the current experience of its inventor, Julia. And the imagined performance also reflects the current 'lively' performance of the boy-actor playing Julia. So there are several elements of truth in Julia's fiction. Above all there is a wonderful accuracy to the statement that the boy-actor drew tears from his 'poor mistress', which in turn made him feel her 'very sorrow', since the fictional boy-actor in the play, the mistress he describes, and the real boy-actor who plays this scene are all one and the same person, sharing the same emotion. In this passage, then, performer and audience are as emotionally attuned as the anti-theatrical lobby said they were. Boy-actor and woman-audience weep for one another in a competitive exchange of sympathy that makes them more or less indistinguishable – although their competition is of a very different kind from the aggressive sort that motivates men. The passage implies that drama and life are so closely bound up with one another that when a play is 'lively acted' it effectively comes alive: it moves and breathes and weeps with the same organs, and for the same causes, as the fictional persons it depicts. This, perhaps, is what Julia meant when she said 'I would always have one play but one thing': one thing, in this case 'very sorrow', being brought into existence and shared by virtue of a player's commitment and mimetic skill. Shakespeare never wrote a more complex analysis of the relationship between actor, audience and dramatic spectacle than this one.

As with the earlier scenes involving Julia, there will clearly be at least two reactions to this revelation of the extent to which drama can participate in life. The anti-theatrical, anti-feminist lobby will be horrified by it, since it depends for its effectiveness and wit on our awareness that the sexes are being richly confused with one another. Supporters of the theatre, on the other hand, will see it as demonstrating drama's capacity to overcome faithlessness, a condition that Valentine describes in the final scene as 'common' in contemporary friendships (5.4.62–3). The latter will note, perhaps, that the imaginary play described by Shakespeare's heroine is a tragedy: a sign of her fundamental seriousness, despite the comic genre in which she finds herself. The former will find their fears cheekily confirmed a little later in the same scene, when the boy-actor expresses his envy of Silvia's picture for the desire its subject has aroused in his master, and boasts of his own ability to make himself as attractive to men as she is. '[L]et me see', he tells himself, looking at the portrait, 'I think / If I had such a tire, this face of mine / Were full as lovely as is this of hers' (4.4.181–3). But in the end, it is those who see Julia's transvestism as a vindication of drama whose perspective seems to be borne out by the play's conclusion.

In the final scene, at the very moment when Valentine gives Silvia to Proteus – the moment that most horrifies modern commentators, and which I have suggested would have horrified Elizabethan audiences likewise – the boy-Julia collapses. He then reveals his identity as Julia, and launches into an explanation of Julia's actions that lays responsibility for them squarely at the feet of treacherous men:

> Behold her that gave aim to all thy oaths,
> And entertain'd 'em deeply in her heart.
> How oft hast thou with perjury cleft the root!
> O Proteus, let this habit make thee blush.
> Be thou asham'd that I have took upon me
> Such an immodest raiment . . .
> It is the lesser blot modesty finds,
> Women to change their shapes, than men their minds.

(5.4.100–8)

Here Julia states unequivocally that her performance as a boy is her way of keeping faith with Proteus's broken oaths: of keeping them alive inwardly, 'in her heart', waiting for the moment when his words can be reunited with their proper meanings, signifiers restored to what they signify. The implication is that drama is a form that nurtures faith (in the sense of mutual trust) in a faithless age, and that attacks on its disguises and 'immodest raiment' are misdirected. These attacks would be better aimed at the changing minds of men like Proteus, whose inconstancy Valentine identifies as the chief defect of the 'time most accurst' in which the play takes place (5.4.71). Theatre defies the curse of the time, restoring what has been rendered double to oneness: the last line of the play celebrates the reunion of the erring characters in 'One feast, one house, one mutual happiness' (5.4.171).

This ending is not, however, as satisfying as my last paragraph makes it sound; and this is largely because of the gulf that has opened up between the sexes in the course of the play. It is difficult to imagine a self-satisfied idiot like Valentine or Proteus settling down in perpetuity with a witty woman like Julia. The men's attitude has been remorselessly parodied by the play's clowns, Launce and Speed, whose names articulate a male lover's agenda: to achieve lance-like penetration as speedily as possible. At one point Launce lists the positive and negative qualities of his own mistress, a milk-maid, reducing her to an inventory of miscellaneous objects whose worth he must carefully calculate before deciding whether she is a 'match' for him (3.1.261ff.). The deciding factor in the list is her wealth; without this, one cannot imagine the disparate items on Launce's list ever getting put together in his head to form a coherent sense of her as a person. Valentine seems equally incapable of keeping an idea of Silvia in his head; in exile he seems afraid that he will forget all about her if they remain apart for too long (5.4.7–12). Proteus's perspective on women is crude enough for him to fall in love at first sight with Silvia's 'picture', as he calls it – her outward appearance, before he has engaged her in more than a line or two of dialogue (2.4.209). The women in the play, on the other hand, have a hearty contempt for the hackneyed views of them held by men. They cross-dress, go travelling, and defy authority, and in doing so they show up the shallowness of the assumptions made about their gender by the anti-theatrical lobby as well as by Proteus and Valentine. Shakespeare's comedy refuses, in fact, to essentialize women, as his men are always trying to do. The term 'woman', it seems, is as flexible, as contingent and as indefinable for him as the term 'comedy'. From time to time in his plays one even gets the sense that the two terms are interdependent, operating as mutually supportive agents in a sustained dramatic assault on male complacency, a perverse reformation unlike anything imagined by either the assailants or the champions of the early modern theatre. But the validity of such a claim must be tested by reading all his comedies, not just one.

SHAKESPEARE'S JEST-BOOK: *THE TAMING OF THE SHREW*

The early plays do not, of course, liberate women from the constraints of Elizabethan patriarchy. Instead they demonstrate the extent to which contemporary anti-feminism, as represented by the attacks on the 'feminizing' effect of the theatre, is governed by convention, as well as the arbitrary nature of the conventions by which it is governed. The most extraordinary of Shakespeare's early exposures of these conventions is the Induction to *The Taming of the Shrew*, a miniature self-enclosed comedy that anatomizes the Elizabethan views on comedy and on women that shape the main body of the play.

In the Induction, an unnamed lord changes places with a tinker in the interests of providing himself with 'sport' (Ind. 1.90). On finding the tinker in a drunken sleep, the lord instructs his servants to dress the sleeper in fine clothes and tell him when he wakes that he has been suffering from delusions for fifteen years, thinking himself a pauper when he has the income of a prince. Now that he has recovered his health, the tinker can finally resume his rightful place in society, with a beautiful wife (played by a page), luxurious possessions, and expensive forms of entertainment at his beck and call. The lord's trick embodies a range of Gossonian anxieties about comedy: its ability to violate the social order by making lords of commoners and women of boys; its delight in sexually arousing its participants – audience and actors alike;

and its blurring of the borders between the real and the imagined. But the trick also shows how the comic theatre shapes itself from fantasies and forms of role-playing that are already endemic in Elizabethan culture. Illusions dominate the minds of men, and Shakespeare's comedy does not generate these illusions so much as open up their operations to the delighted inspection of audiences who have often succumbed to them.

Long before the jest gets under way, Christopher Sly the tinker has had fixed ideas about the lives of the aristocracy. At the beginning of the Induction he lays claim to noble ancestry (the Slys, he says, 'came in with Richard Conqueror' (Ind. 1.4)) and makes allusions to the most aristocratic of theatrical genres, tragedy (he misquotes lines from Kyd's hugely successful play *The Spanish Tragedy* (1589) (Ind. 1.5–9)).[17] His transformation into a lord does not so much take him by surprise as confirm what he has always suspected: that he is a man of equal worth to any member of the ruling classes. After a brief investigation into the state of his faculties ('I do not sleep. I see, I hear, I speak. / I smell sweet savours and I feel soft things. / Upon my life, I am a lord indeed' (Ind. 2.74–6)) he accepts his new circumstances without demur, and sets about playing his part with 'grace' (Ind. 1.130). Sly uses blank verse as readily as any professional improviser and behaves with courtesy to everyone he meets, promising rewards to his faithful servants and seeking the lord's advice as to the polite form of address for his wife. And his treatment of his wife is thoroughly decent. He is astonished that she should call him 'lord' as if she were a servant, and suggests she should say 'husband' or 'goodman' instead (Ind. 2.108–9). He agrees promptly to her request that they defer having sex until he is fully restored to health; and he urges her to sit beside him as his equal during the performance of *The Taming of the Shrew* that follows the Induction. As we watch, it becomes increasingly difficult to reconcile his dignity with the Lord's initial assessment of him as a 'monstrous beast' (Ind. 1.33). Instead, he seems to confirm the existence of a natural courtesy that goes beyond class, making the trappings of power more or less incidental. Shakespeare's clowns have a genius for such levelling performances, from Bottom in *A Midsummer Night's Dream*, who is unphased by his transformation into the paramour of the Fairy Queen, to the Shepherd in *The Winter's Tale*, who discovers at the end of the play that he has always been a gentleman born, despite his humble birth. There is nothing about Sly's behaviour in the Induction to justify the views of the anti-theatrical lobby that comedy's dissolution of class boundaries must lead inevitably to violence, bestiality and social collapse. Instead it suggests that class boundaries are loose ones, determined not by natural differences between one man and another but by the question of whether or not one has the material means to put one's fantasies into action.

This view seems to be confirmed by the fact that the Lord is as inveterate a fantasist as Sly is. Indeed, it is the Lord rather than Sly who seems to embody the fears of the anti-theatrical lobby. He has a special predilection for erotic fantasies, possessing a range of 'wanton pictures' based on ancient myths (Ind. 1.46), with a couch 'Softer and sweeter than the lustful bed / On purpose trimm'd up for Semiramis' from which to view them (Ind. 2.42–3).[18] And he is a connoisseur of erotic theatre. When a troupe of travelling players comes to his house, he remembers one of them chiefly for his performance as the suitor in a romantic comedy; and later he gives detailed instructions to his page on how to mimic the seductive behaviour of ladies (he should greet Sly 'with kind embracements, tempting kisses, / And with declining head into his bosom' (Ind. 1.117–18)). Moreover, the basis of these instructions would seem to be the Lord's imagination. He commands the boy to imitate 'honourable action, / Such as he hath observ'd in noble ladies' (Ind. 1.109–10); but there are no ladies to observe in the Lord's household. His establishment is exclusively male, so that his confidence that the boy 'will well usurp the grace, / Voice, gait, and action of a gentlewoman' presupposes that female characteristics may be acquired by men without any direct input from the opposite sex (Ind. 1.130–1). In other words, men are more interested in their own fantasies of women than in the voices or actions of women themselves. Which is exactly what we deduce from the play that follows – together with the difficulty of sustaining these fantasies through a period of prolonged and intimate acquaintance with their eloquent subjects.

It is of course the Lord who takes control of – and assumes a central role in – the comic fantasy in which Sly unwittingly participates; and it is he who commissions the players to act a comedy for Sly, *The Taming of the Shrew*. But in each case he seems anxious that the 'sport' he instigates may get out of hand. When planning the prank to be played on Sly, the Lord says: 'It will be pastime passing excellent, / If it be husbanded with modesty' (Ind. 1.66–7); and his advice to the players is to avoid going to extremes in their performance:

> But I am doubtful of your modesties,
> Lest over-eyeing of his odd behaviour–
> For yet his honour never heard a play–
> You break into some merry passion
> And so offend him.
>
> (Ind. 1.93–7)

Later, the Lord hopes that his participation in the performance will prevent the comedy from turning ugly: 'Haply my presence / May well abate the over-merry spleen / Which otherwise would grow into extremes' (Ind. 1.135–7). The classical historians of comedy are all agreed that it is prone to excess: the Lord is concerned to ensure that it keeps within the bounds of legitimacy, never disintegrating into discourtesy or obscenity. His protectiveness presumably springs from the sense that decorous behaviour preserves the distinctions between classes that he is temporarily choosing to overthrow, distinctions that it is in his interest to reinstate when the game is over.

But the Lord's anxieties about comic excess seem to be misplaced in this instance. Sly is as keen as he is to keep things modest and orderly. When advised by his supposed wife that sex is not good for his condition, he consents to 'tarry in despite of the flesh and the blood' before sleeping with her (Ind. 2.131). He needs no lessons in good conduct from his Lordship; and neither do the actors who present him with the comedy of Petruchio and Katherina. Like most Elizabethan players, this troupe is fully aware of the history and theory of their profession, especially of stage comedy. According to the Greek physician Hippocrates, as cited by his Renaissance followers such as Laurent Joubert and Andrew Borde, laughter serves to purge the body of its excess humours: humours being the four elements of which the body is composed, which must be kept in perfect equilibrium if a person's health is to be maintained.[19] The messenger who announces the 'pleasant comedy' to be shown by the troupe tells Sly that his doctors have prescribed it in order to 'frame your mind to mirth and merriment, / Which bars a thousand harms and lengthens life' (Ind. 2.138–9). *The Taming of the Shrew*, then, is an energetic substitute for sex, helping Sly to defer it with delight rather than to whip himself up into a sexual frenzy as the theatre-haters would have expected. The play can be read as a witty demonstration of comedy's health-giving properties, illustrating them through its account of a woman, Katherina Baptista, who undergoes comic shock-treatment at the hands of her husband in order to cure her of an excess of choler (the humour that causes anger). Part of her treatment is the denial of sex and food; so that despite the obsession with sex displayed by the men in the play, the comedy protects itself from the charge of promoting lewdness by depicting the determined *suppression* of both male and female bodily appetites. The players who present it would seem, then, to be more practised in the art of moderating their performance than their aristocratic patron, with his penchant for pornography and his Assyrian 'lustful couch'.

The professional expertise of the players raises a question: if the *Shrew* is intended as therapy, at whom is it directed? The play's audience consists of a tinker disguised as a lord and a lord disguised as a servant, and either or both could be its intended patients; but will they both derive equal benefit from the life-extending mirth it brings? The tinker does not seem to enjoy the performance much (he starts to drop off after the first scene), but he approaches it in exactly the right frame of mind. On his tongue the term 'comedy' becomes a statement of egalitarianism, combining with the word 'common' to create a 'comonty' (Ind. 2.140); and he settles down to enjoy this new form of entertainment in defiance of more serious demands on his time ('let the world slip, we shall ne'er be younger' (Ind. 2.145)). Sly, then, is a cheerful soul, unlikely to be much afflicted with melancholia, the disease for which laughter is most often prescribed.[20] The Lord, on the other hand, seems a prime candidate for acute depression. His first thought when he sees Sly in a drunken sleep is 'Grim death, how foul and loathsome is thine image' (Ind. 1.34). And his solitary life as a bachelor, his tendency to lapse into soliloquies and his passion for the theatre, all link him to a far more famous melancholic, Hamlet. Sly's attitude, by contrast, allies him with the commoners who perform the comedy, and with the play's irrepressible protagonist Petruchio. The tinker's metamorphosis, too, is echoed by the many transformations in the *Shrew*, where the servant Tranio becomes his wealthy master while a brace of rich young men become poor teachers to get close to the woman they love. The *Shrew*, then, is Sly's element, however little he may appreciate being immersed in it; whereas the Lord looks comparatively distant from its universe, with his desire for control, his contempt for the lower orders and his quest for exotic modes of self-stimulation. The play's therapy seems more urgently required by the unhappy ruling classes than by the commoners who apply it.

Comedy was said to promote a healthy mind as well as a healthy body: the plays of Plautus and Terence were taught in schools as treasuries of good Latin and even good manners, although sometimes in bowdlerized form, stripped of their erotic elements.[21] Accordingly, the *Shrew* presents itself as a kind of comic schoolroom as well as an alternative health clinic. The action begins in Padua, home to the most celebrated medical school in Europe; and the first character we meet, the wealthy heir Lucentio, announces that he has travelled there with the aim of finishing his education. But although his courtship of Katherina's sister Bianca begins as a wholesome diversion from his studies (as his servant Tranio says, 'No profit grows where is no pleasure ta'en' (1.1.39)), it ends as the whole focus of his attention. The notion of schooling dominates the play, from the lessons in love given to Bianca by Lucentio and Hortensio, who disguise themselves as teachers to gain access to her, to the so-called 'taming school' set up by Petruchio (4.2.55), which claims to give men practical instruction in the art of controlling recalcitrant women. But the education provided by this comedy turns out, in the end, to compete with rather than to complement the formal education provided at Padua for the sons of the wealthy.[22] And this is nowhere more obvious than in the controversial ending, which has proved such a bitter pill for modern audiences to swallow.

In recent years the focus of the comedy has inevitably been Katherina's notorious speech in Act 5, where she recites by rote the

lesson she has had drummed into her in the course of the play. It is a
lesson that could only be applauded by the moralists who railed against
comedy: a paean to patriarchy political and domestic, comparing a
woman's place in the home to a commoner's place in a kingdom:

> Such duty as the subject owes the prince
> Even such a woman oweth to her husband.
> And when she is froward, peevish, sullen, sour,
> And not obedient to his honest will,
> What is she but a foul contending rebel,
> And graceless traitor to her loving lord?
>
> (5.2.156–61)

Gosson's acolytes viewing the *Shrew* could have concluded from this
speech, as some critics have concluded since, that Shakespeare is a
safely conservative thinker, committed to the reformation of the stage
promised by playwrights throughout the 1580s in response to the anti-
theatrical campaign. The Lord in the Induction could have approved of
it too, avowing as it does the futility of seeking 'rule, supremacy and
sway' when you are not born to them. Even Sly could have heard it with
relish; in an anonymous imitation of Shakespeare's play, *The Taming of a
Shrew* (1594), he leaves the Lord's house at the end of the performance
determined to teach his own wife the same lesson.[23] In this speech, in
fact, Katherina articulates the ultimate fantasy of male power, a kind of
moral pornography for patriarchs, the verbal equivalent of the Lord's
dirty pictures.

But the speech is by no means simple to interpret. For one thing, its
lexicon is suspect. By the time he wrote it Shakespeare had probably
already won fame for his depiction of 'foul contending rebels' like Jack
Cade; and in his epic account of the English civil wars now known as
the First Tetralogy, the relationship of king to subject is highly unstable,
so that the terms employed in Katherina's speech (obedience, honesty,
treachery, subject, king) are all hotly contested sites, appropriated by
competing factions for opposing ends. For another thing, the *Shrew* itself
up to this point has repeatedly shown how easy it is to construct and
demolish male fantasies like this one. In the Induction we witnessed the
ready substitution of one 'loving lord' for another, and the construction

of a seemingly obedient wife from an obedient boy. And throughout the *Shrew* itself, women have freely either pandered to or punctured men's perceptions of them according to the whim of the passing moment, as Lucentio knows better than anyone else from his experience with Bianca. Lucentio speaks, then, for most of the men in the cast when he responds to Katherina's speech with scepticism: ''Tis a wonder, by your leave, she will be tam'd so' (5.2.190). The context of her disquisition on female obedience warns him not to take it at face value. And the man who provided him with this lesson in wariness is Katherina's self-appointed tutor and the founder of a distinctly non-Paduan 'taming school': Petruchio of Verona.

It is Petruchio who gives the *Shrew* its wildness, transforming it from a tame 'new' comedy to yet another embodiment of the fears of the anti-theatrical lobby. The methods of his taming school derive not from classical drama but from the tradition of the jest-book, in which the wit of the ruling classes and the learned men who serve them is more than matched by the wit of clowns and women.[24] In his household, as in the jest-books, there is a constant comic skirmishing between the classes, with the insubordinate humour of servants pitted against the ineffectual blows of their employers. The first time we see him, Petruchio is engaged in a war of words with his servant Grumio, a much less accommodating subordinate than Lucentio's servant Tranio; and although throughout the 'taming' of Katherina Grumio aids and abets his master, this preliminary scene establishes his cooperation as both voluntary and contingent, capable of being withdrawn whenever he pleases. Under these conditions, Katherina's absorption into Petruchio's chaotic ménage may not be the capitulation it seems: her cooperation, too, may be contingent. And the instruction offered in this wayward jest-book setting – the instruction that inculcates in Katherina the principles she enunciates in her final speech – exposes those principles as elaborate shams, 'flatt'ring dream[s] or worthless fanc[ies]' like the illusion that Sly is a lord (Ind. 1.43), or the dream of 'love in idleness' that engulfs Lucentio when he first sets eyes on Bianca (1.1.150). Petruchio's household may look like a patriarchal paradise, but it is a seedy, unstable one that – like the spontaneous wit that fills it – may change its character in an instant.

For these reasons, Petruchio's tuition is disturbing not just to modern sensibilities, but to the men and women who comment on it in the course of the play. His behaviour always borders on madness – the kind of excess that the Lord in the Induction was so anxious to avert. The threat of violence underpins his words and actions, and men as well as women view his antics with alarm, afraid that they may overthrow not just petty social conventions but entire moral systems. By the end of Act 3 he has established himself as 'a devil, a devil, a very fiend' (3.2.155); a reincarnation of the demonic Vice, whose willing entry into the 'hell' of marriage with Katherina (1.1.124) – by way of a marriage ceremony in which he blasphemously strikes the priest – summons up the old link between clowning and damnation that had been forged in the Middle Ages.

Petruchio's most alarming trait is the sheer extravagance of his fantasies – he out-fantasizes the most committed dreamer in the comedy – and the rugged determination with which he puts them into practice, stamping his ideal image of a wife on Katherina against all reason. Matched with this imaginative tyranny, his bluntness about his motives for marriage ('I come to wive it wealthily in Padua' (1.2.74)) reveals the extent to which the male rhetoric of love serves as a mask for crude self-interest. The suitors for the hand of Katherina's sister Bianca make her the focus of their dreams, celebrating her as a 'young modest girl' on the flimsiest of evidence (1.1.155), associating her with the classical legends of rape and metamorphosis that figured in the lord's pornographic pictures in the Induction. What she says or does is of no interest to them: they imagine her as they want her to be – as a Europa, an Io, a Minerva, a Helen of Troy – and are shocked when she turns out otherwise. Petruchio, by contrast, starts out with no illusions about Katherina, and forces her into the mould of his perfect woman by making a conscious decision to do what the other men do without knowing it: that is, to ignore her utterly as an intelligent and articulate being. He tells her father that he was first attracted to Katherina by her reputation for 'affability and bashful modesty' (2.1.49) – a reputation that does not exist. Again, after their first fiery exchange he sums her up in ludicrously inappropriate terms, as if he has heard nothing of what she has said: 'thou with mildness entertain'st thy wooers, / With gentle conference, soft and affable' (2.1.245–6). Once he gets her home he sets about corrupting her every sentence, converting what she says into what he wishes to hear, either by pretending to misunderstand it or by depriving her of food, sleep and sex till she speaks as he demands. And by these means he steadily erodes her identity. Her strident voice is reduced, in effect, to silence; her point of view blotted out; her very senses rendered null and void. 'Why, sir', the frustrated Katherina tells her husband at one point,

> I trust I may have leave to speak,
> And speak I will. I am no child, no babe.
> Your betters have endur'd me say my mind,
> And if you cannot, best you stop your ears.
>
> (4.3.73–6)

But stopping his ears is exactly what Petruchio does, and by doing so he seems to reduce Katherina to the status of a child, shaped to the will of men more powerful than herself without the right to answer back.

Once again, this behaviour both does and does not conform to the model of male behaviour favoured by the anti-theatrical lobby. From one point of view, Petruchio is heroically resisting the siren call of sex, refusing to be made effeminate, reducing a woman to her proper place of subservience to male mastery. Gosson's *School of Abuse* enjoined women to stop their ears to the seductive sound of the players' voices, thus protecting their virtue as married wives or virgins in the face of the stage's call to libertinism.[25] Petruchio stops his ears instead to Katherina's 'free ... words' (4.3.79–80), thus protecting his manhood from her efforts to usurp its dominant role. But from another point of view, he is the ultimate exponent of the devilish dramatic art of instilling illusions in his victim's minds. The climactic confirmation of his skills as an illusionist occurs in Act 4 scene 5, when the exhausted, hungry, sleep-deprived Katherina assents to a succession of absurd pronouncements he makes about gender. Desperate to reach the relative comfort and safety of her father's house, she is prepared to say anything he asks her to – for instance, that the traditionally male sun is the female moon – if this will prevent him taking her back to his crazy household:

> Then, God be blest, it is the blessed sun.
> But sun it is not, when you say it is not,
> And the moon changes even as your mind.
> What you will have it nam'd, even that it is,
> And so it shall be so for Katherine.
>
> (4.5.18–22)

Here Petruchio himself has taken on the mutability associated by
Elizabethan misogynists with women, but which the *Two Gentlemen*
identified as a male preserve: giving the same name to different objects,
as Proteus did, and regularly changing his mind on a whim. Soon afterwards the couple meet an old man, whom Petruchio hails as a young
woman of exceptional beauty, comparing her features to yet more of
the luminaries of the night sky ('What stars do spangle heaven with
such beauty / As those two eyes become that heavenly face?'
(4.5.31–2)). Petruchio alters the never-altering heavens and trans-
plants them to the earth, changes woman to man and man to woman,
and drags Katherina into his illusory world along with him: she salutes
the old man as the ultimate object of male desire, a 'Young budding
virgin', and even goes so far as to celebrate the luck of the man 'whom
favourable stars / Allots thee for his lovely bedfellow' (4.5.36–40). If
Petruchio is a patriarch, then the claims of patriarchy – indeed, of all
forms of 'awful rule, and right supremacy' (5.2.110) – are no less irrational than madness.

But in fact, this scene brilliantly undermines any suggestion that
Petruchio stands for the triumph of the patriarchal values favoured by
Gosson and his peers, which they saw as being eroded by the erotic
fantasies purveyed by comedy. The old man is the personification of
patriarchy, Vincentio, father of Lucentio. And as the audience knows,
Vincentio is being impersonated, even as Petruchio and Katherina meet
him, by another old man – a pedant or schoolmaster – in order to further Lucentio's plot to secure Bianca. On his first appearance, then, the
'real' Vincentio is transformed beyond all expectation into a young
virgin, the imaginative object of his son's desire; and thus the instability
of the dominant patriarchal 'reality' in the world of the play is established. The scene ends with Vincentio baffled and amazed by the news

that his son has married Bianca without his consent, and the joke that has just been played on him by Petruchio and Katherina serves to intensify his bewilderment: 'But is this true, or is it else your pleasure, / Like pleasant travellers, to break a jest / Upon the company you overtake?' (4.5.70–2). And in the following scene Vincentio's fear and horror intensifies in the face of another youthful prank. Meeting his son's servant Tranio dressed in fine clothes, he is afraid at first that 'my son and my servant spend all at the university' (5.1.62–3), then terrified that Tranio has murdered his master (5.1.80). Petruchio's prank, then, in which he enlists Katherina, colludes with Lucentio's and Tranio's in its mockery of the older generation. It identifies Petruchio's part in this play, like Lucentio's part and the whole of *Two Gentlemen*, as closely allied with the youthful practice of truancy. And more disturbingly, it makes the orthodox patriarchal position voiced by Katherina in her final speech part of the same tricky comic milieu. We must bear in mind, after all, that the speech occurs in the context of a competition between all three of the young couples who have married in the course of the play. There is simply no way of knowing whether Katherina utters the speech as her contribution to a kind of 'sport' being played out among the young of both sexes, or whether she means it seriously.

Even if she means it, there are elements in the speech that might bear a playful double meaning. When Katherina says, for instance, 'But now I see our lances are but straws, / Our strength as weak, our weakness past compare, / That seeming to be most which we indeed least are' (5.2.174–6), is she telling her fellow women that their strength lies in *feigning* weakness, and in dissimulation (or 'seeming') generally? We do not know: and the point of the play is that the playful role-playing celebrated in comedies is already endemic in the lives of men and women beyond the stage, however vigorously the theatre-haters may protest against it. Patriarchs are performers just as rebellious young people are. The implications of this discovery are as unsettling as they are filled with comic potential.

Katherina's speech, then, is as much a performance as the play put on for the benefit of Sly. And the one thing that is certain about both performances is that they do not belong to the ruling class. Almost twenty years after the *Shrew*'s first performance – not long before John

Fletcher wrote a quasi-feminist sequel to it[26] – a prose pamphlet by the comic dramatist Thomas Dekker seems to invoke the spirit of Sly as an emblem for the democratic practices of the English playhouse. 'The place is so free in entertainment', he writes,

> allowing a stoole as well to the Farmers sonne as to your Templer [i.e. law student]: that your Stinkard has the self-same libertie to be there in his Tobacco-Fumes, which your sweet Courtier hath: and that your Car-man and Tinker claime as strong a voice in their suffrage, and sit to give judgement on the plaies life and death, as well as the prowdest *Momus* among the tribes of *Critick*.[27]

In the version of the *Shrew* that survives, the action of the Induction never ends: Sly and the lord simply disappear from sight, overwhelmed by the vitality of the play the Lord commissioned. As a result, the tinker never ceases to be a 'sweet Courtier', and we are never asked to give our suffrage either to his voice or the Lord's as they 'give judgement' on the play. Katherina's voice is left to speak directly to us, and we have the liberty to read it as we will. Whatever its restrictions, it is a liberty well worth celebrating.

TIME AND TERROR IN *THE COMEDY OF ERRORS*

The comedies discussed so far in this chapter spring from a theatrical tradition one might call the comedy of truancy: a tradition whose history extends from John Redford's *Wit and Science* (*c.* 1531–4) – whose student protagonist gets waylaid by Idleness in the midst of his studies – to Nicholas Udall's *Jack Juggler* (*c.* 1553), where the boy Jack Careaway gets severely punished by the titular Vice for his neglect of his master's instructions, and George Gascoigne's *The Glass of Government* (1575), in which a young man is executed for delinquency. Shakespeare's first comedies cast themselves as erotic digressions from the official curriculum, chunks of leisure time purloined from a schedule that ought to have been wholly devoted to serious study. The idle activities of

FIGURE 4   Title page illustration from the anonymous *The Deceit of Women*
(*c.* 1557), one of the many English texts to participate in the *querelle des femmes*,
a long-running debate about the merits and demerits of women that raged
throughout early modern Europe. Shakespeare draws on the debate in *The
Taming of the Shrew*.

feminized male lovers in *The Two Gentlemen of Verona*, the substitution of disguised lovers for properly qualified teachers in *The Taming of the Shrew*, both offend against the notion that every moment should be taken up with productive labour – a notion that was being relentlessly drummed into the consciousness of Elizabethan readers. For the theatre-haters, the encouragement of idleness by the theatre could never consti-tute 'honest recreation', as Thomas Lodge and the players claimed, because it robbed the bustling city of valuable workers, exhausted their strength in the indulgence of erotic fantasies, and above all consumed an extravagant quantity of that most precious of all commodities: time.[28]

According to the antiquarian William Harrison, Elizabethan England was a nation obsessed with measuring time. The chronological divisions of the day were marked by 'clocks, dials, and astronomical instruments of all sorts, the artificial variety of which kind of ware is so great here in England as no place else (in mine opinion) can be compar-able therein to this isle'.[29] For Harrison, the rich variety of English time-pieces was a sign of the times. 'I will not speak of the cost bestowed upon them in pearl and stone', he writes,

> neither of the value of metal whereof they have been made, as gold, silver, etc. . . . This only shall suffice to note here (as by the way), that as antiquity hath delighted in these things, so in our time pomp and excess spendeth all, and nothing is regarded that bringeth in no bread.[30]

The costliness of English chronometers indicates the new emphasis in Elizabethan England (as Harrison sees it) on the accumulation of capital as the most valuable use of one's waking hours, and on conspic-uous consumption as the best way of dispensing one's wealth. Dials, clocks and astronomical instruments embody the shifts in cultural values that happen over the decades, and that Harrison also charts in his account of how the measurement of time has changed through his-tory, from the days of Julius Caesar to Harrison's own lifetime, when Pope Gregory XIII made 'a general correction of the calendar'.[31] Each new generation seeks to exert its own form of control over how time is measured and how it is spent; and the Elizabethan city authorities were as keen as Gosson to see time properly divided up and productively exploited, in accordance with the proto-capitalist work ethic identified by Harrison.

The busiest period for Elizabethan anti-theatrical polemic – the 1580s and 1590s – witnessed a busy exchange of letters between the city fathers and the Queen's Privy Council, concerning the refusal of the London theatre companies to keep to the days of the week and times of day for which they had been licensed. In this as in all things, complained the Mayor and Aldermen of the city, modern players run 'Contrary to the rules and art prescribed for the makinge of Comedies eaven amonge the Heathen, who used them seldom and at certen sett tymes, and not all the year longe as our manner is'.[32] Performances during working hours or on Sundays, they aver, 'draw apprentices and other servantes from theire ordinary workes and all sortes of people from the resort unto sermons'; while performance 'In the time of sicknes' – during outbreaks of plague – helps to accelerate the spread of infection through the city streets. The mistiming of comedy could prove disastrous not just to business but to the health of the citizens' bodies; and Shakespeare's most sophisticated early meditation on comedy is necessarily also a theatrical disquisition on the political, commercial and moral consequences of good and bad timing.

The title of *The Comedy of Errors* proclaims its reflexive preoccupation with its own genre. It is Shakespeare's closest imitation of a classical comedy, obeying the unities of time, place and action, locating itself in the ancient Grecian world where the plays of Plautus and Terence took place, and deriving elements of its plot from Plautus's *Menaechmi* and *Amphitruo*.[33] At the same time, as I pointed out at the beginning of this chapter, it is no pure comedy, according to the guidelines laid down by Horace and Donatus. A duke presides over the action, so that the play concerns itself, as comedies should not, with the affairs of the ruling classes; and it opens with an imminent execution, a matter far too serious, Donatus would say, for comic treatment. Sidney defined the genre – based on the example of Roman New Comedy – as 'an imitation of the common errors of our life', presented 'in the most ridiculous and scornful sort that may be, so as it is impossible that any beholder can be content to be such a one'.[34] But in Shakespeare's play the term 'errors' seems to take on a weightier set of meanings than Sidney gave it: geographically expanding, in the opening scene, to embrace the wanderings or 'errors' of the unhappy father Egeon in search of his sons, and extending itself morally in later scenes to include both the sexual waywardness of which one of these sons is accused and the demonic possession of which the other is suspected.[35] The errors this comedy contains are, at times, as terrifying for the characters in it as they are ridiculous for the audience, and the relative appropriateness of the various possible reactions to the play's events – terror, delight or laughter – is finally determined by time. It is only at the end of the play that we find out whether the unwinding chain of coincidences will culminate in execution or reunion, misery or happiness. And in Elizabethan England, the happy outcome of a play that calls itself a comedy is by no means a foregone conclusion.

In its stress on precarious comic timing, *The Comedy of Errors* closely resembles Richard Edwards's *Damon and Pythias* (1566) – the first play in English to describe itself as a 'tragical comedy'.[36] At the centre of both plays is a serious meditation on the operations of tyranny, and on time as the tyrant's servant. Shakespeare's play locates itself in Ephesus, a city that has converted itself into a kind of murderous trap for unsuspecting strangers, not unlike Edwards's Syracuse. In response to certain outrages committed by the Duke of Syracuse against merchants from Ephesus, Shakespeare's Ephesians have passed a law that any 'Syracusian born' caught in their territory will be condemned to death unless he is able to pay the extortionate sum of a thousand marks for his freedom (1.1.21). The entire comedy unfolds within the parameters set by this aggressive law, just as the whole of *Damon and Pythias* takes its tone from Dionysius' paranoia concerning foreign nationals. At the beginning a Syracusian merchant is condemned to death for trespassing on Ephesian territory; he is given till five o'clock that afternoon to raise the money that would save his life; and the rest of the play's action takes place in the chronological space between the stranger's sentencing and the time set for his execution.

The question of timing is therefore at the heart of the comedy, just as it was at the heart of Elizabethan anti-theatrical polemic.[37] But where the theatre-haters maintained that comedy was dangerous

because it disregarded the timetables imposed by the city authorities,
Shakespeare's Ephesus is at its most dangerous when it subjects itself
most rigorously to the tyranny of the clock. Amusingly, the city contains within itself all the elements that Stephen Gosson had identified as
the tell-tale signs of comic depravity: Siren-like temptresses, adulterous
romantic liaisons, the breakdown of reason (four of its main characters
are diagnosed as mad), demonic activity, Catholic values (it features an
abbess who challenges the Ephesian civic authorities), thievery, insubordinate servants. But these danger-signs are for the most part illusory,
conjured up by the most harmless brand of errors – the mistaking of
one thing for another which George Gascoigne called 'supposes', and
which may be instantly dispelled with an explanation.[38] The real dangers lie elsewhere: with the officer of the law who arrests a merchant
for debt (a matter of timing, since the period set for repayment of a loan
has expired), then arrests Antipholus of Ephesus for breach of contract;
with the breakdown of the fine business reputation this Antipholus has
acquired among his fellow merchants (again a matter of timing – a
reputation is built up over years of successful business dealings, but can
be lost in an instant by failing to deliver what is promised in the time
agreed); and above all with the state, which ruthlessly punishes 'error'
in the sense of wandering, as well as in its other senses of insanity,
heresy, lawbreaking, or a simple mistake. It is in the two realms most
absolutely governed by the clock, the marketplace and the law, that
the tendency of human beings to tyrannize – to subject each other
to arbitrary rules enforced by violence – manifests itself most starkly.
Fears of whoredom, witchcraft, devilry and the rest are a mere comic
distraction, an idle frolic, compared with the operation of the combined
apparatuses of state control: a remorseless clockwork mechanism
designed to ensure that the lives of men and women run as smoothly
and efficiently as well-oiled cogs, and that those who fail to fulfil their
function are sequestered or destroyed.

Yet after the first scene of the play – which frames the action, just as
the Sly scenes frame the action of the *Shrew* – nobody in *The Comedy of
Errors* seems to be much concerned with the real dangers to life and
liberty posed by the aggressive Ephesian laws. Although the play begins
with a Syracusian merchant being condemned to death for no good

reason, and although in the very next scene his son Antipholus of Syracuse is warned that he too risks falling victim to the same tyrannical treatment, the young man seems more preoccupied with his own state of mind – and with the whereabouts of his money – than with his possible execution. These preoccupations are of course quite reasonable: his well-being really does depend on his continuing mental health and on his having enough to live on. But as the play unfolds, the fears of Antipholus of Syracuse become increasingly extravagant, and come more and more to resemble the fears of the anti-theatrical movement. It is as if an unsuspecting visitor to the city of London has found his way into one of the dangerous foreign comic plots condemned by Gosson, and remembering Gosson's condemnations, fancies himself in imminent danger of succumbing to the various disasters of which he has been warned.

The problem is that both Antipholus of Syracuse and his servant Dromio share their names with their long-lost identical twins, and that they are being mistaken for these twins by the inhabitants of Ephesus. They are walking homonyms or puns, the signifiers of their names denoting more than one object, and as a result all the contracts or agreements drawn up between them and their fellow human beings are thrown into confusion. Error piles on error, and the Syracusians quickly lapse into panic, resorting to supernatural explanations for their disorientation instead of looking for rational causes for these irrational effects. When the first mistake occurs, Antipholus of Syracuse begins to see the city as the theatre-haters saw it, contaminated by the corrupt conjurings of con-artists, players and other illusionists:

> They say this town is full of cozenage,
> As nimble jugglers that deceive the eye,
> Dark-working sorcerers that change the mind,
> Soul-killing witches that deform the body,
> Disguised cheaters, prating mountebanks,
> And many such-like liberties of sin.
>
> (1.2.97–102)

The word 'liberties', amended to 'libertines' by some editors,[39] associates Ephesus with the 'Liberties' of London — the area outside the jurisdiction of the city authorities where many theatres and brothels were located, and the geographical focus of the theatre-haters' venom. In his panic, Antipholus of Syracuse has lapsed automatically into the diction of Gosson, Rankins and their fellow polemicists; and in doing so he marks it as the language of paranoia, and its users as the helpless victims of their own baseless and self-inflicted nightmares.

Accordingly, the Syracusians' view of Ephesus becomes increasingly apocalyptic. At first they think themselves beset with a fairly low grade of illusionist: the brotherhood of 'cony-catchers', as they had been dubbed in the recent popular pamphlets of Robert Greene – bands of ingenious criminals who made it their business to con unwary country-dwellers or 'conies' (rabbits) out of their money.[40] Greene's fascination with these tricksters sprang from his recognition that their imaginative pursuit of gain had much in common with his own profession as poet-playwright, wringing pennies from the public by playing on their dreams.[41] Like Greene, Antipholus of Syracuse at one point allows himself to be seduced by the charms of the Ephesian con-artists, as he thinks them. Finding himself in the attractive position of being asked home by an unknown woman – in fact his twin brother's wife – he quickly accedes to her invitation:

> What error drives our eyes and ears amiss?
> Until I know this sure uncertainty,
> I'll entertain the offer'd fallacy.
>
> (2.2.183–5)

In Act 3 he even allows himself to be erotically aroused by these cunning strangers, just as audiences were said to be stimulated into sexual frenzy by the cleverly staged titillations of romantic comedy. Having fallen in love with his supposed sister-in-law, Antipholus tells her:

> Sing, siren, for thyself, and I will dote;
> Spread o'er the silver waves thy golden hairs,
> And as a bed I'll take thee, and there lie,
> And in that glorious supposition think
> He gains by death that has such means to die.
>
> (3.2.47–51)

But all at once he remembers the punishments that are said to be meted out *after* death to men who become ensnared by the world, the flesh and the devil, as embodied by the illusions of the Elizabethan stage. These perils are recalled by his servant Dromio's encounter with a grotesque kitchen-maid, whose body resembles the world ('she is spherical', says Dromio, 'like a globe' (3.2.114)) – much like the miniature globe of the stage – who knows all his secrets, and who claims to be betrothed to him. This powerful woman's blandishments convince the Syracusians that it is 'high time' they left this haunted city (3.2.156), and that like Ulysses they need to 'stop [their] ears against the mermaid's song' if they are not to be ruined by the place's enchantments (3.2.163). Soon afterwards another supposed 'mermaid' or Siren approaches them, this time a courtesan, come to demand a ring from Antipholus which she has given to his twin brother. The Syracusians convince themselves she is a devil in disguise, an actor, in fact, as Gosson or Rankins might have seen him: 'she is the devil's dam . . . It is written, they appear to men like angels of light' (4.3.50–4); and master and servant spend the rest of the play frantically fending off the advances of the various demons by whom they think themselves besieged. For these two unfortunates from out of town, the time during which they find themselves wrapped up in Shakespeare's elaborate comic plot – like an audience unused to theatrical illusion – becomes at last a spell in purgatory, from which they struggle to free themselves before falling victim to its predatory inhabitants.

Meanwhile, Antipholus of Ephesus, the man whose respectable position in the city is being threatened by the unsuspected presence of his twin, has a rather different experience of the unfolding comedy of errors. This Antipholus imagines himself to be the absolute master of his own time, choosing for himself, for instance, when to come home for dinner – and when to bring dinner-guests home with him – without consulting his wife. As his sister-in-law Luciana sees it, men like him deem that 'Time is their master, and when they see time / They'll go or come' (2.1.8–9). For the Ephesian Antipholus, the errors that arise on the arrival of his twin have nothing supernatural about them. Rather they are a succession of jokes that go too far, bringing the time-wasting of game or comic sport into headlong collision with the valuable time he has allocated to the serious business of commerce. His twin from

Syracuse cracks jokes about time with his servant Dromio; Antipholus of Ephesus would never treat it with such frivolity. When he invites two of his business associates back to his house and finds the door locked against him, his entrance denied – by Dromio of Syracuse – in a series of manically improvised puns and insults, the Ephesian finds himself wholly unable to join in the mistimed mirth, resorting instead to violence in his efforts to force an entrance. One of his business acquaintances persuades him not to raise a public outcry at this particular moment, 'Now in the stirring passage of the day', since if he does,

> A vulgar comment will be made of it;
> And that supposed by the common rout
> Against your yet ungalled estimation,
> That may with foul intrusion enter in,
> And dwell upon your grave when you are dead;
> For slander lives upon succession,
> For e'er hous'd where it gets possession.
>
> (3.1.100–106)

For this businessman, getting involved with the comic poses a serious threat to a merchant's future prosperity in the shape of his 'estimation' among his colleagues; a view shared by the Mayor and Aldermen of the Elizabethan City of London. Later, this view is confirmed for Antipholus of Ephesus when he falls victim, as he thinks, to another mistimed jest. Angelo the goldsmith has borrowed money from a merchant and the time comes when the debt is called in: 'You know since Pentecost the sum is due', says the merchant, 'Therefore make present satisfaction' (4.1.1–5). Angelo has given the Ephesian Antipholus a chain, as he thinks, worth exactly the amount that he owes the merchant; unfortunately, however, it was Antipholus of Syracuse who received the chain, and his twin knows nothing about it. As a result, Angelo's attempts to recover the money from Antipholus of Ephesus seem to both parties like a second instance of comedy run mad, a new intrusion of laughter into the sacrosanct territory of the marketplace. 'Fie, now you run this humour out of breath', cries Antipholus, 'But sirrah, you shall buy this sport as dear / As all the metal in your shop will answer' (4.1.57–83). The Ephesian twin never succumbs to the terror that grips his

Syracusian counterpart; instead he repeatedly invokes the machinery of his country's legal system to back him in his efforts to defend his turf. When his attempt to bail himself out of debtor's prison fails (he has asked the wrong Dromio to fetch him the bail money), and his threat to sue Angelo seems likely to prove empty, he turns for justice to the Duke himself, with whom he has unexpected leverage. The Duke is beholden to him, says Antipholus, 'Even for the service that long since I did thee / When I bestrid thee in the wars, and took / Deep scars to save thy life' (5.1.192–4). In this final scene, the ultimate source of the Ephesian twin's confidence is revealed: he has a direct link to the head of state, and any debts he owes will finally be discharged, he feels sure, by the authority that owes him a still more substantial debt.

In fact, both the Antipholus twins have more in common with the Duke of Ephesus than we might think. All three share the tyrant's glib assumption that their authority may be upheld with violence (the Duke's execution of Egeon, Antipholus of Ephesus' battering at the door of his house and threats of battery against those within, the two Antipholus's repeated pummelling of the Dromio twins). And all three consider themselves to have the right to an absolute command over time. As we have seen, the Duke deems it his function to set a term on Egeon's life, while Antipholus of Ephesus resents all incursions on his business timetable as challenges to his authority. But it is Antipholus of Syracuse – the twin in the precarious position of being a stranger in Ephesus – who offers perhaps the most intriguing illustration of the relationship between power and comic timing. A hopeless melancholic, he entertains a secret fear that he may lose his identity in his endless quest for his twin ('I to the world am like a drop of water, / That in the ocean seeks another drop' (1.2.35–6)). And he fends off these anxieties with the therapeutic treatment recommended by the best physicians: laughter. His servant Dromio can instantly lift him out of his depression 'with his merry jests' (1.2.21), like the 'heart-easing Mirth' of Milton's *L'Allegro*.[42] But Dromio does more than this: he also acts as a guarantor of his master's identity. Dromio is 'the almanac of my true date', as Antipholus puts it (1.2.41); that is, he was born in the same hour and place as Antipholus; and for Renaissance astrologers the date and time of a man's birth were who he was, marking forever his preordained place in the cosmos. In other words, Dromio is the subject whose unwaveringly consistent nature ensures the stability of power-relations within the miniature state of Antipholus' itinerant household; the North Star, as it were, that enables his master to hold his course. His 'merry jests' are the badges of his servitude, identifying his kinship with the clever slaves of Roman New Comedy: so that they serve not only to relieve his master's melancholy but also to confirm his social status as a man of substance in command of other men. Despite the lurking presence of melancholy, Antipholus' household seems as tightly organized as the Ephesian state: no wonder he does not feel threatened by the harsh Ephesian law when he first hears about it.

This, then, is why the Syracusian Antipholus is so much more disconcerted than his Ephesian twin when he finds himself subject to a series of mistimed jests on the part of his servant, the man who effectively defines him in his wanderings. The bulk of these jests arise from the repeated mistaking of one Dromio for the other; and Antipholus of Syracuse finds it as hard as his twin does to see the funny side of things when he thinks his control over time is being seriously challenged. 'Come, Dromio, come', he warns, 'these jests are out of season, / Reserve them till a merrier hour than this' (1.2.68–9); and later he tells him that careful observance of the demands of the social hierarchy is essential to good comic timing:

> Because that I familiarly sometimes
> Do use you for my fool, and chat with you,
> Your sauciness will jest upon my love,
> And make a common of my serious hours;
> When the sun shines let foolish gnats make sport,
> But creep in crannies when he hides his beams.
> If you will jest with me, know my aspect,
> And fashion your demeanour to my looks,
> Or I will beat this method in your sconce.
>
> (2.2.26–34)

The Syracusian traveller is here elaborating a familiar commonplace from the early modern rhetorics and conduct-books: that wits and clowns must either adapt themselves to the demands of person, time and place, or else reap the painful consequences.[43] But he is doing so in somewhat grandiose terms – 'know my aspect' makes him sound like a god or a planet – and backs his words with violence, beating Dromio whenever he steps out of line. And the logic that permits him to beat his slave for a mistimed prank is the same logic that permits the Ephesian authorities to put Antipholus to death for being in the wrong place at the wrong time. Throughout the play, his bantering with his servant – which converts itself so easily into 'battering' (2.2.36) – stands in danger of being converted into a still more violent assertion of power, state execution, to be visited, like Antipholus' blows, on the head of its victim (at the end of the play the condemned Syracusian merchant Egeon is led onto the stage accompanied by 'the headsman and other officers', ready to carry out his decapitation). By claiming absolute power over the organization of his servant's time, Antipholus implicitly lends his support to the view of the Ephesian state that it has the right to cut short the life-span of any innocent traveller who falls into its power – that is, to set the deadline for death.

The connection between Antipholus of Syracuse and the Duke is reinforced by their similar ability to convert currency into violence. The Duke sets a price of a thousand gold marks on Egeon's head, while the traveller beats a thousand red and purple marks into Dromio's head when he thinks the servant has lost a thousand marks in gold with which he has been entrusted. By changing marks into marks, currency into a cudgelling, barter (as well as banter) into battery, Antipholus proclaims his complicity with the savage economy of Ephesus, which weighs summary execution against sums of money. The arbitrary nature of this economy – the fact that it signally fails to distribute cash where it is most needed – seems to be symbolized by the coincidence that the sum Antipholus of Syracuse gives to Dromio for safekeeping is exactly the sum his father needs to buy his life. There seems no possible way, within the Ephesian social system, for the son's money to meet the father's need; and this suggests that there is something profoundly flawed about the hostile state in which they find themselves.

It is a woman who most clearly identifies the inequity on which the Ephesian state is founded. In terms that anticipate two of Shakespeare's later comedies – *The Merchant of Venice* and *Measure for Measure* –

Adriana, the wife of Antipholus of Ephesus, draws attention to the imbalance that is enshrined in Ephesian culture and legislation. Complaining of her husband's consistent disregard for reasonable time-keeping, she asks her sister Luciana: 'Why should [men's] liberty than ours be more?' (2.1.10); and when Luciana responds with the hackneyed Pauline opinion that the male of all species is 'master' to the female (2.1.24),[44] Adriana retorts that their different views on men are based on their unequal experience of them (Luciana is unmarried). A just measure of other people's griefs can only be obtained by imagining oneself into their position:

> A wretched soul bruis'd with adversity,
> We bid be quiet when we hear it cry;
> But were we burden'd with like weight of pain,
> As much, or more, we should ourselves complain.
>
> (2.1.34–7)

Adriana's comment applies as much to her husband's attitude to her complaints as it does to her sister's. When she upbraids her husband (as she thinks) for taking excessive liberty with time – and perhaps with other women's bodies – she asks him to put himself in her place for a moment:

> How dearly would it touch thee to the quick,
> Shouldst thou but hear I were licentious?
> And that this body, consecrate to thee,
> By ruffian lust should be contaminate?
>
> (2.2.129–32)

His response, she feels sure, would be a savage outburst of violence – tearing the skin from her face and cutting the wedding-ring from her hand. And she reminds him that technically, according to their wedding vows, they are indeed one person, so that any infidelity on his part is a betrayal of himself, since it betrays his wife, who is his own flesh. If Antipholus of Syracuse is searching for his other self – his twin, flesh of his flesh, and born in the selfsame hour – Antipholus of Ephesus has found himself a replacement twin, as it were, in the form of a wife, but is failing to honour his commitment to treat her (on one level, at least) as his equal. Instead he is substituting other women for her, by being, as she thinks, unfaithful. And unfortunately, the other Antipholus – Antipholus of Syracuse – helps to confirm her view that men are willing to substitute any bedfellow for their legitimate partner. Mistaken for his brother, he is wafted into Adriana's household, where he immediately turns his attentions on Adriana's sister: 'mine own self's better part', he calls her, and urges her to 'Call thyself sister, sweet, for I am thee' (3.2.61–6). The inequity that allows a man greater freedom with his time than a woman also allows him greater freedom to transfer his allegiances from one person to another; and Adriana's and Luciana's discovery of this fact exposes a dangerous inconsistency at the heart of Ephesian culture, one that threatens to overthrow all the complex web of agreements on which it is founded – and by which it is funded. Men are masters of their time, masters of their households, and part of an all-male hierarchy topped by the master or 'head' of the state. They enforce their mastery by staking claim to other people's heads, such as the head of Egeon and the heads of the two Dromios; and St Paul in the letter to Ephesians describes the husband as the wife's 'head' – an act of head-swapping that makes her head effectively redundant.[45] Men's claim to absolute power extends itself to a claim to absolute freedom from responsibility, a right to renege on all agreements with their inferiors. Such lopsided freedom is tantamount to tyranny, and tyranny invariably leads to self-destruction, the final breakdown of all the chains of command on which it depends.

The issue becomes clearer if we look at another of the biblical texts on which The Comedy of Errors is based. Much has been made of the play's debt to the letter from St Paul to the Ephesians, and there is no doubt of the relevance of Paul's observations on marriage to the quarrel between Antipholus of Ephesus and Adriana. But the play is equally preoccupied with the most celebrated biblical text on the subject of time: the opening verses of Ecclesiastes chapter 3. 'To every thing there is a season', the chapter runs,

> and a time to every purpose under the heaven: a time to be born, and a time to die; a time to plant, and a time to pluck up that which is planted; a time to kill, and a time to heal; a time to break

down, and a time to build up; a time to weep, and a time to laugh;
a time to mourn, and a time to dance.

At a crucial moment in *The Comedy of Errors* Antipholus of Syracuse
quotes this passage to Dromio, his bondsman: 'Well, sir, learn to jest in
good time; there's a time for all things' (2.2.63–4). Antipholus clearly
takes the words to imply that good working relations between servant
and master depend on the servant's careful conformity with his master's emotional schedule. 'If you will jest with me', he goes on, in the
passage we have already noted, 'know my aspect, / And fashion your
demeanour to my looks, / Or I will beat this method in your sconce'
(2.2.32–4). But the statement that there is 'a time to every purpose
under the sun' need not be the sole property of tyrants, appropriated by
them to justify their monopolistic regulation of timetables and calen-
dars. When the writer William Harrison complains that in Elizabethan
England 'pomp and excess spendeth all, and nothing is regarded that
bringeth in no bread', this implies that there are other ways of spending
and measuring time besides those privileged by men greedy for wealth
or jealous of power. Harrison tells us, for instance, that daylight may be
divided either into two parts – morning and afternoon – or into four: the
'ruddy, shining, burning, and warming seasons'; or every twenty-four
hours may be divided into four segments, each dominated by one of the
four 'humours' of which the human body was composed (blood, choler,
bile and phlegm).[46] The night, too, could be divided into either four or
seven watches as well as into hours.[47] In *The Comedy of Errors*, a variety
of alternative time-schemes competes with the schedule set by the
Ephesian authorities (who include masters and husbands as well as
princes and justices). And it is at the moment when all these different
time-schemes converge, bringing all the different interests of the current inhabitants of Ephesus into fruitful combination, that a possible
issue offers itself: a way out of the labyrinthine prison that the play is
threatening to become.

Men's and women's bodies run to timetables beyond the control of
tyrants. They feel hunger, which must be satisfied if they are not to perish, as Dromio of Ephesus points out when he is sent to call his master
to dinner: 'Methinks your maw, like mine, should be your clock, / And

strike you home without a messenger' (1.2.66–7). And they have a built-in redundancy that manifests itself in time as they grow to maturity and then fall into decay. Adriana reminds us of this when she complains that Antipholus of Ephesus has stopped fancying her because his actions have aged her: 'Hath homely age th'alluring beauty took / From my poor cheek? then he hath wasted it' (2.1.90–1). His own looks have decayed with time – and perhaps also, she implies, through licentious living ('He is deformed, crooked, old, and sere, / Ill-fac'd, worse-bodied, shapeless everywhere' (4.2.19–20)). At the end of the play Egeon is afraid that time has altered him so much that his own son will not know him, and he will lose his life because of it: 'careful hours with time's deformed hand / Hath written strange defeatures in my face' (5.1.299–300). Here is a range of rivals to man's mastery over time: the respective powers of hunger, sex, grief and age to inscribe themselves on a man's or woman's body. And there are other time-schemes still, we learn, that claim precedence over any man-made chronologies. The play is filled with anachronistic references to the Christian Day of Judgement, when God will separate the good from the wicked at the point when all times end. And in the very first scene a time-scheme is set in motion that will reach a natural conclusion at this apocalyptic moment.

As we have seen, the first scene winds the clock of tyranny, in the form of the sentence of death passed on Egeon. But it also winds another clock, whose operation is embedded in the narrative Egeon tells to explain his presence in Ephesus. This narrative implies that human lives run to an inscrutable timetable set by hidden and possibly malevolent controllers, variously identified as Fortune and the fates. Each stage of the old man's story is governed by a series of improbable chances that lead him inexorably to the moment when he is sentenced to death; chances whose chronological relationship to one another is scrupulously recorded: 'From whom my absence was not six months old' (1.1.44); 'That very hour' (1.1.53); 'My youngest boy ... / At eighteen years became inquisitive / After his brother' (1.1.124–6); 'Five summers have I spent in farthest Greece' (1.1.132); 'here must end the story of my life' (1.1.137). And at the end of the story Egeon's audience, the Duke of Ephesus, professes himself amazed at the extent to which the tale reveals man's ultimate powerlessness to master time. Egeon is one 'whom the fates have mark'd / To bear the extremity of dire mishap' (1.1.140–1) – that is, he is the victim of catastrophic mistiming; and it is in response to his record of extraordinary misfortune that the Duke decides to put off his execution till the end of the day on which he tells his story. The execution cannot be deferred any longer than this, insists the Duke, without 'our honour's great disparagement' (1.1.148). But even this limited deferral means that Shakespeare's comedy occupies a period of time stolen against all odds, as it were, from the official schedule.

As we have seen, this theft of precious hours and minutes is precisely what the London city authorities objected to in contemporary comedy. But where they imply that the purloining of time is a peculiarly modern form of insubordination, contrary to the unspecified 'rules and art prescribed for the makinge of Comedies eaven amonge the Heathen', Shakespeare implies both that it has been practised since ancient times and that it provides an essential countercheck to the various brands of absolutism that have sprung up in the course of history. In fact, it is as a direct result of this deferral or theft – this bending of a government's rules – that his comedy steals its happy ending, as it were, from under tyranny's nose. In the fifth act, Antipholus and Dromio of Syracuse flee for sanctuary to a priory, representative of an ecclesiastical challenge to the monolithic power of the secular state, and presided over by a woman who poses a challenge to the monolithic power of patriarchy. And it is at the door of the priory that all the tangled skeins of time are unravelled – necessitating as they come apart the abandonment of the sentence of death passed on Egeon. All characters are reunited with their proper bodies – their own and those of their partners – and retrieve their lost identities; words are restored to their agreed meanings, as names are finally returned to their owners; and the business of Ephesus is able, in theory, to start again – though we have no way of knowing whether it can now operate on a more equitable footing. We may hope so, since blame is apportioned equally among all the characters at the end of the play – or rather, no one is blamed at all: the abbess describes the comedy as 'this sympathised one day's error' (5.1.398), a mistake shared out among all of its participants. Besides, it is the abbess who invites the whole cast to a 'gossips' feast' in the closing lines, taking over the Duke's role as time's organizer (5.1.406). And it is the servants who get the last word in the performance, as the Dromio twins refuse to let one of them take precedence over the other – for the time being at least – by leaving the stage first: 'We came into the world like brother and brother, / And now let's go hand in hand, not one before another' (5.1.425–6). The end of this tragicomedy is decidedly comic, and offers a disarmingly convivial take on the theatre-haters' fear that comedy might usurp the prerogatives of traditional authorities. In the first act, Dromio of Syracuse served as a wholesome remedy for depression, lightening his master's humour with his 'merry jests'. In the last, the abbess warns Adriana – and the rest of the characters, and the theatre-haters in the audience – that recreation (sexual, comic, theatrical) is a necessity, not a luxury:

> Sweet recreation barr'd, what doth ensue
> But moody and dull melancholy,
> Kinsman to grim and comfortless despair,
> And at her heels a huge infectious troop
> Of pale distemperatures and foes to life?
>
> (5.1.78–82)

In view of the theatre-haters' contention that comic recreation spread disease and brought with it a host of hellish moral consequences, the abbess's statement is bolder, as well as more witty, than we might think.

Shakespeare's early plays set up comedy as a countercheck to tyranny; the tyranny of man over woman, master over servant, the law over natural justice, a despot over his subjects. In acting as a countercheck, however, the comic renders itself vulnerable to the charge of committing treason against divinely sanctioned authority; and Shakespeare builds the notion of betrayal into his plots as zealously as he interweaves it with the notion of liberation and the struggle of the subject to achieve free speech in defiance of the many restraints set on the human tongue. These topics are central both to contemporary theories of the theatre and to Elizabethan anti-theatrical polemics; and they remained the driving force behind Shakespeare's comic writing for the rest of his career. His early plays are not his only comic manifestos –

nearly all his excursions into the comic mode seem to rewrite the terms in which it engages with its audience – but they set the tone for what came later. Or rather, they establish the complex interplay of tones, the playing off of 'sweet recreation' against 'dull melancholy' and even 'grim and comfortless despair' that unites all his various productions, whatever their genre. And they predict with astonishing accuracy his continuing preoccupations. *The Comedy of Errors* holds the seeds of *Measure for Measure* and *The Tempest*; the *Shrew* anticipates *Much Ado* and *The Merry Wives of Windsor*; *The Two Gentlemen* foreshadows *Cymbeline* and *The Winter's Tale*. It is as if his interest in comic disruptions of standard time impelled him repeatedly to revisit times past and subject them to further, yet more outrageous disruptions as the time of his own ending drew inexorably closer.

Chapter Two

COMIC CONVERSATION AND ROUGH JUSTICE

THE POLITICS OF COMIC LANGUAGE

In *The Comedy of Errors*, the twins Antipholus of Syracuse and Antipholus of Ephesus share the same name, the same face and (presumably) the same taste in clothes, and their twin servants too are as identical in name as in appearance. The unexpected convergence of these two sets of homonyms unleashes demons in the imaginations of everyone in Ephesus, confronting them with their worst fears and most destructive paranoias. It threatens, too, to tear apart the complex verbal network of agreements and contracts essential for the operation of a mercantile society. These are drastic consequences for what is in effect a meeting between two puns: living embodiments of the tendency of single words to embrace multiple meanings.[1]

But the pun had been politicized long before Shakespeare's comedy gave it a new and unsettling physical manifestation. The Tudor humanist Sir Thomas Elyot, who wrote an influential textbook for aspiring politicians – *The Book Named the Governor* (1531) – had a lawyer's suspicion of the verbal ambiguity that is exemplified by wordplay. He devotes a chapter of his book to 'fraud and deceit, which be against justice', and his definition of these terms centres on the difference between what he calls 'simplicity' – a clear, limited set of meanings mutually understood between all parties in a bargain – and ambiguity or subtlety, the favourite qualities of traitors and clowns. 'Truly', he writes,

in every covenant, bargain, or promise ought to be a simplicity, that is to say, one plain understanding or meaning between the parties. And that simplicity is properly justice. And where any man of a covetous or malicious mind will digress purposely from that simplicity, taking advantage of a sentence or word which might be ambiguous or doubtful or in something either superfluous or lacking in the bargain or promise, where he certainly knoweth the truth to be otherwise, this in mine opinion is damnable fraud, being as plain against justice as if it were enforced by violence.[2]

The passage is replete with dramatic possibilities. Who is to judge, for instance, whether people who take advantage of an ambiguity in a given phrase 'certainly know the truth to be otherwise', or whether they are digressing from simplicity 'of a covetous or malicious mind'? These questions are easily answered in the case, say, of Richard III, whose delight in ambiguities is plainly reinforced by violence. Think of his exploitation of an ambiguous prophecy, concerning the danger posed to the English crown by a man whose name begins with the letter G.[3] Richard may well suspect that the prophecy applies to himself (his title at this point is Duke of Gloucester), but he encourages the King to imagine it applies to his elder brother George, with the result that George is locked up in the Tower of London and eventually murdered. But how far does Portia, for instance, in *The Merchant of Venice* – who takes advantage of an ambiguity in the contract between Shylock and Antonio to save Antonio's life – deviate from contractual simplicity 'of a covetous or malicious mind', motivated by the racism that is endemic in Shakespeare's Venice? And what are the implications of her exploitation of ambiguity for the agreements that bind Venetian society in the play? In the world of Shakespeare's plays, Elyot's simplicity is elusive, fragile, constantly under assault. Those who lay claim to it – like Richard III, who tells a gathering of his enemies that 'I do not know that Englishman alive / With whom my soul is any jot at odds, / More than the infant that is born tonight' (2.1.70–2); or Don John in *Much Ado about Nothing*, who describes himself as 'a plain-dealing villain' (1.3.29–30) – are invariably the most dangerously fraudulent figures of all, doing violence to men and women as freely as they do violence to words.

But all this is surely getting too serious for a discussion of Shakespeare's comedies. After all, the courtier-poet George Puttenham pointed out that the same tricks of language could have entirely different effects in different contexts: what was deadly in one place could be delightful in another. Speaking of the various rhetorical means by which words with one set of agreed meanings may acquire a quite different set – figures of speech, such as metaphor, allegory, irony and hyperbole – Puttenham describes these as:

> abuses or rather trespasses in speach, because they passe the ordinary limits of common utterance, and be occupied of purpose to deceive the eare and also the minde, drawing it from plainnesse and simplicitie to a certaine doublenesse, whereby our talke is the more guilefull and abusing.[4]

For this reason, he says, the Greek judges known as the Areopagites banned figures of speech from their courts of law 'as meere illusions to the minde, and wresters of upright judgement'.[5] In poetry, on the other hand – and like Sidney he thinks of drama as poetry – verbal ambiguity and the power of persuasion need not be taken seriously:

> because our maker or Poet is appointed not for a judge, but rather for a pleader, and that of pleasant and lovely causes and nothing perillous, such as be those for the triall of life, limme, or livelyhood; and before judges neither sower nor severe, but in the eare of princely dames, yong ladies, gentlewomen and courtiers, beyng all for the most part either meeke of nature, or of pleasant humour, and that all his abuses tende but to dispose the hearers to mirth and sollace by pleasant conveyance and efficacy of speech, they [i.e. figures of speech] are not to be accompted vices but for vertues in the poetical science very commendable.[6]

For Puttenham, the comic spaces dominated by high-born women and courtiers are 'nothing perillous', so that the verbal tricks distrusted by the Areopagites may be freely deployed in this safe environment. But he goes on to point out – as Castiglione did in *The Book of the Courtier* – that even here the purveyors of 'mirth and sollace' must be careful to avoid 'any foule indecencie or disproportion of sound, situation, or sence', keeping within the bounds of decorum.[7] Decorum is 'a speciall regard to all circumstances of the person, place, time, cause and purpose he hath in hand';[8] but the allocation of the proper words to the proper circumstances is a ticklish matter, to which Puttenham devotes many pages in the last part of his book *The Art of English Poesy*.[9] In the end he concludes that decorum is a matter of instinct, impossible to define and easily violated. And the anti-theatrical lobby, of course, went further. For them, the comic spaces dominated by wordplay – however courtly these spaces might be – are 'perillous' precisely because they demolish categories and overthrow convictions, turning vices into virtues, feminizing men and endowing women with 'masculine' authority. Any theatrical event was a 'triall of life, limme, or livelyhood', and must be reacted to with the ferocity of an Athenian judge confronted by an ill-judged *jeu de mots* in the middle of a murder trial.

Shakespeare's mature comedies are 'ambiguous or doubtful', to use Elyot's phrase, digressing from simplicity in order to explore the area where the serious and the amusing, the political and the trivial overlap and cross-contaminate. They are richly stocked with courtiers, as though to take advantage of the status of the court from Puttenham's perspective, as a place where 'mirth and sollace' may be freely and safely indulged in. But they also demonstrate Shakespeare's awareness that nothing involving the ruling classes can ever be wholly frivolous, since they hold power in their hands and can unleash it at will when the mood takes them. As in Puttenham's courtly poetic environment, women dominate these dramatic spaces; but they are very far from being content to remain the 'ears' or 'hearers' to which they are reduced by Puttenham, or to allow themselves to be described as 'neither sower nor severe'. They serve instead as judges, weighing up the evidence for and against the men who woo them.[10] They even (in *The Merchant of Venice*) find their way into the civic law-courts in disguise, openly defying the Areopagites' ban on 'meere illusions to the minde' from their legal processes. In these plays, too, the courtiers of both sexes are not allowed to indulge themselves in isolation from other social classes. Many other forms of discourse intersect with the rhetoric of the court, challenging its claim to supremacy in the comic arts and recalling its aristocratic users to a sense of their responsibilities within a complex wider community.[11] Clowns, fools, pedagogues, petty officials and others present a range of alternative perspectives on words and their uses, mounting a potent challenge to the courtiers' arrogant assumption that they alone possess the key to language. The question with which Dogberry greets his fellow members of the Watch in *Much Ado about Nothing* is the question the lower classes are always asking: 'Are you good men and true?' (3.3.1); and it connotes their role in many of the comedies as a kind of unruly jury, always testing and unsettling the judgements of their superiors.[12]

Shakespeare's friend, the great comic dramatist Ben Jonson, said in the prefatory epistle to his play *Volpone* (1607) that it is 'the office of a comic poet to imitate justice, and instruct to life, as well as purity of language, or stir up gentle affections'.[13] *Volpone* ends with the trickster of the title being sentenced to the severest of punishments – imprisonment, leading to sickness and probably death – by a panel of corrupt Venetian judges. This is an imitation of justice as it is dispensed in the law-courts of early modern Europe, where bribery and self-interest rather than impure or ambiguous language inhibit the proper conduct of trials. Shakespeare's comedies imitate justice in a different way. They often end in trials, though these are rarely set in courtrooms or presided over by conventional judges. And the trials never end in a simple sentence – or in any other manifestation of 'the purity of language'. Rather, they form part of ongoing conversations: the verbal give-and-take by which communities cooperate, which militates against linguistic imprisonment of any kind and offers us many alternative far-from-simple sentences to choose from. It is as meditations on the art of conversation that I shall be considering the plays in this chapter.[14]

FEMINIZING COMEDY: *LOVE'S LABOUR'S LOST*

The title of *Love's Labour's Lost* boldly proclaims its status as a time-wasting comic performance, irresponsibly substituting itself for the 'ordinary' labour of craftsmen and agricultural workers, schoolmasters and priests, and offering nothing of substance in return. The phrase can be taken as a foreshadowing of the play's ending, when four courtiers, whose courtship of four visiting ladies is the theme of the comedy, find their labour frustrated, their suits bereft of a final answer. Alternatively, it may recall the critique of all sexual passion made by poet-haters and many pedagogues in Shakespeare's lifetime, for whom love's labour is *always* lost. In either case, the phrase pays wry tribute to the loving labour that has gone into the play's composition. The play is a rhetorical firework display, the most dazzlingly inventive burst of verbal pyrotechnics in the Shakespeare canon, and it is typical of the comedy's preoccupation with various forms of deflation that its name should reflect the worthlessness of the hours of work needed to bring it into being.[15]

But the title has further resonances. The 1598 quarto calls the play *Loues labors lost*, which allows one to punctuate it *Love's Labours Lost*; and the plural noun recalls the most famous and arduous working period of all: the twelve-year-long labours of Hercules. Hercules was one of the most contradictory heroes of the early modern period, identified at once with brute force, with intellectual and verbal prowess, and with the comic humiliation of the dominant male.[16] As an intellectual giant, he makes an apt if somewhat overblown emblem for the ambitions of the King of Navarre and his courtiers at the opening of the play. The nobles plan to set up a 'little academe' in their court and to live for three years in studious isolation, waging 'war against . . . affections / And the huge army of the world's desires' (1.1.9–13). Hercules, too, was said to have striven against sensuality in his quest for enlightenment. 'In his infancie', wrote Abraham Fraunce in 1592, 'he strangled two snakes; the meaning is, that he began even then to repress wantonnesse';[17] and his later labours were similarly interpreted by Fraunce as representations of the perennial struggle of the spirit against the flesh.

But Hercules was also an embodiment of the irrepressible force of sensuality. In his *Apology for Poetry*, the poet Sir Philip Sidney recommended as a good subject for a comic picture or text the image of the hero dressed as a woman and labouring at the spinning wheel, a delightful and risible instance of the 'strange' power of love.[18] Whether or not Shakespeare had read the *Apology* by the time he wrote *Love's*

FIGURE 5   Geofroy Tory (1480–1533), 'Hercules Gallicus, Hercules François', from *Champ Fleury* (1529). The 'French' Hercules, who conquers men and women of all classes with his eloquence, seems to haunt Shakespeare's first comedy set in France, *Love's Labour's Lost*.

Labour's Lost, the play looks very much like an ebullient response to Sidney's call for a work of comic art based on the humiliation of Hercules. Abraham Fraunce takes the story of Hercules in drag for an allegory of the difficulties of the intellectual life courted by Shakespeare's courtiers. 'Yet alas', he writes,

> he that overcame all, was at last overcome himselfe: He that mas-
> tred men, was whipped by a woman, and enforced by her to
> spinne and handle a distaffe in stead of an Iron clubbe: so doth
> wantonnes effeminate the most warlike hearts, and so much
> harder it is, to resist pleasure, then not to be overcome by payne.[19]

The King and courtiers of Navarre succumb to affection not 'at last' but at once, metamorphosing into lovers with astonishing speed when their all-male enclave is approached by a diplomatic mission led by the Princess of France. Thenceforth all the men's intellectual energies are redirected to courting their female visitors; and the men place their trust in the persuasive power of eloquence – another of the areas where Hercules was said to reign supreme. The hero is often painted, says Fraunce, with 'smal chaynes or wyres drawen from his toung, to other mens eares: signifiyng, that his sweete toung wrought more, then his strong body'.[20] But the courtiers get nothing with their eloquence but a comprehensive lashing from the tongues of the women, the verbal equivalent of the physical whipping Hercules got from his queenly mistress. More even than *The Two Gentlemen of Verona*, then, the play seems to confirm the view of the theatre-haters that comedy encourages the subjection of its male spectators to sexual desire, rendering them limply effeminate by fixing their attention on the female, and urging them to waste their physical and intellectual energies in the labyrinthine ingenuities of modern-day romance.

In fact, however, the play is another of Shakespeare's brilliant refutations of the crude misogyny that underpins this jaundiced view of comedy. In it Shakespeare mocks the inflated pretensions of men raised in the exclusive environments of the universities and law schools: men like the poet-playwrights Lyly, Greene, Nashe and Marlowe, as well as the theatre-hater Gosson.[21] Formal education, Shakespeare's play implies, is no preparation for life, since it courts a simplicity that does not exist beyond the monastic seclusion of pedagogic institutions. Navarre's desire to found an academy sounds laudable enough in his opening speech, inspired by the hope that 'Th'endeavour of this present breath may … make us heirs of all eternity' (1.1.5–7), and described in one of the loveliest lines Shakespeare wrote ('Our court shall be a little academe, / *Still and contemplative in living art*' (1.1.13–14, my emphasis)). But the glorious vision is soon dissipated by the silly terms in which Navarre's three courtier-companions assent to his proposal that they abandon things of the flesh. 'Fat paunches have lean pates', quips Longaville (1.1.26), and 'To love, to wealth, to pomp I pine and die', murmurs Dumaine (1.1.31), the facile music of their speeches making nonsense of their exalted intellectual goals and betraying the fragility of their promise to shut themselves away from the temptations of the flesh. The wittiest courtier, Berowne, declares that if this promise involves any serious privation then he 'swore in jest' (1.1.54), and the phrase clearly applies equally to his glib-tongued colleagues. And Berowne goes on to demonstrate in a single brilliant speech how easily the argument for acquiring knowledge through abstinence and the study of books may be countered with an argument for acquiring knowledge through the study of a woman's eyes (1.1.72–93). In this first scene, then, the Herculean trajectory of the courtiers' academic careers is acted out in miniature, beginning with heroic labour and ending with a humiliating but delightful decline into total subjection to the emotions. As with the *Two Gentlemen*, the course of the play is driven not by the Siren-like influence of the women feminizing the men, but by the men's inherent slipperiness, their readiness to allow the pleasure of the moment to shape their actions regardless of promises, laws or responsibilities of any kind – to dissolve all bonds in the interests of instant self-gratification.

The men in the play are, in fact, childish. Berowne's objection to the academy springs from his conviction that the courtiers' adolescent ebullience will not abide the impositions that have been laid on it. His view is borne out in Act 4 Scene 3, when the courtiers find they are all in love after eavesdropping on one another as they lament their amorous condition. 'Sweet lords, sweet lovers', cries Berowne,

> O, let us embrace!
> As true we are as flesh and blood can be,
> The sea will ebb and flow, heaven show his face;
> Young blood doth not obey an old decree.
>
> (4.3.210–13)

The lines mark a final divorce between the kind of promise made at the beginning of the play and the passionate ebb and flow of the young male body. It is worth noting, too, that they express the men's youthful addiction to irrationality in the favourite medium of courtiers and children, rhyme, which is traditionally opposed to reason; there is more rhyme in this play than in any other by Shakespeare. The courtiers' love of rhyme declares their delight in the music of their own tongues, an aspect of their adolescent pleasure in sensory titillation of all kinds.

But for much of the comedy the men seem hardly even to have attained the comparative maturity of adolescence. In the first scene, Navarre compares the cynical Berowne, with his scepticism as to the value of the academic enterprise, to 'an envious sneaping frost, / That bites the first-born *infants* of the spring' (1.1.100–1). The phrase implies both that the project is in its infancy and that the men engaged in it are babies, playful *putti* whose futile efforts to mimic the solemnity of their elders should be smilingly cherished, not suppressed. In the final scene, Berowne claims that 'love is full of unbefitting strains, / All wanton as a child, skipping and vain' (5.2.756–7), and the comparison makes it clear that the courtiers' view of courtship is as infantile as their view of learning. In between, the courtiers squabble, roll around laughing on the ground, dress up in disguise and swap dirty jokes with the enthusiasm of schoolchildren. It is appropriate, then, that their first effort to make a public display of their affection – a masque they put on for the ladies' entertainment, where they don the guise of Russians to pursue their suit – should be fronted by a child: a precocious page called Moth, who delivers some verses to introduce the masque and is taunted by the audience into forgetting his lines (5.2.158–74). And it is apt, too, that this same boy should play Hercules in the entertainment put on for the courtiers themselves in the final act. If the courtiers' academic project was Herculean in scope, by the end it has been cut down to size, rendered absurd by its association with a mythical hero who seems quite unable, in this play, to sustain his status as an adult.

Hercules is twice invoked as a precedent for the nobles' abandonment of their academic enterprise. He is mentioned first by the extravagant Spanish soldier Armado, whom the courtiers have persuaded to join their academy as a butt for their boyish laughter. Finding himself in love with a dairymaid, Armado is delighted when Moth reminds him that Hercules too was a lover: 'Most sweet Hercules!' (1.2.65). Later Berowne too invokes the hero, as part of his gloriously elaborate defence of the courtiers' perjury in abandoning their vow to abstain from women. 'For valour', he cries, 'is not Love a Hercules, / Still climbing trees in the Hesperides?' (4.3.314–15). The internal rhyme in the second line renders the couplet childish – like the activity of climbing trees itself – despite the fact that it alludes to one of the hero's most celebrated labours. But by this stage of the play Hercules has already been twice infantilized. Armado has maintained that 'Cupid's butt-shaft is too hard for Hercules' club' (1.2.171–2) – a phrase that makes it sound as though the hero has come off worse in a comparison of penises with a pre-pubescent boy. And Berowne has mocked his fellow-courtiers for falling in love by comparing them to a succession of famously solemn adults, Hercules among them, who have succumbed to second childishness:

> To see great Hercules whipping a gig,
> And profound Solomon to tune a jig,
> And Nestor play at push-pin with the boys,
> And critic Timon laugh at idle toys.
>
> (4.3.164–7)

This hardly makes the courtiers' descent into love sound heroically Herculean, a valorous feat like the stealing of golden apples from the garden of the Hesperides. Instead it is no more serious or emotionally engaging than a game, an act of truancy that supplants time spent labouring to improve the intellect with time wasted fiddling with mindless 'toys'. For the men in this play, Hercules is constantly being supplanted by the infant god of love, 'This wimpled, whining, purblind, wayward boy, / This Signor Junior, giant dwarf, Dan Cupid' (3.1.178–9); and their Cupid is more notable for his infancy than for his godhead.

Inevitably, though, the courtiers wish to segregate themselves from the charge of childishness, and their preferred means of doing this is to expose people of lower classes to humiliating ridicule in the hope of making them look small. As I have mentioned, they first invite the Spaniard Armado to join their academy as a target for their mockery, a means of enhancing their self-esteem by comparison with his more obviously misguided sense of self-importance. He is, Navarre says, 'One who the music of his own vain tongue / Doth ravish like enchanting harmony' (1.1.164–5), and the description is clearly meant to guarantee that the courtiers are not what he is. Obligingly enough, Armado begins the play looking more ridiculous than they do. In a letter to Jaquenetta, for instance, he compares himself to the Nemean lion – the first of the monsters to be slain by Hercules – thus making a beast of himself where he means to appear heroic. One cannot imagine Berowne, say, belittling himself so brazenly. But as time goes by the distance between Armado and the courtiers rapidly shrinks. Both share an obsession with Hercules and a delight in the music of their own vain tongues; both fall in love and resort to absurd lengths to justify their apostasy; and both rely on the unreliable page-boy Moth, who advises his master Armado on matters of the heart and who later speaks the prologue to the courtiers' Russian masque. Clearly, then, the courtiers are not as superior to Armado as they would like to think; and by the end of the play the Spaniard's stature – and even Moth's – has risen far above theirs, by dint of their very efforts to diminish him.

Derided by the women they hoped to impress, repeatedly beaten in their verbal games by people of both sexes who do not have their educational advantages, the courtiers resort in the final act to the crude expedient of disrupting a performance put on for them by Armado, Moth, and members of the local community. The play is about the heroes known as the Nine Worthies, and Hercules appears among them in the form of 'a babe, a child, a shrimp' (5.2.585) – performed by Moth – as he was when he strangled the serpents of wantonness. But the boy Moth plays the hero's part with aplomb, while the courtiers who once aspired to Herculean heroism behave like naughty boys, giggling, jeering and showing off throughout the performance. One of the Worthies is acted by a schoolmaster, Holofernes: and it is the schoolmaster who is subjected to the most relentless barrage of the courtiers' mockery as he tries to play his part. But it is also the schoolmaster who delivers the most stinging rebuke to the courtiers. 'This is not generous, not gentle, not humble', cries Holofernes (5.2.624), enraged by their refusal to let him discharge his role; and his unexpected use of the word 'humble' to describe the proper behaviour of the nobility helps remind us of the collaborative nature of theatre. The dramatic arts depend on the observance of an unspoken pact between actors and audience, a promise that the audience will remain both generously participatory and humbly receptive throughout the show. The theatre is in fact the ritualized equivalent of a conversation – the verbal give and take between all classes that is necessary for the smooth running of any society; and the courtiers' inability to adopt the receptive posture necessary for the enjoyment of a play exposes to public view the serious flaw in their attitudes to every kind of linguistic exchange.

There is, in fact, something seriously amiss about the courtiers and their constant banter; a seriousness that is pointed up by the lurking presence of Hercules in the play. For Hercules was not, of course, a purely comic figure. He had been the subject of many classical tragedies; and he was also the embodiment of tragicomedy.[22] The circumstances of his conception formed the subject of the most famous tragicomedy of all, Plautus' *Amphitruo*, on which Shakespeare drew in *The Comedy of Errors*.[23] And his most comic adventure – when he dressed up as a woman for the love of Iole (in other versions, the Amazon Omphale) – is taken by Ovid in the *Heroides* to be the direct cause of his death: learning of his bondage to a domineering mistress, his wife Deianira tries to win him back by sending him a shirt dipped in the poisonous blood of Nessus, under the mistaken impression that the blood is a love-potion.[24] *Love's Labour's Lost*, too, is a tragicomedy, because the boyish escapades of the courtiers are led by a King, whose games with words cannot fail to have serious consequences. For anyone else in a monarchy to say that an oath of chastity constitutes 'Flat treason 'gainst the kingly state of youth' might be amusing – as it is when Berowne says it in his defence of the courtiers' perjury in Act 4 (4.3.289). But a king who assents to such a proposition is treacherously setting aside his responsibilities as leader, removing the grounds for any simple understanding between himself and his subjects, as Elyot might have seen it.[25] And the King in Shakespeare's play has close associations with a real-life monarch: Henry of Navarre, the fallen Protestant hero.[26]

Celebrated as the great hope of European Protestantism, Navarre became King of France in 1589 and converted to Catholicism in 1593 (*Love's Labour's Lost* is usually dated 1594–5).[27] Like Hercules he was unfaithful to his wife; but for his English admirers his infidelity to the Protestant church was vastly more significant. By this act of apostasy he destroyed the basis of faith itself, leaving his former co-religionists – in England as elsewhere – bereft of the means to ascertain the sincerity of even the most solemn protestation. Shakespeare's Navarre shares his namesake's cavalier attitude to his promises. In the opening scene he berates his companion Berowne for saying he 'swore in jest' when he promised to abjure the company of women – for failing, that is, to take his promise seriously. But later it is the King himself who begs Berowne to find the courtiers an excuse for their breach of faith ('good Berowne, now prove / Our loving lawful and our faith not torn' (4.3.280–1)) – a plea predicted by Berowne in the opening scene, when he maintained that 'These oaths and laws will prove an idle scorn' (1.1.294). In the fourth act of the play, in fact, the jests of Berowne are enlisted to support the King's violation of his own royal statutes. And in the process they acquire a political and social weight that belies their apparent lightness, rendering it as potentially dangerous as it is entertaining.

The full weight acquired by the lightness of this ruling elite is only revealed in the final act. In the meantime, however, two very different social groups help the audience take stock of the social implications of the courtiers' jesting. The first is composed of the noblewomen of France, led by their Princess, who arrive at Navarre in the second act on a diplomatic mission. The second comprises a motley collection of humbler characters – Armado and Moth, Holofernes the schoolmaster, Nathaniel the priest, constable Dull, the dairymaid Jaquenetta and the peasant Costard – five of whom join together to perform the play of the Nine Worthies in the final scene. Both groups are quite as passionate about wordplay as the courtiers – even the aptly-named Dull has a linguistic riddle to share with his friends (4.2.35ff.) – and both are as excited by the delights of sex and of theatrical performance. But both groups, too, have what one might call a groundedness: a consciousness (or in some cases more of an instinct) that words are worthy of respect as the sole available means of designating things and actions, of making commitments and articulating convictions; while at the same time things, actions, commitments and convictions have an existence that is somehow independent of the words used to express them.

This groundedness manifests itself in a number of ways, some of them surprising. Constable Dull, for instance, who muddles words constantly, is nevertheless certain that he represents or stands for something of value; and this certainty sustains his conviction that there is substance behind his own muddled words. Approaching the courtiers he declares: 'I myself reprehend [the King's] own person, for I am his grace's farborough' (1.1.181–2); and his consciousness of his own official function as a representative of royalty does indeed 'reprehend' a King who has forgotten his kingly duties, placing the faithful Dull 'far' from the King's infidelity. The peasant Costard, meanwhile, whom Dull arrests for breaking the King's commandment – he has been 'taken with a wench' (1.1.274) – points out when he is punished for it that 'I suffer for the truth, sir, for true it is, I was taken with Jaquenetta, and Jaquenetta is a true girl' (1.1.296–7). His direct confession contrasts with the King's hypocrisy in passing a law he knows no one will keep; just as Costard's honest act of sex contrasts with the courtiers' prurience (they listen to his case with voyeuristic attentiveness, and are therefore as 'taken' with Jaquenetta as he is). Despite his penchant for malapropisms, Costard's motto is 'truth is truth' (4.1.50), and he repeatedly serves as truth's unexpected instrument. It is Costard and Jaquenetta who expose the courtiers' faithlessness by delivering a misdirected letter to Berowne at the very moment when Berowne is berating his companions for falling in love. The missive is a love-letter from Berowne to Rosalind; Costard rightly describes it as 'Some certain treason' (4.3.187), a betrayal of the courtier's word of honour; and Costard's betrayal of Berowne, who has entrusted the letter to him, betrays a truth that Berowne had hoped to keep concealed from his courtly companions. Costard, then, possesses the politically explosive knowledge that when the ruling classes betray themselves and others, treachery to them is an act of faith; and the clown articulates this when the king orders him off stage so that the courtiers can discuss their lovesickness: 'Walk aside the true folk', he says, 'and let the traitors stay' (4.3.209). Costard and Dull are the servants of an authority higher than any aristocracy: the consensual 'simple understanding' that is a prerequisite for the aristocracy's existence.

The schoolmaster, the priest, and Armado, for all the absurdity of their pedantic obsession with neologisms and petty grammatical quibbles, have an acute sensitivity to the social responsibilities of the eloquent speaker, as the courtiers do not. Returning from a material and intellectual feast – a platonic symposium of the kind the nobles' academy never yields – Nathaniel tells Holofernes admiringly: 'I praise God for you, sir. Your reasons at dinner have been sharp and sententious, pleasant without scurrility, witty without affection, audacious without impudency, learned without opinion and strange without heresy' (5.1.2–6). Holofernes's careful navigation between the perilous rocks of rhetorical 'abuses', as Puttenham calls them, renders his later mistreatment at the hands of the courtiers all the more painful. The same is true of Armado's zealous cultivation of chivalric courtesy. For him an insult is an assault on a man's dignity, something to be avoided by the courteous speaker even if the man insulted is long dead, and is being represented on stage by someone of inferior status. As the courtiers mock him for his efforts to act Hector of Troy in the Play of the Worthies, Armado tells them: 'Sweet chucks[,] beat not the bones of the buried. When he breathed, he was a man' (5.2.659–61). For Armado, Costard, Holofernes and the rest, a word and what it represents – in rhetorical terms, *verbum* and *res*,[28] or in theatrical terms, a role played by an actor and the historical person on which the role is modelled – are by no means identical. But they all understand and respect the convention that allows one to stand for (or 'pursent', or 'parfect') the other (5.2.488, 500); a convention the courtiers signally fail to appreciate.

The women, too, respect the communal agreements that govern words. For them as for Elyot, a given word should have only a limited range of meanings if there is to be any 'understanding between the parties' in a linguistic community – although they are happy to play fantastic verbal games when the moment is right. The 'groundedness' of these women consists in their consciousness of where they are, the ground on which they stand, topographically and morally speaking as well as verbally. They readily assent to the King's request that they remain in a field beyond the court of Navarre, so that he will not have to violate his oath to let no women into his court. Later, when he tries to persuade them to enter the court despite his promise ('The virtue of your eye must break my oath' (5.2.348)), the Princess insists on staying where she is: 'This field shall hold me, and so hold your vow' (5.2.345). At the same time, the women know that the field is a playground, a place of 'pastimes . . . and pleasant game' where words may legitimately be subjected to an infinite variety of acrobatic jugglings (5.2.360). For most of the play, the space the women occupy resembles an Elizabethan playhouse, an area devoted to pleasure beyond the purlieux of the serious business of the city, and they take full advantage of its delightful amenities. But they always retain their sense of the city's presence just outside the playhouse walls, ready to reassert its authority over the performers when the period of play is over. So unlike the courtiers, the women are not taken by surprise when the mood of the comedy changes in the final scene. And this is the moment when the men and women of the play discover that they have been living in separate universes.

At the end of the play of the Nine Worthies a messenger enters to announce that the time of play is over: the princess's father has died. As soon as the news arrives, the Princess – now Queen of France – declares her intention to leave for home, where new duties await her. She accompanies the declaration with an apology for the verbal 'boldness' the women have displayed during their visit: 'excuse or hide / The liberal opposition of our spirits, / If over-boldly we have borne ourselves / In the converse of breath. Your gentleness / Was guilty of it' (5.2.728–32). The women's witty conversational exchanges were stimulated, she implies, by the men's cheerful example. The time of merry-making is over, and she expects the courtiers of Navarre to respond to her altered mood with as much sensitivity as she has responded to theirs.

But the King's reply to this statement displays instead his *inability* to adapt himself to another person's mood or behaviour. In an effort to retain the hold he thinks he has gained on the Queen's affections, he executes an elaborate rhetorical manoeuvre whereby he hopes to persuade her to accept his love despite the unexpected onset of grief: 'since love's argument was first on foot', he says, 'Let not the cloud of sorrow jostle it / From what it purposed' (5.2.743–5). Not surprisingly – given the poor taste of such a rhetorical manoeuvre at such a time – the Queen fails to understand him ('I understand you not. My griefs are double' (5.2.748)), and Berowne proceeds to explain, in the still more convoluted terms of Petrarchan love, that the men truly meant their protestations of affection. From one point of view, his explanation looks something like the Queen's excuse for the women's verbal boldness: if the men's amorous and witty behaviour has 'misbecomed' their 'oaths and gravities', the fault is the women's, since their 'heavenly eyes' forced the men to commit these 'faults' (5.2.762–6). But the Queen's suggestion that the men's 'gentleness' or courtesy made the women 'overbold' is very different from Berowne's claim that the women's eyes made the men commit 'faults'. The distance between the two positions is confirmed by the end of Berowne's speech, where he struggles with serpentine ingenuity to transform the courtiers' vices into virtues, their falsehood into truth:

> We to ourselves prove false
> By being once false for ever to be true
> To those that make us both – fair ladies, you.
> And even that falsehood, in itself a sin,
> Thus purifies itself and turns to grace.

(5.2.768–72)

The linguistic glibness that enables Berowne to convert a thing into its opposite – especially when wrong is being transformed into right – goes right to the core of Elizabethan anxieties over the comic. Jesting verbal transformations are all very well in a context consensually understood to be frivolous – when pleading 'pleasant and lovely causes and nothing perillous', as Puttenham said – but once these jests are used to seal what the Queen calls 'a world-without-end bargain' (5.2.785) – marriage, or the union of the kingdoms of France and Navarre – they must inevitably destroy the integrity of any agreement. The Queen has no choice but to consign the men's professions of love to the idle time of play or sport, which must be segregated from the time of serious business if understanding between the parties is to be restored. The women read the men's protestations, she says, as 'courtship, pleasant jest and courtesy, / As bombast and as lining to the time' (5.2.776–7). A real agreement has to be made in a different spirit, matching words to deeds, offering appropriate guarantees in support of offers 'made in heat of blood' (5.2.796). 'Your oath I will not trust', the Queen tells the King (5.2.790), while Catherine tells Dumaine, 'I'll mark no words that smooth-faced wooers say' (5.2.819). Instead the women propose a failsafe method for lending substance to the men's words: to subject them to the test of time, matching their Herculean rhetoric to a suitably Herculean 'trial', a twelve-month period of labour in the form of withdrawal from the frivolous courtly pursuits that have been their exclusive medium till now. Only after all the seasons of the year have been dedicated to love – the solemn seasons as well as the festive ones – can the men's declarations be taken seriously. Only by living for a year in solitude can they learn what it means to be sociable.

It is the wittiest of the courtiers, Lord Berowne, who is subjected to the most Herculean twelve-months' labour: that of cracking jokes to the terminally ill, striving 'To move wild laughter in the throat of death' (5.2.846). This is impossible, Berowne protests, since 'Mirth cannot move a soul in agony' (5.2.848). The lord must voluntarily submit to the consequences of the worst possible comic timing; and in the process he is to learn what the Renaissance termed the art of 'civil conversation'. Conversation in the period meant more than simply talk: it embraced the notion of the fundamentally collaborative nature of society, where knowledge, trade, law, conquest and laughter are all necessarily the products of dialogue, an unending series of exchanges and negotiations between classes, genders and peoples as well as between persons of the same class, nation and gender.[29] The Italian diplomat and intellectual Stefano Guazzo devoted an entire book to the topic (*Civil Conversation*, translated into English in the 1580s), which moves easily between the intellectual conversation enjoyed by the aristocratic members of the Italian Academies and the pleasurable knowledge to be gained from conversations between the sexes.[30] Berowne's year-long labour is to 'Visit the speechless sick and still *converse* / With groaning wretches' (5.2.842–3); to inhabit, that is, an environment where his own voice is the only articulate sound to be heard among cries of agony, and where his wit falls on ears that have been 'deafed' by pain (5.2.855). In this way he will learn, says Rosaline, that conversation is a two-way traffic, demanding a respectful sensitivity to the nature and situation of one's interlocutors rather than a singular, Herculean eloquence. 'A jest's prosperity lies in the ear / Of him that hears it, never in the tongue / Of him that makes it', Rosaline points out (5.2.852–4), echoing the view of the rhetorician Thomas Wilson that 'the measuryng of an oracion, standeth not in the speaker, but in the hearers'.[31] Civil conversation, like theatre, is a collaborative activity, and both are spoiled by speakers who insist on spouting monologues for their own private amusement.

The courtiers are inevitably disappointed by the ending of *Love's Labour's Lost*. 'Our wooing doth not end like an old play', complains Berowne; 'Jack hath not Jill. These ladies' courtesy / Might well have made our sport a comedy' (5.2.865–7). His view of the comic ending, then, is as trivial as his view of love. Like the King he had hoped that a happy ending could be patched up 'at the latest minute of the hour' (5.2.782), each courtier leaving with a consort on his arm, regardless of the misunderstandings and confusions that propelled the comic action. Meanwhile, the women's refusal to be bound by the length of a conventional stage performance may be taken as a cheeky response to the complaints of the Mayor and Aldermen of London regarding comedy's encroachment on time set aside for other things. Indeed, this play encroaches more than any other comedy, since it imaginatively extends its action throughout the year, refusing to be restricted to the festive occasions with which comic performances were traditionally associated.[32] And the women's ascendancy in the final scene wittily recalls the theatre-haters' view that comedy feminizes its male participants by exposing them to love-stories driven by sensuality rather than good sense.

Amusingly, though, the women's refusal to bow to male pressure is driven by a desire to *avoid* being reduced to the status of erotic objects, as they were in the minds of the theatre-haters. It is the *men* in this play who are identified as dangerous spreaders of plague, infected as they are by the twin diseases of verbal ostentation and sexual desire; the women have the job of curing them with health-giving comic laughter. They are the agents of what Rosaline calls 'reformation' (5.2.859), the process of cleaning-up to which comedy must periodically be subjected. And they accomplish this reformation by way of a final mutation of the meaning of the play's title. The twelve-months' labour they impose on the men is an extended gestation period, like the ten months that elapsed between the conception of the hero Hercules and his difficult birth.[33] The men are contracted, as it were, to suffer agonizing contractions in the process of their own rebirth: a labour that may or may not end with a gain rather than a loss. At one point in the play the Princess observes that the best form of humour is that which is born of bathos, 'When great things labouring perish in their birth' (5.2.518). This is, as Berowne ruefully notes, a 'right description' of the courtiers' academic ambitions and their Russian masque, as well as of the performance to which Rosaline is ostensibly alluding, the play of the Worthies (5.2.519). But the twelve-months' labour imposed by the women promises a live birth instead of a still one, a heroic outcome instead of a dud. In *Love's Labour's Lost*, comedy needs to be feminized – taken out of the hands of men – if it is to grow up and acquire new life.

SLIPPERY SENTENCES: *THE MERCHANT OF VENICE*

Love's Labour's Lost avoids tackling the full social and political consequences of the connection between breaking one's word and the pleasures of wordplay. *The Merchant of Venice*, by contrast, tackles head on the topic of the joke as a form of treason or fraud, whose effects may be damaging or pleasant depending on the nature of the relationship between joker and audience. Of all early modern literary theorists, Sir Philip Sidney puts it best.[34] For Sidney there are two reactions to comedy: laughter and delight. Delight is produced by things that please or attract us (a beautiful woman, the happiness of our friends and country); laughter by things we find disgusting or absurd ('deformed creatures', 'a matter quite mistaken'). Delight springs from sympathy with the subject of the comic narrative; laughter from hostility to that subject, a desire to mark our distance from the victims of our derision. Delight is enjoyed in silence; laughter is raucous and abrasive, gathering together crowds of onlookers to share in its ritual exclusion of the people it mocks. *The Merchant of Venice* plays laughter off against delight, and in doing so reconstitutes comedy as an astonishingly subtle instrument for the analysis of the verbal bonds that bind communities together – all too often at the expense of a perceived outsider.[35] After it, Shakespeare's use of the comic mode was never the same again.

In the *Merchant*, the most obvious outsider is a Jew named Shylock, who is excluded by virtue of his religion from conversation (in its broad Elizabethan sense) with the dominant Christian community in Venice.[36] His verbal exchanges with Christians are limited to the vocabulary of commerce, and the only other form of discourse they offer him is invective. The Christian sense of humour is deadly for him in a number of ways. Its punning ability to render words ambiguous threatens the verbal simplicity that is necessary for financial transactions and binding

FIGURE 6   Hans Holbein (1497–1543), 'Death and the Merchant' from *The Dance of Death* (1538). Holbein's grinning Death seems to be enjoying a joke at the merchant's expense, as Shylock does at Antonio's.

promises or 'bonds'. Its delight in time-wasting play runs counter to the merchant's need to take careful account of time, especially when calculating due interest on loans. And its invective dehumanizes him, threatening to place him outside the protection of the law, like an animal or an evil spirit. It is in direct response to these elements in Christian humour, each of which poses a specific danger to his 'life . . . or lively-hood' (as Puttenham puts it), that Shylock himself resorts to humour, proposing what he calls a 'merry bond' (1.3.172) – lending a Christian money with a pound of flesh as surety – as a means of bringing home to Antonio's community a sense of the physical and psychological pain inflicted on the Jews by mockery. Shylock's deadly 'merry bond' is a joke of the kind he has been taught by its victim, Antonio; it demonstrates how he has profited from the schooling afforded him by the dominant religion in Venice. As he puts it, 'The villainy you teach me I will execute, and it shall go hard but I will better the instruction' (3.1.66–7). It therefore ranks alongside the murderous school founded by Aaron and Tamora in *Titus Andronicus* as Shakespeare's most terrifying confirmation of the horrific effects of comic excess.

Shakespeare's Venice is a society founded on comedy. Its religion, even, is comic, since it involves the invention by God's son of an ingenious way to circumvent the severe judicial system propounded in the Old Testament, by substituting himself for sinning humanity in a kind of stupendous practical joke.[37] In Christ's case this substitution is unproblematically benevolent, a means of redeeming the irredeemable against all expectation. But in the case of Shakespeare's Venetian Christians, slippery substitutions – of one person for another, of one word or interpretation for another – may be marks either of generosity or enmity, kindness or treason. The substitution of Antonio for Bassanio as guarantor for the latter's loan, for instance, is a sign of Antonio's love for his friend, an enactment of the scriptural precept that one man can show no greater love than to lay down his life for another. Whereas the substitution of the terms 'devil' and 'dog' for the proper term to describe Shylock – 'man'; or Shylock's enforced conversion to Christianity, which may be described as an arbitrary substitution of the term 'Christian' for 'Jew'; these are shocking signs of the Christian ability to erase its enemies altogether, to blot out their existence by the deft deployment of language. The most attractive aspect of Christianity – its ability to set aside the letter of the law and embrace transgressors unconditionally – is also the aspect of it that is most open to abuse, making it impossible to determine the system of values Christians stand for, and next to impossible to resist their verbal assaults. Their capacity spontaneously to undermine or alter the 'worth' of a thing makes the position of non-Christians in a Christian society alarmingly precarious.

The play opens with a scene that demonstrates the centrality of laughter to the Christian community in Venice. One of its members, Antonio, is sad, and cannot explain his sadness. His merchant friends speculate that he is anxious because of the ease with which his own value may be altered at the whim of the weather: a ship bearing his goods may strike a rock in a storm, and what he is 'worth' may be altered at a stroke. They describe Antonio's anxiety in terms that suggest the frivolity of their faith. As one of them says, if he himself had entrusted all his wealth to a ship religion would afford no solace:

> Should I go to church
> And see the holy edifice of stone
> And not bethink me straight of dangerous rocks,
> Which touching but my gentle vessel's side
> Would scatter all her spices on the stream,
> Enrobe the roaring waters with my silks,
> And in a word, but even now worth this,
> And now worth nothing?
>
> (1.1.29–36)

The easy transformation of the church into a dangerous shoal is both wittily imaginative and disturbing, suggesting as it does how easily commerce might supplant faith as a Venetian Christian's chief priority. It is worth noting, too, how the injury to the vessel foreshadows the injury Shylock later plans to inflict on Antonio, opening up his 'side' to allow the treasure of his blood to spill freely forth. The Venetians' witty language can alter values or 'worth' at will, and this attribute of theirs is what Shylock's 'merry bond' aptly satirizes, by suggesting that flesh be substituted for cash as interest for his loan to Antonio, then insisting on the impossibility of substituting anything else for human flesh.

But this first scene also demonstrates the Christians' intolerance for anyone who does not share their lightness, their refusal to let themselves be weighed down by solemnity. When Antonio denies that his sadness springs from commercial reasons or from love, his friends assume he is sad for no reason at all: 'then let us say you are sad /

Because you are not merry; and 'twere as easy / For you to laugh and leap, and say you are merry / Because you are not sad' (1.1.47–50). Like Berowne turning black to white and dark to light, these Christians can alter solemnity to cheerfulness at a breath, making both equally insubstantial. Soon afterwards Antonio's friend Bassanio comes in; and his remarks on entry suggest that shared laughter is a test of faith between friends, and the sign, therefore, of a strong commercial alliance. 'Good signiors both', he calls to the departing merchants Salerio and Solanio, 'when shall we laugh? say, when? / You grow exceeding strange' (1.1.66–7). A failure to laugh together is a sign of 'strangeness' – of growing foreign, of declaring your severance of quasi-familial ties with the man whose company you are avoiding (are they avoiding Bassanio because, as we shortly learn, he is in debt?). Again the sense is that friendship and strangeness, like sadness and laughter, are terms that may be easily interchanged – that they may be fallen into and fallen out of with alarming rapidity in this community. Of course, Bassanio may not mean what he says literally; he may not really be implying that Salerio and Solanio have become strangers to him. But the fact that he can say it lightly, in jest, gives us a worrying insight into the shiftiness of Christian Venice.

Bassanio's friend Gratiano accuses Antonio of being too preoccupied with the 'world' (1.1.74) – that is, with material things, especially money – and so introduces one of the three terms that will haunt the play: the world, the flesh, the devil. Antonio's reply – that he counts the world 'A stage, where every man must play a part, / And mine a sad one' (1.1.78–9), implies that he sees material or 'worldly' things – even his own melancholy – as transient and therefore finally of little import-ance, in comparison, one presumes, with the life eternal. This serious allusion to the lightest of entertainments, the theatre, shows that even the fleeting things delighted in by his friends may be exploited to convey weighty meanings. But any weighty meaning in his words is utterly ignored by Gratiano, who launches at once into an encomium of cheer-fulness, praising folly (it lengthens life where melancholy shortens it) and condemning those who look miserable 'With purpose to be dress'd in an opinion / Of wisdom, gravity, profound conceit' (1.1.91–2). For Gratiano, conspicuous wisdom like Antonio's is nothing but a fashion statement, a question of how you choose to look, and will inevitably be exposed as folly at one time or another. By the end of the scene Antonio seems wholly isolated in his commitment to one unwavering principle, his love of Bassanio. His love offers a firm 'warranty' to the unstable Bassanio (1.1.132) – who has childishly frittered away the money he borrowed from Antonio in the past – and the merchant is offended when Bassanio suggests he might not wish to hazard more of his money by lending it to his prodigal friend. 'You know me well,' he tells Bassanio, meaning that Bassanio knows full well that Antonio values friendship above financial profit (1.1.153). And with these words Antonio sets himself up as an unmoving measure of worth, the one stable element in the ever-shifting Christian world.

Except that he is less stable than he appears, as we learn in scene 3, where he accompanies Bassanio to Shylock's house to borrow money from him. Shylock is fully conscious of the way the Christian perception of 'worth' alters with every breath; he is therefore unwaveringly materialist in his assessment of the 'worth' of Christians. For him, Antonio is a 'good man' only in the narrow sense that he has money enough to repay Bassanio's debt at the time agreed; he is a good risk, in other words (1.3.15–17). But not a certain one: as Shylock points out, his wealth rests on the unsteady foundation of a fleet of ships. And Antonio himself is directly responsible for diminishing the value of certain financial transactions: by lending money without charging interest, he has lowered 'The rate of usance here with us in Venice' (1.3.43). Antonio's financial stability, then, is not guaranteed; and his moral position, it turns out, is no more stable than his finances. He has attacked Shylock for his faith and for his commercial practices; has called him 'dog'; yet here he is, asking to make use of Shylock's services to borrow money, something that would be impossible if Shylock were not a man, a money-lender, and a merchant whose faith may be trusted. Shylock delightedly exposes the logical inconsistencies in Antonio's position ('Hath a dog money? is it possible / A cur can lend three thousand ducats?' (1.3.119–20)) before announcing, to everyone's surprise, that he will follow his example by lending him the money without interest. But given the slipperiness or looseness he has identified at the heart of Christian culture, his declaration that 'This is *kind* I offer' (1.3.141) is as ambiguous as anything a joking Christian might say. 'Kind' fuses the most familiar modern meaning (generous, bene-volent) with others (natural to me; akin to you). And since Christians are so slippery, a declaration of kinship with them may easily mean that one is committing oneself to the kind of verbal trickery they delight in – including the deployment of ambiguities as a means of taking advan-tage of one's enemies.

So it proves. Shylock's merry bond cuts straight to the heart of the question of likeness or difference. In Venice, the value of a man's flesh is negotiable. As Shylock says, it is of no value at all as food, unlike the flesh of 'muttons, beefs, or goats' (1.3.166); so exacting this forfeiture will gain him nothing. On the other hand, Christians eat food that Jews consider equally inedible, such as pork. And Shylock has already declared that if he can take advantage of Antonio he will 'feed fat the ancient grudge I bear him' (1.3.45); a phrase that inaugurates the succession of cannibalistic allusions that run through the play. If Shylock were really a dog – or a wolf, as Gratiano later describes him – his desire for Antonio's flesh would be less horrific than it is, exempt from the taboo of cannibalism. In fact, however, the flesh he demands is effectively his own. It is the material he shares in common with his enemies, as he explains to Antonio's merchant friends after his daugh-ter's elopement with a Christian: a Jew's flesh is 'hurt with the same weapons, subject to the same diseases, healed by the same means, warmed and cooled by the same winter and summer', as a Christian's is (3.1.56–9). His demand of a pound of flesh is therefore a complex rebuke to the Christian community for their blithe and damaging lack of concern for the relationship between the words they use and the living, breathing bodies that are affected by them.

At the same time, Shylock's merry bond renders him vulnerable to the same charge as the Christians: that of blurring distinctions between people, words and things to the extent of losing sight of meaning. When we first meet him, Shylock identifies a clear physical break between himself and his Christian clients. 'I will buy with you, sell with you, talk with you, walk with you, and so following', he tells Bassanio, 'but I will not eat with you, drink with you, nor pray with you' (1.3.34–6). After drawing up the merry bond, however, he feels compelled to accept

Bassanio's invitation to dinner, thus marking his own voluntary erosion of distinctions between himself and the Christian community (2.5.11ff.). And in accepting the rules of games that are his enemies' natural medium, he renders himself more vulnerable to their tricks than ever. Launcelot Gobbo tells him that the Christians have 'conspired together' to entertain him with a masque during the dinner to which he has been invited (2.5.22); Shylock immediately expresses his distrust of the 'shallow fopp'ry' of such comic shows (2.5.35), instructing his daughter Jessica to shut up the 'ears' or windows of his 'sober house' to prevent it from being contaminated by sounds of laughter from the street (2.5.34–6).[38] And Shylock's suspicion of comic festivities turns out to be well founded. There is indeed a conspiracy afoot, of which the masque is an integral part; under cover of the noises and disguises that are the stuff of festive games, the Christian Lorenzo elopes with Jessica. Shylock's yielding to the Christians in the matter of jesting with them – however aggressively – and eating with them – however reluctantly – turns out to be hugely costly to him; marks the beginning, in fact, of their forcible absorption of him into the body of their community.

The Christians, then, have a double capacity both to distinguish themselves from their enemies by calling them names (dog, devil, etc.) and to erase distinctions when it serves their interests to do so. One of the wittiest expressions of this dual capacity is the first speech of the Christian servant, Launcelot Gobbo, in which he debates with himself whether to run away from his Jewish master, Shylock (2.2.1–30). Such a breach of contract would, he thinks, be devilish: it is the 'fiend' who 'bids me pack', his conscience that bids him stay. But he is able to reconcile himself to the devil's counsel by casting Shylock in the role of 'a kind of devil'; which enables him to conclude that the 'fiend' who urges him to run away is offering more 'friendly' council than his conscience. The slippage between 'fiend' and 'friend', and Launcelot's ability to shift the location of the devil at will, offers a perfect summary of the power accorded to Christians by their embracing of ambiguity.

It also predicts the extent to which they are ready to play games with their own faith. Later in the same scene, Bassanio begs his friend Gratiano to restrain his exuberant sense of humour when they visit

Belmont, where Bassanio hopes to impress Portia with his credentials as a prospective husband (2.2.171–9). Gratiano answers by identifying sobriety and piety – as he had earlier identified wisdom – as fashion statements, reassuring Bassanio that he will 'Wear prayer-books in my pocket, look demurely … Like one well studied in a sad ostent / To please his grandam' (2.2.183–8). And this light attitude to faith is detectable in even the most solemn Christian protestations. At the climax of the trial scene, for instance, Bassanio tells Antonio that he would sacrifice his life, his wife and all the world 'Here to this devil' to save the life of his friend (4.1.285). If one takes the word 'devil' here seriously, this implies that one man's physical survival can outweigh the salvation of two souls and even of the world itself, a notion hardly compatible with orthodox Christian doctrine. Gratiano, meanwhile, says that he is half prepared to give up his religion altogether in his efforts to account for Shylock's cruelty: 'Thou almost mak'st me waver in my faith, / To hold opinion with Pythagoras, / That souls of animals infuse themselves / Into the trunks of men' (4.1.130–3). Later Gratiano wishes his wife's soul in heaven in exchange for Antonio's life, a wish that elicits a sardonic comment from Shylock on the misfortune of women like Jessica who are married to 'Christian husbands' (4.1.293). Christians bandy people's souls around like a juggler's balls, and forfeit their own at a whim. In the final act, not knowing the identity of the lawyer to whom he gave away a ring, Bassanio swears 'by my soul / No woman had it, but a civil doctor' (5.1.209–10) – an oath that in theory condemns him to damnation, since the doctor who had it *was* a woman (Portia) in disguise. Antonio then declares of Bassanio that 'I dare be bound again, / My soul upon the forfeit, that your lord / Will never more break faith advisedly' (5.1.251–3): this despite the fact that Bassanio has twice at least broken faith, both advisedly and by accident, in the course of the play. For Christians, a light attitude to words seems to entail a light attitude to salvation, with potentially disastrous effects on their position at the final Day of Judgement.

As with *Love's Labour's Lost*, it is the women in this play who prove most sensitive to the implications of verbal lightness. This is hardly surprising, since their lives and livelihoods are most at risk from men's failure to keep faith. Jessica's position is especially precarious, as a woman who is neither Jew nor Christian, neither unmarried nor married with parental consent; and this precariousness declares itself in the many jokes about infidelity – personal and religious – that bedevil her conversations with her Christian lover and his friends. It is fortunate for her, then, that she finds shelter in the predominantly female sphere of Belmont. If the male sphere of Venice represents Elizabethan anxieties over the reconciliation of faith with comedy, Belmont represents an effort to formulate a new comic mode, able to salvage a kind of fidelity from the damage that is always being done to it by cruel pranks and hostile laughter. It is a highly provisional, compromised kind of faith; but one that seems well adapted to dealing with the Protean verbal shape-shifting that is the province of Shakespeare's male lovers and husbands. If there is anywhere in Shakespeare's universe where Lorenzo may be forced to keep faith with Jessica, it is in the house where Portia holds ambiguous sway.

Like Venice, Belmont is nominally governed by laws devised by men: in this case, the rules concerning the caskets bequeathed to Portia by her late father. Each of Portia's suitors must choose one of three caskets, and his choice of casket determines his 'worth' by testing his attitude to worth itself. Those who think the right chest must of necessity be constructed of valuable materials show an addiction to worldly wealth that makes them unworthy of Portia's hand. This, at least, was Portia's father's view, and Portia agrees to be bound by the test he set, much as the tricky men of Venice agree to be bound by the Venetian legal system. But for Portia the circumventing of uncongenial legislation is a fundamental characteristic of youth, whether male or female. '[T]he brain may devise laws for the blood', she says, 'but a hot temper leaps o'er a cold decree, – such a hare is madness the youth, to skip o'er the meshes of good counsel the cripple' (1.2.17–20). Her father's test may have been devised as a trap ('meshes') for his mad young hare, a means of controlling her passions; but leaping over such controls is the special business of comedy, and in this play Portia is comedy's cleverest adept. She combines brains and a sense of humour with her youthful 'hot temper'; and like the women in *Love's Labour's Lost*, she is both the mistress of spontaneous comic improvisation and the architect of the play's ambiguous comic ending. It is controversial, perhaps, to claim that Portia has absolute control over her destiny, and it is not something that can finally be proven. We have no way of knowing what would have happened if the wrong man had chosen the right casket – would Portia then have submitted to her father's 'cold decree' as readily as she does when the man she fancies chooses correctly? But one thing is certain: she has as much of a hand in ensuring that Bassanio chooses the right casket as she does in ensuring that Shylock's merry bond is waived, or that she has her husband where she wants him in the final act.[39]

Like the male Venetians, Portia is wedded to laughter; and she refuses to be wedded to a man who cannot laugh. As she lists her suitors in the play's second scene, it becomes plain that she is more interested in their wit than in their other qualities, dismissing them one by one for dullness in a series of comically acerbic character sketches. The Neapolitan talks only of his horse, the County Palatine 'hears merry tales and smiles not' (1.2.46–7), and the Frenchman combines the worst properties of the other two (1.2.56–62). The Englishman can speak nothing but his own language, and 'who', she asks, 'can converse with a dumbshow' (1.2.71)? The Scotsman is quarrelsome, the German a drunkard. And the Prince of Aragon is an arrogant fool, whose self-satisfaction gets an appropriate reward when he finds the portrait of a 'blinking idiot' in the casket he chooses (2.9.54). In each case she discards conventional marks of manhood – fighting, riding, heavy drinking, a good physique – as an inadequate basis for what Love's Labour's Lost calls a 'world-without-end bargain'. Her rejection of the Prince of Morocco is consistent with her rejection of the other nations she lists. The Prince's stress on his own Herculean qualities (2.1.32–6) (Bassanio, by contrast, is described as Herculean by Portia (3.2.53–60)), his willingness to be guided by appearances despite his claim that he is not ('A golden mind stoops not to shows of dross', he says, as he rejects the leaden casket (2.7.20)), his incapacity to see Portia in any terms but of physical 'fairness' (2.7.43) – which leads him to transform her metaphorically into a gold coin (2.7.55–9) – all indicate that he is no more her equal in wit than any of his predecessors. When she discards him with a casual show of racism ('Let all of his complexion choose me so' (2.7.79)) she is commenting as much on his internal composition – his temperament – as on the colour of his skin.[40] The question then arises: what is different about Bassanio's mind from that of his rivals? Why is Portia prejudiced in his favour?

The answer, it seems, lies in his intelligence (he is a scholar as well as a soldier, as Nerissa reminds her), his wit, and his readiness to be taught by her – to be her student rather than her instructor. Delighting in his company, Portia tells him that she could 'teach' him 'How to choose right', but will refrain from doing so from reluctance to break her oath (3.2.10–11); and later Bassanio says half jokingly that she 'Doth teach me answers' as they converse (3.2.38). Later still, this is literally what she does in the matter of the caskets. She commands music to be played and a song sung: a song whose first three lines rhyme with 'lead' (the metal of which the right casket is made), and whose sense sets Bassanio's thoughts on the track to choosing correctly (3.2.63–72). If fancy begins and dies in the eyes, as the song says, then something more lasting than visual attraction must underpin any long-term relationship. Once this lesson has been learned, the choice of the lead casket over the gaudy gold and silver ones is inevitable. Bassanio chooses accordingly, then justifies Portia's good opinion of him by turning to her for ratification of his choice, 'As doubtful whether what I see be true / Until confirm'd, sign'd, ratified by you' (3.2.147–8). Portia's father may have set the rules of the game by which her husband wins her, but it is Portia who chooses both to abide by these rules, and ingeniously to circumvent them without breaking them, so as to ensure that the right husband will be the winner. And her tuition of Bassanio, paired with his willingness to be taught by her, suggest that he will never be the dominant partner in this marriage. Portia's father instructed Portia, Portia instructs Bassanio, so that in Belmont, at least, the balance of power between men and women seems to be more or less even – if not weighted slightly towards the latter.

Portia arranges that this shall remain the case even after Bassanio has chosen correctly; even after she has given herself to him and designated him her lord. Once Bassanio has won her she rhetorically swaps the roles of instructor and instructed, describing herself like the conventional virgin bride, 'an unlesson'd girl, unschool'd, unpractised', and going on to say that she is:

Happy in this, she is not yet so old
But she may learn: happier than this,
She is not bred so dull but she can learn;
Happiest of all, is that her gentle spirit
Commits itself to yours to be directed,
As from her lord, her governor, her king.

(3.2.159–65)

But this declaration of total submission, which echoes Katherine's final speech in the *Shrew*, is qualified by the fact that Portia draws up her own prenuptial contract, giving Bassanio a ring 'Which when you part from, lose, or give away, / Let it presage the ruin of your love, / And be my vantage to exclaim on you' (3.2.172–4). So she recaptures the initiative even as she seems to surrender it. And Portia never actually displays the submission she professes. As soon as she hears that Antonio is in trouble, that the 'dearest friend' to her new fiancé risks death for his sake (3.2.291), she is both generous and curt in issuing her instructions to Bassanio: 'First go with me to church, and call me wife, / And then away to Venice to your friend: / For never shall you lie by Portia's side / With an unquiet soul' (3.2.302–5). Bassanio rushes back to Venice with her 'good leave' (3.2.322), and it is she who lays down the terms of the couple's parting, as she did of their union. Long before she adopts the disguise of a lawyer, Portia has manifested her capacity for circumventing the letter of the law in her own interests. And she has also laid down wayward laws of her own: rules designed to be broken, which appraise men's faith more accurately than any rule devised to be followed and rigorously policed.

Portia's bonds, unlike Shylock's, betray a profound suspicion of words as guarantors of fidelity. She is as conscious as Lorenzo that they are the playthings of the Venetian men. As Lorenzo puts it when subjected to a display of Launcelot's wit, 'How every fool can play upon the word! I think the best grace of wit will shortly turn into silence, and discourse grow commendable in none only but parrots' (3.5.42–5). Accordingly, Portia does not invest much faith in Bassanio's verbal protestations. When he declares he loves her she replies in light-hearted mood, 'I fear you speak upon the rack / Where men enforced do speak any thing' (3.2.32–3). The forms of expression she prefers are non-verbal ones: actions, such as keeping a ring safe; or music, such as the melody she has her musicians play as Bassanio makes his choice, or the tune that accompanies her return to Belmont in the final act. It is from Bassanio's actions – his facial expression – that Portia learns the seriousness of the contents of the letter he receives from Venice telling him of Antonio's danger. And it is from her knowledge of Bassanio won through action that she claims to derive her understanding of Antonio's character:

> for in companions
> That do converse and waste the time together,
> Whose souls do bear an egall [i.e. equal] yoke of love,
> There must be needs a like proportion
> Of lineaments, of manners, and of spirit;
> Which makes me think that this Antonio
> Being the bosom lover of my lord,
> Must needs be like my lord.
>
> (3.4.11–18)

Antonio being Bassanio's second self, and Bassanio being Portia's, she knows him as well as she knows herself without the need of verbal affirmations. So too when she finally welcomes Antonio into her house she tells him that her regard for him 'must appear in other ways than words' (5.1.140). For her, an 'egall yoke of love' connects like-minded people regardless of what they say, manifesting itself in deeds, behaviour, performance. Friends waste time together, converse, and share in all the delights associated with comedy. Such people literally live in harmony, dancing to the same tune, moved by the same melodies; their friendship is a miniature model of society as a whole, which is ideally in its turn an imitation of the harmonious cooperation of the heavens, where 'There's not the smallest orb ... But in his motion like an angel sings, / Still quiring to the young-ey'd cherubins' (5.1.60–2). So Lorenzo tells Jessica in the final act, articulating his sense that communities large and small are held together not by a spoken language but by an unheard set of musical vibrations shared among 'immortal souls' (5.1.63).

But in certain respects Portia's attitude to non-verbal communication differs crucially from Lorenzo's. For Lorenzo, music is an almost infallible means of telling friend from foe, those 'inside' a given community from those beyond its pale. For him, an appreciation of music draws men and women together just as the playing of the mythical musician Orpheus was said to draw animals, plants and stones together in sociable groups. The 'man that hath no music in himself', by contrast – a man like Shylock, who bid Jessica shut up his house's 'ears' against the 'vile squealing of the wry-neck'd fife' (2.5.30) – has no place in civil society, being fit only 'for treasons, stratagems and spoils', all actions tending to undermine social cohesion (5.1.83–5). For Portia, on the other hand, music is a fundamentally ambiguous art, whose meaning changes with its context. It differs from words mainly in that there is no mistaking its ambiguity; words purport to represent their users' meanings with accuracy, whereas music responds to the mood and circumstances of its hearers. When calling for music to accompany Bassanio's choosing of the casket, Portia offers two different interpretations of the melody, each dependent on Bassanio's failure or success. If he loses, it will be his swan-song, the prelude to his symbolic death (3.2.44–5); if he wins, it will become a sign of communal celebration, 'the flourish, when true subjects bow / To a new-crowned monarch' (3.2.49–50). Returning to Belmont in the final act Portia hears the music of her house again, this time by night, and is struck by the unusual beauty it gains from its nocturnal setting. 'Nothing is good (I see) without respect', she observes, 'Methinks it sounds much sweeter than by day'; and this in turn leads to the biblical thought, reminiscent of *The Comedy of Errors*, of 'How many things by season, season'd are / To their right praise, and true perfection!' (5.1.99–108).[41] For Portia, music undoubtedly speaks to the hearts and minds of its hearers, but its meaning differs radically from one moment or 'season' to the next. In this it resembles jokes, such as Shylock's jesting bond, which may be funny when first proposed but becomes hideously serious when the time comes to collect his forfeit. Hence music's close affinity with comedy, an affinity recognized by the anti-theatrical lobby (Gosson describes the musician's art as 'chayned in linkes of abuse' with the comic theatre).[42] Portia's sensitivity to music, which is as far beyond Lorenzo's as

Lorenzo's pleasure in laughter is beyond Shylock's, identifies her as this comedy's presiding genius.

The moment of greatest bliss in the play, when a man and a woman declare their love for one another, comes at the music-measured moment (or 'season') when Bassanio chooses the right casket. At this point of emotional intensity Bassanio himself recognizes that words cannot express his feelings for Portia, any better than they can describe the likeness of her he finds in the casket. He tells her he feels like a victorious athlete who 'thinks he hath done well in people's eyes, / Hearing applause and universal shout' (3.2.142–3), but needs his thoughts confirmed by someone else before he can accept his interpretation of what he hears. When Portia confirms her feelings for him, he remains speechless with Sidneian delight, experiencing

> such confusion in my powers,
> As after some oration fairly spoke
> By a beloved prince, there doth appear
> Among the buzzing pleased multitude,
> Where every something being blent together,
> Turns to a wild of nothing save of joy
> Express'd and not express'd.
>
> (3.2.177–83)

The sense of collective, consensual understanding communicated through Bassanio's metaphors at this climactic moment marks it as the high point in the fortunes of the male Venetian community in the play. In the end, the metaphors imply, the power and success courted by men need be expressed through nothing more than cheerful noises, the laughter-track of a sitcom, the choreographed applause of a politician's supporters. Portia is more cynical. She demands that he keep the ring as a guarantee that this harmonious moment will last; and it is she who hatches the plot that ensures Bassanio will *fail* to preserve that moment by giving the ring away. The plot involves adopting the disguise of a youth 'between the change of man and boy' (3.4.66) – the slipperiest and most indefinable age in a male life, characterized by the elaborate sexual lies he tells about 'How honourable ladies sought my love, / Which I denying, they fell sick and died' (3.4.70–1). In doing so she identifies masculinity in the play as a contested site, less complacently consensual than men like Bassanio and Lorenzo like to think. It is in this ambiguous form that she enters the Venetian court of justice to defend Antonio from Shylock; and it is in this form that she stages a comic performance to probe the very heart of Venetian culture, high-lighting the centrality of laughter to the Christian community there – for better and for worse.

In the court scene (Act 4, scene 1), Shylock's attack on Christian humour reaches its climax. His 'merry bond' ceases to be funny for any-one but himself at the moment when he shuts down all communication with the Christians who are its targets. In Act 3, scene 3 he meets Antonio, who is being led to jail as a debtor, and tells him 'I'll have my bond ... I will not hear thee speak ... I'll have no speaking' (3.3.4, 12, 17), thus shattering the verbal basis on which the tricky Christian comic world operates. Puns and other forms of verbal play presume that speaking goes on forever, and that the meanings of words are always shifting in response to new situations, always opening up new possib-ilities to be exploited at will by the fertile wit. Shylock blocks these avenues of verbal possibility at a stroke: the stroke of his watch, as it were. In Act 3 he reminds Antonio of the cause of his resentment of him: 'Thou call'dst me dog before thou hadst a cause, / But, since I am a dog, beware my fangs' (3.3.6–7). In the court scene, on the other hand, Shylock claims that his desire for Antonio's flesh has no cause at all; that it is driven by precisely the sort of irrational prejudice that sets the laughter-loving Christians against the Jews. He can 'give no reason' for it 'More than a lodg'd hate, and a certain loathing / I bear Antonio' (4.1.59–61). It cannot, therefore, be argued with; and not all the inventive wit they bring to bear on him can undermine his determina-tion to put it into legal practice. When the joker Gratiano asks 'can no prayers pierce thee?' Shylock answers 'No, none that thou hast wit enough to make', and thus reduces the joker to hackneyed execrations on the Jew's 'currish spirit' as a feeble substitute for piercing witticisms (4.1.126–33). The metamorphoses wrought by wit have come to an end, and the Christians are left to flail around helplessly in the search for 'some power to change this currish Jew' (4.1.290). Meanwhile Shylock declares 'There is no power in the tongue of man / To alter me'

(4.1.239–40). This infidel's faith is unshakeable; his integrity inviolable; and in his triumph he reproves Gratiano for his incivility in terms lifted straight from the lexicon of the anti-theatrical moralists: 'Repair thy wit good youth, or it will fall / To cureless ruin' (4.1.141–2).

Shylock's attack on Christian laughter consists (among other things) in an exposure of the superficiality of its claims to be genial. At the beginning of the trial the Duke tells Antonio that he has 'come to answer / A stony adversary, an inhuman wretch / Uncapable of pity' (4.1.3–5); yet on Shylock's entry the Duke makes a characteristically Christian volte-face, pretending to have accepted Shylock into the comic community from which he has just barred him. The Jew's joke *is* indeed a joke, the Duke suggests – like all jokes, dependent on violating expectation; and this is how the Duke expects it to end, or so he says. 'Shylock,' he says,

> the world thinks, and I think so too,
> That thou but leadest this fashion of thy malice
> To the last hour of act, and then 'tis thought
> Thou'lt show thy mercy and remorse more strange
> Than is thy strange apparent cruelty ...
> We all expect a gentle answer Jew!

(4.1.17–34)

But barely concealed beneath this show of appeasement is what the Duke *really* thinks of Shylock: that any show of mercy from this 'stranger' would be far more strange than his cruelty, and that as a Jew he is incapable of acting 'gently' – that is, like a gentile. He does not *really* expect Shylock to be merciful; so that when Shylock proceeds to violate the supposed expectation of mercy, nobody is surprised. Shylock's insistence on having justice according to the strict letter of the law – his legalistic refusal of ambiguity – is therefore both a joke and not a joke: it both does and does not violate expectation; and as such it lays bare the true relations between Christians and Jews in Venice, which has been repeatedly obfuscated by Christian verbal evasiveness. In the courtroom scene Shylock stages the war between comedy and its enemies, which is couched in clever words but waged in deadly earnest. Comedy's enemies said it could have tragic consequences: Shylock exposes these consequences through the remorselessness with which he forces Antonio to expose his flesh in readiness for the sacrificial incision.

When Portia enters, by contrast, she embodies comedy in its most dangerous form, as the moralists saw it. She is a woman who smuggles herself into the male sphere, thus feminizing it; a boy actor in drag; a prankster in the law courts, who plays with the letter of the law and makes it 'light'. It is therefore an act of brazen impudence that Shakespeare should put the most serious theological argument in the play into her mouth: the famous speech about the quality of mercy. This is the quality that overthrows the logic of the law, teaching all human beings to imagine themselves into the position of others less fortunate: 'we do pray for mercy, / And that same prayer, doth teach us all to render / The deeds of mercy' (4.1.198–200). And when Shylock refuses to be persuaded into being merciful, he is forcefully shown the meaning of mercy through a succession of legal tricks that are closely akin to witticisms: first the injunction that he shed no blood when he cuts his pound of flesh; then the insistence that he take no more nor less than a pound; then the revelation that he stands in danger of execution himself for conspiring against a Venetian's life, and must therefore beg for mercy on his own behalf: 'Down therefore', Portia concludes, 'and beg mercy of the duke' (4.1.361). Christian humorists are past masters at transforming others into their own likeness: it is therefore a triumph of Christian comedy that Shylock is finally forced into accepting his transformation at their hands, and turn Christian despite his rooted hostility to the religion.

There is of course something deeply disturbing about this transformation of the man who has resisted all transformation, all compromise. To be forced into bending is a form of torture; and the crowing responses of the Christian onlookers to Shylock's humiliation – perfect exemplars of Sidneian laughter – seem far nastier than Shylock's solitary crowings over Portia's earlier legal pronouncements in his favour (and Gratiano is the first to admit that Shylock has taught him how to crow (4.1.339)). The crucial Christian concept of sacrifice – that a man lay down his life for his friend, as Christ did – seems mocked when Shylock is forced to lay down his livelihood for his enemy (even if he is later forgiven part of his debt by the same enemy). The court scene, then, is an uncomfortable blend of comic indoctrination, of the sort playwrights claimed to offer, and less than comic warpings of Christian doctrine, of the sort comedy's enemies claimed the genre encouraged. One could hardly imagine a more striking or complex demonstration of the ambiguity of Elizabethan attitudes to the comic.

Portia's subsequent testing of her new husband Bassanio participates in this ambiguity. At the centre of her joke, like Shylock's, is the question of likeness and difference; this time not between cultures or religions but between the sexes. During the courtroom scene the Christian males in the play indulge in some serious bonding. Antonio waxes competitive as he prepares to die for Bassanio: 'Commend me to your honourable wife', he tells him, 'And when the tale is told, bid her be judge / Whether Bassanio had not once a love' (4.1.271–5). The implication is that any love a woman can give him is nothing compared with Antonio's; and Bassanio responds by overthrowing the values to which he committed himself in Belmont: 'life itself, my wife, and all the world, / Are not with me esteem'd above thy life' (4.1.282–3). Shylock's action has shocked the Christian men out of laughter, and in their seriousness they show their true colours, uniting against all who are not themselves – whether strangers or women. And Portia is as conscious of this as Shylock is. In a moment of wonderful irony she and the Jew express identical sentiments on the subject, as Shylock comments on the disloyalty of Christian husbands and Portia tells Bassanio that his wife would give him 'little thanks' for his willingness to sacrifice her for Antonio (4.1.293, 286). For this brief moment Shylock and Portia stand together as wondering witnesses to the inconsistency of Christian males.

But Portia's wittiest comment on male bonding occurs when she engages in it herself in male disguise, demanding Portia's ring from Bassanio as a reward for saving Antonio, and in doing so transforming herself into her own rival – a counterpart of Antonio, who held himself up as an example of true love to rival Bassanio's wife. Portia couches her demand of the ring in terms that explicitly invoke the perennial struggle between men's loyalty to each other and their love for women. S/he tells Bassanio that 'if your wife be not a mad-woman, / And know how well I have deserv'd this ring, / She would not hold out enemy for ever / For giving it to me' (4.1.443–6); and for a moment the spectre of woman as the enemy of Venice – another Shylock – is held up to her spectators, to complement her moment of solidarity with Shylock earlier in the scene. Antonio compounds the effect when he urges Bassanio to 'Let his deservings *and my love withal* / Be valued 'gainst your wife's commandement' (4.1.448–9). The battle lines are drawn; Bassanio's claim to be willing to learn from Portia comes up against his eagerness to 'teach' the young judge the extent of his gratitude (4.1.437–8); and the innate misogyny of the Christian male tips the balance in the judge's favour. Once again, under pressure the supposedly genial and even-handed Christians revert to type, and give all their loyalty to those they think to be like them. The prospects for that union between different beings known as marriage – which is supposed to end comedies happily – are scarcely promising.

Except, of course, that Portia is the 'man' who saves her husband's best male friend, and who claims the reward for doing so – in defiance of any 'mad-woman' who might resent his insistence on taking the ring. In giving up the ring to the young judge, Bassanio is once again succumbing to the persuasive charms of his wife – proving himself teachable, tractable, not obstinate like Shylock. Taken from this point of view, Portia's test is a joke; her ability to give and take a ring is a 'merry bond' to rival Shylock's, which exposes the shifty values of Christian men as Shylock's did, but without resorting to near tragedy to bring it off. Unlike Shylock's bond, her test is founded on the wordless understanding that has been established between her and Bassanio at the casket scene; its implications can therefore be more easily laughed off. And her response to what she pretends to believe is Bassanio's infidelity – a variation on Shylock's 'the villainy you teach me I will execute', where she tells him 'I will become as liberal as you' by giving another man free access to her body (5.1.226) – need not be taken seriously because we know that Bassanio has *not* in fact been unfaithful.

At least, not sexually speaking. But there is also an aspect of Portia's test that is quite as unsettling as the outcome of Shylock's bond, because it calls into question the grounds of Bassanio's capacity to keep faith. Depending on how it is spoken, one phrase she utters may or may not ring disconcertingly in the audience's ears long after the end of the play: 'Even so void is your false heart of truth' (5.1.189). The relation-ship between Bassanio's words and his heart is by no means certain, and though Portia freely pardons his fault, the play ends with no guar-antee that it will not recur. In other words, the institution of marriage has faultiness built into it; and the sexual joke that ends the play, when Gratiano declares that 'while I live, I'll fear no other thing / So sore, as keeping safe Nerissa's ring' (5.1.306–7), articulates in its jokey fashion an anxiety that the comedy has served to intensify rather than dissi-pate: an uncertainty about the grounds of bonds between men and women.

Just as infidelity lurks in the pledge of faith that is marriage, so too at the end of the play infidelity has been introduced into the Christian faith itself. The infidel Shylock has been turned Christian, admitted into the religion to which he is hostile, and the last we hear of him is that he has also been forcibly incorporated into his daughter's marriage contract with Lorenzo: Nerissa presents the newly-weds with 'a special deed of gift' from the 'rich Jew', which consists 'After his death, of all he dies possess'd of' (5.1.292–3). Shylock, then, participates in the comic closing celebrations against his will; so that a tension between gen-erations is added to the tensions between husband and wife, and the familial marriage circle represented by the ring appears quite as unsafe as Gratiano jokily suggests it is. Even the unexpected restoration of Antonio's goods to him, when he learns from Portia that against all expectation 'my ships / Are safely come to road' (5.1.287–8), is patently the result of a lottery: his trade as a merchant is just as hazardous as the commitment of one's body and soul to another human being in marriage. What the play seems to be saying, then, is that comedy is dangerous – just as dangerous as litigation, commerce and matrimony; and that like these it tests and unsettles our assumptions about faith and trust. The theatre-haters are right to fear it, since comedy teaches the necessity to live with fear, to reconcile oneself to it, to incorporate it into one's routines and contracts. At the end of *The Merchant of Venice* Shylock has been made part of the community that despised him; no longer a stranger, a devil or a dog, but a member of the family, the provider of its living. It is hard to imagine a more ingenious disturbance of the comic 'happy ending'.[43]

Chapter Three

LIGHTNESS, LOVE AND DEATH

LIGHT TRAGEDY: *ROMEO AND JULIET*

One love story haunts Shakespeare's plays more than any other. It is a contemporary story, unburdened by the weight of a classical past; and it comes from Italy, bringing with it all the conflicting notions of stylishness, impromptu violence, artistic flare, political instability, eroticism and religious oppression to which English Protestant travellers and translators had connected Italian culture since the break with Rome. It is a story, too, that mingles frivolity with solemnity, light with dark, as richly as the *Merchant* and with bloodier results; a working model, in fact, of the disastrous effects of mingling dramatic genres. In Shakespeare's version, the narrative begins in comic mode, full of laughter, innuendo, flashing blades and dazzling repartee. Yet it transforms itself into tragedy with a smoothness and ease that suggests this might be the outcome of any of the so-called 'comedies' given the slightest adjustment in timing, the slightest slippage in the cogs that drive the plot. It is the story of Romeo and Juliet, and it provides the starting-point for this chapter on Shakespeare's obsession with the sometimes appalling weight of comic lightness, above all in the context of love.[1]

From the beginning of Shakespeare's career the tragedy of the Veronese lovers lurks in the background of his comic narratives, threatening to unbalance them with its Italian excesses.[2] As we have seen, *The Two Gentlemen of Verona* is an early version of it; but it is present, too, in *A Midsummer Night's Dream* and *Much Ado About Nothing*, *Troilus and*

Cressida and *Measure for Measure*. The tragedy of love *Othello* is terminally infected by it, and an equally virulent though mutated strain of
the Romeo virus breaks out in *Antony and Cleopatra*. It is not hard to see
why the narrative should have distributed itself so irresistibly through
so many plays. It reminds us of love's energy, its funniness, the way it
anarchically reinvents the world in defiance of all attempts to reduce
things to order and immobility. And it reminds us too of love's propensity for falling foul of authority. This aspect of lawless desire forges
an unbreakable link between it and the theatre, and especially with
comedy. For the theatre-haters, the promulgation of such desire is one
of the theatre's principal functions, and their treatises trace the tragic
progress of this particular form of lawlessness from its origins in Italy to
its devastating incursions into early modern English culture. *Romeo and
Juliet* enacts those tragic effects. And it embodies, too, the ongoing conflict between the imaginative community of the playhouse, with its
high passions, wily plots, and addiction to laughter, and the society
beyond the playhouse doors, which was so reluctant to acknowledge
the legitimacy of theatrical representations of its follies and inconsistencies.

Yet the tragic ending of *Romeo and Juliet* seems to derive its impetus
from a rather different conflict. The lovers die as victims of a clash
between the imperatives of heterosexual love and the age-old alliance of
masculinity with violence;[3] an alliance Shakespeare invokes by intro-
ducing two major innovations into the plot, neither of which has any
equivalent in earlier versions of the story. The first is the killing of
Romeo's friend Mercutio, the act that prompts Romeo to kill Tybalt in
revenge and get himself banished from Verona. The second is the
sword-fight between Romeo and Paris, Juliet's fiancé, at the entrance to
Juliet's tomb, where Romeo stabs his rival, to his instant regret, before
taking his own life with poison. In Shakespeare's Verona violence
between men breaks out with startling suddenness, as if in conscious or
unconscious rivalry with the build-up of sexual excitement between the
lovers. And from this point on in Shakespeare's theatrical career, sword-
fights between men are always interrupting the intimate verbal and
physical encounters between men and women. The male lovers in
A Midsummer Night's Dream stumble through a forest at midnight,

swords drawn, thirsting after one another's blood; in *Much Ado about
Nothing*, the lover Benedick is sent by Beatrice to prove his commitment
to her by killing his best friend Claudio; in *Twelfth Night* the lover Viola
in boy's disguise gets forced into a duel with Sir Andrew Aguecheek, an
abortive combat that is later brought to a bloody conclusion by Viola's
brother Sebastian; and in *Othello* Desdemona's supposed lover Cassio is
horribly maimed in a night-time brawl by the villain Iago.
Responsibility for such outbreaks of male violence, as well as for the
erotic context that engenders them, was laid by the theatre-haters at
the playwrights' door; indeed, they claimed that the doors of playhouses were invariably the starting point for the periodic riots that
broke out in the London streets. At first sight, then, it looks as though
the love of Romeo for Juliet and the aggression of the Veronese men
spring from the same anarchic source, and that both are disastrous
instances of the uncontrolled emotion that is always getting fanned into
flame by the early modern theatre.

Elizabethan London was certainly a violent place, and the ubiquity
of deadly weapons made its violence always potentially mortal. William
Harrison comments on the fact with consternation in his *Description of
England*. 'Seldom', he writes,

> shall you see any of my countrymen above eighteen or twenty
> years old to go without a dagger at least at his back or by his side,
> although they be aged burgesses or magistrates of any city, who
> in appearance are most exempt from brabbling and contention.
> Our nobility wear commonly swords or rapiers with their
> daggers, as doth every common servingman also that followeth
> his lord and master. Some desperate cutters we have in like sort
> which carry two daggers or two rapiers in a sheath always about
> them, wherewith in every drunken fray they are known to work
> much mischief; their swords and daggers also are of great length
> and longer than the like used in any other country, whereby each
> one pretendeth to have the more advantage of his enemy. But as
> many orders have been taken for the intolerable length of these
> weapons, so I see as yet small redress, but where the cause thereof
> doth rest, in sooth for my part I wot not.[4]

Here, the elderly burgesses wielding knives anticipate the brawling
fathers of Romeo and Juliet, and the sense of omnipresent steel makes
London sound as volatile as Verona. Moreover, the theatre-haters were
partly right: theatre men *did* seem particularly prone to stabbings, both
on the stage and off it. Marlowe's friend the poet and playwright
Thomas Watson killed a man in a sword-fight in 1589, four years before
Marlowe – who was involved in the same skirmish – died from a dagger-
blow to the eye in Deptford.[5] In 1598 Ben Jonson killed the actor Gabriel
Spencer in a duel, despite the fact that Spencer's sword was 'ten inches
longer than his'.[6] The clown Richard Tarlton was a Master of Fence,
and backed up his displays of wit on stage with aggressive displays of
swordsmanship on the streets of London. As Tarlton's case suggests,
fencing with swords was closely associated, both metaphorically and in
practice, with verbal fencing. It is partly for this reason that Stephen
Gosson in *The School of Abuse* brackets fencing masters with poets,
playwrights and musicians as teachers in the wayward institution of
his title, instructing vulnerable English youngsters in the dark arts
necessary for a dissolute life. Contemporary fencers, he claims, like
men trained in the arts of language, use their skill for their own self-
aggrandisement rather than for the benefit of their country: they think
themselves 'no men, if for stirring of a strawe they proove not their
valure uppon some bodyes flesh'.[7] *Romeo and Juliet* presents us with a
world like this one, where manhood is proved in violence on the body.
The play begins with two young men of the house of Capulet bragging
about their plans to kill the men of the rival house of Montague and
rape their women with the help of their 'naked weapons' (1.1.34); and
soon afterwards the Capulets graduate from trading insults with their
enemies to trading blows. All Shakespeare's later engagements with
desire occupy some point on this continuum, where words transform
themselves into swords and the male tool of sexual pleasure spontaneously converts itself into an instrument of death. Nowhere, however,
is he more explicit than in this play on the catastrophic consequences of
defining masculinity, both verbally and physically, in terms of blood-
shed.[8]

   Sparring brings men closer together, whether in affection or in
enmity. They jostle for power by joshing one another on their sexual

inadequacies and triumphs. They exploit women as a means of defining their relationships with other men, verbally invading women's bodies with the same freedom they propose to themselves in invading one another's bodies with their swords. And by probing the hidden desires of their friends they affirm their mutual intimacy, as when Romeo's cousin Benvolio inquires into the cause of Romeo's melancholy in the play's opening scenes, or when his friend Mercutio imagines him and other men having sex with his first love Rosaline. There seems remarkably little difference between this friendly joshing and the insults that provoke mortal combat. When Tybalt calls Romeo 'boy' (3.1.65), an affront to his sexual maturity that triggers a fight to the death, he seems to insult the young man rather less than Mercutio does in earlier scenes when he pretends to conjure up phallic spirits in the circle of Rosaline's vagina (2.1.23–7), or when he tells Romeo that 'this drivelling love is like a great natural that runs lolling up and down to hide his bauble in a hole' (2.4.91–2). The proximity between rapier wit and violence with rapiers is, indeed, attested by Mercutio; at one point in a jocular slanging-match with Romeo he cries out like an exhausted duelist, 'Come between us, good Benvolio, my wits faints' (2.4.67–8). Young men kill each other with swords, yet their sword-fights, like their word-fights, serve as a perverse expression of sympathy, a painful alternative to homoerotic foreplay. It is for this reason, perhaps, that Juliet considers Romeo's killing of her cousin Tybalt as an act of infidelity, and invokes the vocabulary of the abandoned woman as soon as she hears about it: 'O serpent heart, hid with a flowering face. / Did ever dragon keep so fair a cave?' (3.2.73–4). It is for this reason, too, that Romeo's second homicide of the play – his killing of Paris – is prefaced by a declaration of love for his rival ('By heaven I love thee better than myself' (5.3.64)), and followed by the honourable interment of Paris in Juliet's tomb, where Romeo himself intends to lie, as 'One writ with me in sour misfortune's book' (5.3.82). Romeo's love affair with Juliet takes place in a milieu where sexual attraction between men and women forms an integral part of the discourse of affection between men. And like mutual male affection in this fictional Verona, it seems inevitable from the beginning that at one stage or other the love of men for women will be marred by sudden violence.

This inevitability is confirmed by the fact that the older men who rule Verona have not yet lost their taste for the heady fusion of sex and violence they enjoyed in their youth. In the first scene old Capulet, Juliet's father, calls for his sword, eager to join in the fray stirred up by his younger relatives, while his wife urges him to call instead for a crutch, as a more appropriate emblem of his geriatric impotence (1.1.75–6). Next time we see the old man he is indulging in a spot of imaginative voyeurism, as he pictures to himself the sexual arousal of young Paris at a party full of female 'stars' he has thrown in his honour:

> Such comfort as do lusty young men feel
> When well-apparell'd April on the heel
> Of limping winter treads, even such delight
> Among fresh female buds shall you this night
> Inherit at my house.
>
> (1.2.26–30)

Paris is old Capulet's chosen son-in-law and inheritor, just as Juliet is an extension of his ageing body, 'the hopeful lady of my earth', as he calls her (1.2.15); and the party is one of Capulet's efforts to rejuvenate himself through interference with the next generation. Before Romeo and Juliet's first meeting, then, the lexicons of love and sex have been contaminated by their exclusive deployment in the service of male desire, and much of the young couple's energy is expended in an effort to find a language of their own, a discourse of desire that is free from damaging associations with power-games and blood-lust.

At the same time, the young and old men in the play are always trying to reabsorb Romeo into the all-male community by making him speak as they do. As we have seen, men's language in the play is full of barbed jests, which can abruptly gain real barbs or points as hot air gives way to cold steel. These jests are a way of bonding – but they are also a way of identifying those who cannot bond, as with Shylock in *The Merchant of Venice*. Romeo's exclusion from male company at the beginning of the play is signalled by his heaviness: he is too serious about Rosaline, and Mercutio strives throughout the first three acts to recall him to the verbal and sexual lightness that is the medium of male friendship. When at last the younger man begins to jest again – ironically, after he has dismissed Rosaline from his mind and fallen far more seriously for Juliet – Mercutio is delighted. 'Now art thou sociable', he cries, 'now art thou Romeo' (2.4.89), and he welcomes him back into his proper sphere with a veritable barrage of witticisms. Male identity depends on a man's capacity to share a joke with his male friends, and an inability to do so, it is implied, may have serious consequences. It is Romeo's too-serious response to Tybalt's jibes that prompts Mercutio to fight with Tybalt on Romeo's behalf, unable to comprehend his friend's 'calm, dishonourable, vile submission' to one of the hated Capulets (3.1.72). The lightness with which he undertakes the quarrel stakes Mercutio's claim to manhood, a manhood Romeo has forfeited through his solemn declaration of love for his enemy. But when Mercutio is killed in this light quarrel, lightness turns to 'lightning', the word Benvolio uses to describe the ensuing battle between Romeo and Tybalt that ends in Tybalt's death (3.1.173). Male lightness, then, can be a ritual as oppressive as forced marriage, and as likely to prove destructive to its participants.

The chief emblem of male lightness in the play is its imaginary monarch, the fairy called Queen Mab. Mercutio invents her at the point when Romeo is at his most 'heavy' or despondent, having dreamt that something bad will happen at the Capulets' party, 'Some consequence, yet hanging in the stars' which will end in 'some vile forfeit of untimely death'(1.4.107–11). Mercutio's fairy-tale attempts to defuse this moment of foreboding by comically demonstrating that dreams are not to be taken seriously. Instead, Mercutio maintains, they are the playgrounds of men's and women's appetites and cravings, all of which may be reduced to the diminutive dimensions of the supernatural sovereign. Queen Mab's smallness gives her access to the most intimate parts of the human body and mind, and as she steers her tiny wagon through the various nocturnal visions these engender she erases all qualitative distinctions between one dream and the next. For her, the devoted lover's dream of passion has no greater or lesser value than the courtier's of preferment, the lawyer's of fees, the parson's of accumulating benefices, or the soldier's dreams of 'cutting foreign throats' and of heavy drinking (1.4.82–8). For Mercutio, Romeo's infatuation with

Rosaline is, like other obsessions, 'as thin of substance as the air' and 'more inconstant than the wind' (1.4.99–100), and no weight need therefore be attached to any forebodings he may have about it. But Mercutio himself has already shown how the dreams of Queen Mab may turn to nightmare, as he describes the soldier starting awake at the imagined sound of a drum – a forecast of Mercutio's death-by-lightness. In this play, the light has a way of turning heavy, and the 'inconstant' of getting fixed in grooves that lead inexorably to the grave. Like other ladies of the night, Queen Mab brings 'plagues' and 'misfortune' to her sleeping clients as well as delight (1.4.75, 91), and it is not long before we learn that laughter shares in her duplicity, her volatile fusion of daylight brilliance and nocturnal gloom.

As well as turning heavy, light has a way in this play of turning dark – sometimes for a while, sometimes forever. At the beginning it seems that light and dark may be exchanged on a whim, as part of the flashy verbal game that is always afoot in Verona. Romeo creates an artificial night in his bedroom, where he may nurse his yearning for the indifferent Rosaline – a night that seems to his father 'black and portentous' (1.1.141); but soon afterwards Old Capulet is gleefully lighting up the dark with the beauty of the youngsters who attend his party, while Mercutio illuminates the night with his fairy fable. At the end of the first act, however, Romeo sees a vision of light in darkness – Juliet at the party – that overwhelms, for him, all other sensory perceptions, and becomes the touchstone by which the properties of light and darkness will henceforth be measured. On seeing her he at once decides that she is qualitatively different from everyone else: 'It seems she hangs upon the cheek of night / As a rich jewel in an Ethiop's ear – / Beauty too rich for use, for earth too dear' (1.5.45–7). This is ironic, since Benvolio first encouraged him to attend the party in order that he should *cease* to see any single woman as uniquely excellent, since when 'weigh'd' against other women in the 'crystal scales' of Romeo's eyes 'she shall scant show well that now seems best' (1.2.96–101). Instead, Romeo thinks himself to have seen 'true beauty' in Juliet (1.5.53) – beauty that extinguishes all its rivals, and is set apart from anything earthly (the implication is that it will only come into its own after leaving the earth at death). Where he was expected to reunite himself with the levity of his companions, he finds himself more alienated from them than ever, more serious than ever in his devotion to just one woman, more fixed than ever in his affections. Where he was expected to find a diffused everyday lightness, he finds instead a concentrated brilliance that plunges everything else in gloom.

From this moment on, Romeo and Juliet become denizens of the night, meeting under cover of darkness, their relationship barred from exposure to daylight, which in turn gets clogged and burdened with the weight of authority – especially that of oppressive parents and the heavy-handed Veronese state. The famous balcony scene, their second meeting, takes place at night, as does the consummation of their clandestine wedding, Juliet's consumption of the sleeping draft that confirms her commitment to Romeo, and the lovers' eventual death. (The marriage itself takes place by daylight, in accordance with Friar Laurence's hope that it will serve as a means of publicly uniting the lovers' feuding families.) Yet despite being wedded to the dark Romeo and Juliet are the lightest of lovers, whose perennial attractiveness stems partly from their youthful love of laughter. Their situation is deadly; yet they are always playing games with it, then getting caught up short by the seriousness of things, then leaping into playfulness again. Romeo's name, for instance, marks him as the enemy of Juliet's family, and in the balcony scene she first toys with the notion that he might change it as easily as he might make a pun; is then filled with horror at the frivolity with which he treats the risk of death; and finally finds herself comically unable to stop repeating his name, no matter how dangerous such repetition may be, no matter how true it is that 'bondage is hoarse and may not speak aloud' (2.2.160). Romeo, meanwhile, trifles with the notion of lightness in celebration of his release from the leaden weight of his attraction to Rosaline. When Juliet asks him how he got into her garden he answers that he fluttered in on 'love's light wings' (2.2.66); to which Juliet replies bluntly and reprovingly 'If they do see thee, they will murder thee' (2.2.70). Juliet's own natural buoyancy is inhibited at first by her fear that he may think her 'light' – that is, sexually 'easy' – if she assents to his suit too readily (2.2.99). But urgency, and the fact that Romeo already knows her mind (he overheard her talking to herself about her love for him at the beginning of the scene) make it impossible, in the end, for her to be other than bluntly honest: 'therefore pardon me', she concludes, 'And not impute this yielding to light love / Which the dark night hath so discovered' (2.2.104–6). Hereafter their exchanges are as light as the objects – flowers, birds, hearts and souls – to which they are always alluding, and as full of affectionate wit as the exchanges of the Veronese men are full of wittily articulated aggression.

For Juliet in the balcony scene, love strikes with unnerving speed, like the proverbial bolt from the blue. 'It is too rash, too unadvis'd, too sudden', she worries, 'Too like the lightning, which doth cease to be / Ere one can say "It lightens" ' (2.2.118–20). The metaphor of the lightning makes love's rapidity potentially lethal; and sure enough, the speed of events precipitated by love accelerates as the play goes on, bringing it into a collision course with the ponderous solemnity of the older generation. Juliet contrasts 'wind-swift Cupid', the young god of youthful desire, with the plodding pace of the elderly, 'unwieldy, slow, heavy, and pale as lead' (2.5.8–17) – a contrast that ushers in the funniest scene in the play, when she waits on tenterhooks for her aged nurse to tell her the outcome of a crucial interview with Romeo. Friar Laurence warns Romeo to move 'Wisely and slow' since 'they stumble that run fast' (2.3.90). Yet when Juliet hurries to her marriage the Friar himself describes her as the incarnation of lightness, incapable of being weighed down by good advice: 'A lover may bestride the gossamers / That idles in the wanton summer air / And yet not fall; so light is vanity' (2.6.18–20). This youthful lightness as manifested in speed rushes the young couple into chronological spaces that older men consider their own. It is aged male authority that determines when the young are ripe for marriage, when crimes are to be punished, when debts must be paid and when the time has come for death; and as the lovers thrust themselves into each of these spaces – through marriage, manslaughter, disobedience – old age becomes increasingly intolerant of their incursions into its territory, increasingly unable to take their youthful impetuosity lightly.

Romeo's love for Juliet speeds up his fatal reaction to Mercutio's murder: 'O sweet Juliet', he says, 'Thy beauty hath made me effeminate' (3.1.114–15), and he hurries to restore himself to manly status by stabbing Tybalt. But the reaction of age and authority is just as hasty, as if they aim to stop the career of rebellious youth in its tracks by sudden action: the Prince of Verona banishes Romeo 'Immediately' (3.1.188), without more than a cursory inquiry into the circumstances of the killing. Soon afterwards, Juliet's impatience to consummate her marriage ('Gallop apace, you fiery-footed steeds … And bring in cloudy night immediately' (3.2.1–4)) is more than matched by her father's impatience for her to marry Paris – yet another manifestation of old Capulet's eagerness to rekindle his failing vitality at the expense of the young. The last two acts are filled with competing allusions to haste on the part of the lovers and the older generation, as Friar Laurence sends a messenger 'with speed' to tell the banished Romeo of Juliet's predicament (4.1.123), old Capulet brings forward her wedding day from Thursday to 'tomorrow' (4.2.37), Juliet fears that she will wake from her death-like sleep before the Friar arrives to comfort her, and Romeo commissions a fast-working poison from an apothecary, telling him to give him a dram so powerful 'that the trunk may be discharg'd of breath / As violently as hasty powder fir'd / Doth hurry from the fatal cannon's womb' (5.1.63–5). In *The Comedy of Errors* and *The Merchant of Venice*, a subject's time was governed – at least in theory – by the law, whose inexorable operations could be averted only by comic improvisation. In *Romeo and Juliet* nobody governs time, least of all the civic authorities, and the old and the young struggle to seize control of it through a series of ever more drastic pre-emptive strikes.

The lovers continue to improvise jokes and puns right up to the last minute of their lives, as if to confirm the kinship between the lightning speed of love and the sudden flash of wit – the 'quick answer' so beloved of Renaissance connoisseurs of laughter. Each new crisis gives them a new chance to display their skills as improvisers. When Romeo is grieving over his exile he cannot restrain himself from asking the nurse: 'what says / My conceal'd lady to our cancell'd love?' (3.3.97–8). Then as he and Juliet part after consummating their marriage they quibble over definitions of night and day – is the light in the East the dawn or some nocturnal meteor, is the bird they hear a nightingale or a lark? – with yet more dazzling ingenuity, before realizing that their playfulness could cost Romeo his life ('*Juliet*: O now be gone, more light and light it grows. *Romeo*: More light and light: more dark and dark our woes' (3.5.35–6)). As the tragedy hurries towards its end the encounters between light and dark, humour and sorrow become increasingly shocking. Romeo tells us he feels unusually light-hearted ('My bosom's lord sits lightly in his throne' (5.1.3)) when we know he is about to get news of Juliet's death. Later he observes 'How oft when men are at the point of death / Have they been merry! Which their keepers call / A lightning before death' (5.3.88–90); and as if to confirm this principle he himself cracks jokes before his suicide, pretending to be jealous of an 'unsubstantial Death' whose adulterous lust for Juliet's corpse makes it necessary for her husband to stay by her side forever (5.3.102–8). Soon afterwards Juliet emerges from her trance to find him dead beside her. She comically chides him for his bad manners in drinking all of the poison that killed him, leaving 'no friendly drop / To help me after' (5.3.163–4); then ends her life with a dagger thrust as sudden as a well-timed jest. The terminal humour of these young lovers confirms the dire warnings of Elizabethan moralists against the fatal combination of theatrical levity and desire. Friar Laurence seems to summarize the moralists' position when he tells Romeo, who is distraught because of his exile, that desire has bereft him of all reason: 'Thy wit ... Like powder in a skilless soldier's flask / Is set afire by thine own ignorance, / And thou dismember'd with thine own defence' (3.3.130–4). In this play, laughter may be explosive, and the military metaphor suggests that its explosiveness may have devastating consequences for the state as well as for individual subjects.

Yet the tragedy militates against the heavy morals with which the story of the Veronese lovers had been laden by its English narrators. William Painter, who translated the tale in his story-collection *The Palace of Pleasure* (1566–7), tells us that it shows 'what secret sleights of love, what danger either sort incurre which mary without the advise of Parentes'.[9] Arthur Brooke, whose poem *The Tragical History of Romeus and Juliet* (1562) served as Shakespeare's chief source, cites it as evidence of the dastardly doings of the Catholic religious orders, especially 'superstitious friers' who encourage 'auriculer confession (the kay of whoredome, and treason)'.[10] Shakespeare's play, by contrast, represents the world as a complex moral mixture, resistant to such simplistic diagnoses; and at the centre of this moral complexity is Friar Laurence, the lovers' confessor. The old man first appears in the half-light between night and day, signalling his morally ambiguous position as a representative of ecclesiastical authority who engages in clandestine practices of dubious legality (marrying two young lovers against their parents' wishes). He is gathering herbs, and observes how these share his own ambiguous nature:

> O, mickle is the powerful grace that lies
> In plants, herbs, stones, and their true qualities.
> For naught so vile that on the earth doth live
> But to the earth some special good doth give;
> Nor aught so good but, strain'd from that fair use,
> Revolts from true birth, stumbling on abuse.
> Virtue itself turns vice being misapplied,
> And vice sometime's by action dignified.
>
> (2.3.11–18)

For this religious man, the material and moral universe is filled with punning double meanings, and the signs it contains are always altering their significance as a result of tiny alterations in the timing of words and actions. Like Friar Lodowick in *Measure for Measure*, he strives throughout the play to direct the course of these duplicitous events towards a happy ending. He tells Romeo that the boy's secret marriage to Juliet 'may so happy prove / To turn your households' rancour to pure love' (2.3.87–8); and after Tybalt's death his predictions of future happiness grow yet more sanguine. Romeo must go into exile, he insists,

> till we can find a time
> To blaze your marriage, reconcile your friends,
> Beg pardon of the Prince and call thee back,
> With twenty hundred thousand times more joy
> Than thou wentst forth in lamentation.
>
> (3.3.150–4)

But the Friar's efforts to procure this cheerful homecoming grow increasingly contrived, increasingly enmeshed in the moral duplicity of which he spoke. He first resorts to a twisted prank – the simulation of

death – to help Juliet evade the sin of bigamy; and he then urges the
parents of the 'dead' girl to put their faith in a happy ending of a very
different order, the reception of their daughter's soul into heaven
(4.5.67–83). He attempts, in other words, to use grief to bring about
mirth, and the procedure seems so indirect that Juliet herself begins to
doubt him, fearing that he has given her poison instead of a potion so as
to clear himself of guilt for his part in her clandestine marriage
(4.3.24–7). She dismisses her fears at last and drinks the potion; but the
Friar's own philosophy dictates that her seeming escape will lead at last
to entrapment, and that any mirth she achieves with his help will end
in tears. It is appropriate, then, that the Friar should end as the
tragedy's chief narrator, telling the tale of Juliet's life and death amidst
a scene of carnage that is precisely the reverse of the happy ending he
had hoped for, and accusing himself of guilt for the lovers' death even
as he protests his innocence. Under these conditions, blame for the
tragedy can hardly be levelled at one particular figure or generation in
the play. 'All are punish'd', as the Prince points out (5.3.295), from
the Friar to the lovers to the Prince himself; and this collective sharing-
out of punishment parodies the communal merry-making that closes
conventional comedies.

Grief is the proper reaction to such an ending. Yet Juliet famously
took pleasure in a certain kind of grief – the 'sweet sorrow' of leaving
one's lover (2.2.184); and throughout the play the heaviness of grief is
strangely fused, like love and violence, with the lightness of laughter.
On the eve of Juliet's counterfeit death, her father tells his wife that his
'heart is wondrous light' (4.2.46), as if in mockery of the grief it will
shortly be charged with. Once the death is discovered, this grief is
mocked again by the nurse's overblown lamentations, which pastiche
the tragic laments penned by Shakespeare's contemporaries ('O woe! O
woeful, woeful, woeful day' (4.5.49)). Later the Capulets' clownish servant Peter asks some musicians to help him mourn by playing 'some
merry dump' in place of the wedding tunes for which they were hired
(4.5.104). Even when the young lovers are *really* dead the older generation find themselves infected with comedy as if by a virus bequeathed to
them by their children. Old Capulet complains that the dagger with
which Juliet stabbed herself has 'mista'en', having 'mis-sheathed' itself

in his daughter's bosom (5.3.203–5). The Prince tells old Montague that he has got 'early up / To see thy son and heir now early down' (5.3.208–9), and Montague responds by berating Romeo for being rude enough 'To press before thy father to a grave' (5.3.215). In the final scene the lovers' deaths are described by the Prince as hemmed in with 'ambiguities' (5.3.217), and they sow ambiguities in their wake, half-laughing expressions of grief that voice their families' amazement at their spontaneous improvisation of a scenario that so thoroughly violates the expectations of the old.

But this is an indictment of the old, not the young: those who have abandoned humour – or who claim a monopoly over it – not those who have lived by its wayward dictates. The lovers' deaths are brought about by a succession of moments when their elders succumb to solemnity. When old Capulet insists that his daughter marry Paris and adds 'I do not use to jest' (3.5.189), and when he sets a date for the wedding which will not admit of the temporal flexibility that is the stock-in-trade of comedy, he is signing her death warrant. The older generation are insistent on adhering to the dictates of the law, yet at the same time willing to stretch and twist those dictates whenever this serves their interests. And the Veronese law itself is an unwieldy instrument, unable – in contrast to the laws of Venice, Ephesus or Vienna – to find a means of circumventing its own crude prescriptions when occasion demands. It is the voice of the law, Prince Escalus, who defines the blade-wielding badinage between Montagues and Capulets as an act of rebellion ('Rebellious subjects' (1.1.81)), and who demands that the brawl cease at once 'On pain of torture' and 'on pain of death' (1.1.86, 103). Later the Prince appears in a gentler light as he commutes the sentence passed on Romeo for killing Tybalt from death to banishment; but to a theatre audience even this commutation seems heavy-handed, especially when Romeo dies as a result of misunderstandings arising from his situation as an exile. Old Capulet, meanwhile, who breaks the law in the play's first scene, is quick to invoke the immemorial law of patriarchy when his daughter defies him. Forgetting what he said in the first act – that Juliet's consent must be sought before she is engaged – the old man loses his temper and tells her to agree to marry Paris or 'hang! Beg! Starve! Die in the streets!', stripped of her rights as his only heir

(3.5.192). Old Capulet, in other words, gets heavy with his daughter when she fails to accommodate his light-hearted offer to the man he favours – an offer that is presented to her as a means of alleviating her 'heaviness' over the death of Tybalt (3.5.108). By the time he is celebrating his light-heartedness on the eve of her death, it is clear that what makes him cheerful is obedience – the acknowledgement by the young of the full weight of his authority. Juliet's apparent demise underscores the perversity of this form of cheerfulness. What is cheering for him is deadly for her, and how better to point this out than by having his preparations for her wedding party transformed into funeral arrangements, so that in an instant (as Capulet puts it) 'all things change them to the contrary' (4.5.90)?

The old man shares his self-serving intransigence with the young men who are close to him. His kinsman Tybalt, for instance, takes with murderous seriousness the enmity between the rival houses that old Capulet can lay aside whenever it suits him to do so. He is a youth with no sense of humour, who means what he says when he insults Romeo's masculinity, just as he fights strictly according to the rules laid down in the most fashionable duellists' handbook – much to Mercutio's disgust (2.4.19–36). Like his elderly kinsman, however, Tybalt can lay aside the rules of fencing when he wants to: he stabs Mercutio treacherously 'under Romeo's arm' (3.1.89–90), thus violating in an instant all the codes he claims to live by. Count Paris, Capulet's favourite, is just as humourless as Tybalt, though more wedded to the letter of the law: it is in seeking to 'apprehend' Romeo for returning illegally from exile that the young man meets his end (5.3.69). In the case of these two youths – one related to old Capulet, the other to the Prince – obedience to the precepts of their elders proves as damaging as the lovers' adolescent rebelliousness.

Like the great educators of the humanist movement, the theatre-haters attempted to drive a wedge between generations, lending authority to the old and urging subservience on the young. *Romeo and Juliet* explodes these distinctions and displays the destructiveness of trying to enforce them. In this play, the young and the old are inextricably bound up with one another: they share the same qualities of passion, inconsistency, obtuseness, rashness, bull-headedness and the love of laughter.

But the old and those who serve them too easily forget their bond with youth, and too readily discard the generosity that characterizes certain branches of the comic. In Act 1 this generosity is summed up in old Capulet's party, to which he welcomes the disguised Romeo with heart-felt enthusiasm, and at which he restrains his nephew Tybalt from destroying the festive atmosphere by harming this uninvited guest. But the party he later prepares for Juliet's wedding to Paris substitutes duress for delight, oppression for inclusiveness, and so exploits the light-ness of laughter as an instrument of patriarchal tyranny – with tragic results. It is not comedy that does this but the abandonment of certain comic principles: the capacity to accommodate sudden change, to cir-cumvent legal and moral prescriptions, to reinvent yourself spontan-eously whenever the need arises. In Shakespeare's Verona, maturity, authority and obedience are vastly more hurtful to the well-being of the state than that bugbear of the theatre-haters, love.

LUNACY AND LITTLENESS IN
A MIDSUMMER NIGHT'S DREAM

A Midsummer Night's Dream is the principal companion-piece of *Romeo and Juliet* among the comedies. It announces its link with tragedy by invoking the tale of Pyramus and Thisbe, Greek lovers whose parents disapproved of their union and who ended up dead through a succes-sion of unfortunate accidents. Like *Romeo and Juliet* it plays dazzling verbal games with light and dark, night and day, sex and violence, the rigidity of male authority and the flexibility of the comic. The difference is that *Romeo and Juliet* ends with the entrapment of its young lovers in the darkness of the tomb, the official burial ground for disobedience and desire, while the *Dream* ends with the temporary liberation of laughter, love and youth from all entrapment. This section considers how it achieves this liberation.

The play opens with the setting of two deadlines. The first is the date of Theseus' wedding to the Amazon Hippolyta, four days from the moment when the scene begins – a time that seems interminable to Theseus. The second is the date by which Hermia must decide whether

she will marry Demetrius, the man her father favours; or whether she
will choose instead to enter a religious order or to die – two fates that
Theseus seems to think the same. The second of these two deadlines
threatens to launch us into a tragedy much like Juliet's; but the possibility of a tragic outcome seems also to be averted by the fact that this
second deadline is imposed so soon after the first. Just as Theseus
is yearning for some pleasure to take up the time before the wedding
('Go, Philostrate', he cries, 'Stir up the Athenian youth to merriments; /
Awake the pert and nimble spirit of mirth; / Turn melancholy forth to
funerals' (1.1.11–14)), Hermia's furious father bursts in with a complaint against his disobedient daughter, as if in answer to the Athenian
ruler's prayer. The time-scale of the death-dealing law and the time-
scale of 'the pert and nimble spirit of mirth' have been fused, and it is
hard to believe that the second will not cancel out the first in
Shakespeare's Athens.

At the same time, we quickly learn that the comic world of
A Midsummer Night's Dream is no less unsettling than the tragic universe of *Romeo and Juliet*. In this play, people get their kicks from other
people's pain. Theseus' forthcoming marriage to Hippolyta, which he
contemplates with such delight, was brought about by violence:
'Hippolyta', he tells her, 'I woo'd thee with my sword, / And won thy
love doing thee injuries' (1.1.16–17).[11] The festive happy ending of his
particular comedy, then, has its roots in the destruction of the Amazon
people, and Hippolyta seems unable or unwilling to put this fact behind
her – unlike Theseus, she is certain the time till their wedding will pass
swiftly (1.1.7–11). Later, Puck derives unmitigated pleasure from the
sight of four lovers quarrelling in the forest, a sight that ends with two
men chasing each other through the trees with murderous intent; while
one of the lovers, Helena, has no difficulty in believing that the other
three should have teamed up together to mock her cruelly 'for your
merriment' (3.2.146). In the play's final act the court of Athens finds
itself weeping tears of laughter at a tragic performance: as Philostrate
puts it, 'more merry tears / The passion of loud laughter never shed'
(5.1.69–70). Their laughter seems to stem from the same roots as their
delight in blood sports. Theseus and Hippolyta give fulsome praise to the
'musical ... discord' and 'sweet thunder' of Spartan hounds (4.1.117);

and the fairies share the taste of the royal couple, esteeming the murderous 'jangling' of lovers as 'sport' to be voyeuristically pursued to its bloody climax (3.2.354). Laughter, pain and death seem to be bound up together in this play as intimately as they are anywhere else in the work of Shakespeare.

Disturbingly present in the play, too, is the notion – familiar since *The Two Gentlemen of Verona* – that men and women inhabit separate communities, and that these two communities spend much of their time effectively at war. Titania keeps the little Indian boy who is coveted by Oberon in memory of the boy's mother, with whom she shared an intimate bond summed up in a wistful anecdote of a day spent by the sea (2.1.123–37). Her fidelity to this bond between women is what sets her at odds with the Fairy King, with disastrous effects on the seasons. Hippolyta, as an Amazon warrior, personifies a tradition of active female resistance to male influence, one that has been aggressively suppressed by Theseus. And we learn, too, of a 'fair vestal' (2.1.155–64) – a mythical counterpart of Elizabeth I – whose potent resistance to Cupid's arrows seems to involve her in the same combat between the sexes. Hermia and Helena, we learn, once shared an attachment as strong as that of Titania and the boy's mother. Hermia recalls their former friendship with fondness (1.1.214–16), and it is on the strength of it that she tells Helena of her plans to elope from Athens. And although their bond has been severed by the middle of the play, after Helena has betrayed her friend's confidence and the women have descended into mutual acrimony, the aggression of men against women which is its corollary remains present throughout the action. As Helena follows Demetrius into the forest he threatens her with violence ('if thou follow me, do not believe / But I shall do thee mischief in the wood' (2.1.236–7)); and when Lysander falls out of love with Hermia his fiancée is afflicted by nightmares of his delight in seeing her suffer: 'Methought a serpent ate my heart away, / And you sat smiling at his cruel prey' (2.2.148–9). The hostilities between men and women find their most painful outlet in the games men play with women's affections: the savage 'jests' Helena and Hermia believe are being played on them in Act 3, scene 2, and the tasteless prank Oberon plays on Titania, drugging her into infatuation with a monster. These jests are extensions of the still more cruel games which, we learn, were played before the play began, when Demetrius courted Helena and then abandoned her, or when Theseus raped one woman (as Oberon tells us) and abandoned three others (2.1.77–80). The name of Helena recalls another famous victim of Theseus' aggression, Helen of Troy;[12] and at one point Hermia invokes yet another instance of the disastrous male practice of 'sporting' with female affection – Queen Dido, whose abandonment by Aeneas led to her suicide (1.1.173–4). Shakespeare's story takes place in a context where relations between the genders have been permanently blighted, marred by primitive impulses to hurt and shame, unprotected by any consistent standards of civility.

But this is also a play that refuses to take the threat of this context too seriously, or to let the weight of male oppression crush its commitment to lightness. Above all, it resists the kind of confinement that killed the Veronese lovers. The title of *A Midsummer Night's Dream* declares its equal affinity with darkness and light: the gloom of night when fears are at their height and the most innocuous of objects provokes panic ('in the night . . . How easy is a bush suppos'd a bear!' (5.1.21–2)); and the brightness of the dream-state, when sexual desire can be indulged without guilt, transformations accomplished without terror, and laws both scientific and natural may be breached without incurring retribution. The constant interplay between light and dark is itself a kind of lightness, demonstrating the impossibility that the latter should ever overwhelm the former. And in this play, the boundaries of any given night cannot be marked with any precision. The specificity of the title, which locates the action in the shortest night of the year when quasi-pagan festive celebrations took place all over England, is belied by the chronological confusion that reigns over the plot. It is not clear whether midsummer's night is the night of the lovers' flight from Athens, which takes up Acts 2, 3 and the beginning of Act 4, or the night of Theseus' wedding, which takes up Act 5. These two nights seem magically to contain the four nights that are supposed to elapse between the first scene and the marital ceremony. Comedy in this play disrupts the smooth running of the official clock, as *Romeo and Juliet* could not, and so brings all things under its aegis: makes them light, as it were, however heavy or sombre they may seem on first inspection.

The moon dominates proceedings: a moon that changes constantly, and that is always present even when it is invisible. Time in Elizabethan England was often counted in moons, as the first scene reminds us ('but O, methinks, how slow / This old moon wanes!' (1.1.3–4)); and the quality of time counted in moons is very different from that of time as measured by clockwork. Revels in this play are always by moonlight; and the moon-goddess Diana is invoked repeatedly, whether in the person of Titania (who shares one of Diana's names), or by direct or indirect allusion. She is the presiding deity of this particular piece of night-time revelry, and her influence is not restricted to the night – any more than Elizabethan plays were confined to nocturnal performances (indeed plays in public playhouses were *never* performed at night). Accordingly, we are reminded that the moon is also present in daylight, sometimes on the other side of the earth. Both Oberon and the first fairy tell us that fairies can travel round the planet 'Swifter than the wandering moon' (2.1.7, 4.1.96–7); and Hermia says she would as soon believe Lysander could leave her as that 'This whole earth may be bor'd, and that the moon / May through the centre creep, and so displease / Her brother's noon-tide with th'Antipodes' (3.2.53–5) – an event that seems to become entirely feasible when she learns that Lysander has indeed left her. The moon has influence over the seasons of the year, as we learn when she turns 'Pale in her anger' at the quarrel between Oberon and Titania, which makes the spring, summer, autumn and winter 'change / Their wonted liveries' in response to her rage (2.1.103–13). Yet even this sometimes fearsome goddess has a lighter side. The humblest of mortals can become her paramour, as Bottom does when he sleeps with the moon-queen Titania in a cheerful pastiche of the love-affair between Diana and the shepherd boy Endymion.[13] And mortals may mimic the moon herself, as Starveling does when he trots on stage with his lantern, dog and bush of thorns. For Elizabethans, the moon had a direct effect on the human brain, causing it to expand and contract at different times of the month and infecting every man and woman with potential lunacy.[14] Under these circumstances, not even rooted enmity lasts long, depending as it does on an implacability that is foreign to the human body and mind; and though love may not be constant, there will always be plenty of it about, since it is kin to moon-bred madness (as Theseus famously points out in the final act (5.1.4–22)).

The moon's changing light is just one of its qualities. The other is its changing size; so it is hardly surprising if this moon-governed play should be full of sudden spurts of growth and shrinkage. Shakespeare has sometimes been credited – if this is the right word – with diminishing the ancient fairies, which in Medieval times had been as tall as ordinary men and women, into the tiny sensual munchkins that so tickled the Victorian fancy.[15] Titania, whose name, as we have seen, allies her to the terrifying moon-goddess mentioned in Act 5 – the 'triple Hecate' who appears in person in *Macbeth* (3.5 and 4.1) – presides over a train of fairies small enough to think cowslips tall, to wear bat-wing coats, to feel threatened by newts, beetles and spiders, and to do battle with bees. It was for the diminution and defilement of the ancient gods and goddesses that poets were condemned by their classical adversaries. Gosson wrote a whole essay focusing on the poet's and playwright's willingness to countenance the saucy sexual doings of the pagan gods, and his argument takes up a theme developed at length in Plato's *Republic*, from which poets were banned for – among other things – their blasphemous temerity in forging pornographic fantasies about boys, girls, beasts and deities.[16] Titania's world is so small, however – so preoccupied with harmless objects like bee-stings, butterflies' wings and flowers – that her own sexual scandal, her falling in love with an ass-headed mortal, scarcely seems to warrant the solemn treatment the theatre-haters would have given it. Her double change of status, meanwhile, from goddess to fairy and from queen to laughing-stock, parallels the equally rapid shifts of status among mortals. Helena is transformed, through the operation of an enchanted plant, from an ugly 'monster' (as she thinks herself (2.2.93–6)) to an Olympian in a few short lines: 'O Helen', cries the converted Demetrius, 'goddess, nymph, perfect, divine!' (3.2.137). Meanwhile Hermia experiences a reverse transformation, from a goddess as bright as Venus (3.2.60–1) to a woman whose defining characteristic is her smallness, described variously as 'puppet', 'dwarf', 'minimus', 'bead' and 'acorn' (3.2.288–329).

The little Indian boy over whom the fairy monarchs quarrel undergoes a similar shrinkage, from the 'rich' cause of his mother's big belly and the alteration of the seasons (2.1.131) to a trifle small enough to be carried by a fairy to Oberon's bower, once Titania's attentions have shifted to Bottom (4.1.58–60). And the whole night's adventures in the woods dwindle in the penultimate scene of Act 4 to the size of a land-scape seen at a distance: 'These things', says Demetrius, 'seem small and undistinguishable, / Like far-off mountains turned into clouds' (4.1.186–7). In the final act, the craftsmen of Athens stage a tragedy in the full awareness that size and status are both relative. The court ladies, they believe, will be frightened by the 'smallest monstrous mouse that creeps on floor' (5.1.217), and it is incumbent on the actors to ensure that their fear of the monstrous does not diminish their pleasure in the dramatic performance they are about to witness. They do so by making every aspect of their play minute: from the 'monstrous little voice' with which Bottom proposes to play the part of Thisbe in Act 1 (1.2.49) to the tiny roar he promises to emit as Lion (1.2.68–9); from the name of King Ninus, which the actors pronounce 'Ninny' (3.1.91), to the many curtailments with which the play is filled, as actors announce their departure or death with equal equanimity and abrupt-ness. If Mercutio's Queen Mab aimed to show Romeo that his love of Rosaline was less serious than he thought it, the tininesses of *A Midsummer Night's Dream* render all solemnity suspect, an error in judgement that lends undue weight to that which might as easily, and more safely, be taken with a pinch of salt, a leavening of laughter.

The implications of this triumph of comic littleness and lightness are nevertheless serious ones. Drama in this play is the province of the humblest members of a commonwealth, the craftsmen who are at home neither in the forest nor the court, neither in Oberon's domain nor Theseus'.[17] Yet these commoners move with consummate ease between both spheres, protected by their confidence in their own iden-tity. The 'mechanicals' have a better idea of the magical illusion of drama than anyone else in the play; it both exhilarates and disturbs them. Preparing their play, they are certain that their performance will utterly possess the imaginations of their audience – hence their intro-duction of safety measures (the prologue, the lion's speech) to protect their audience from suffering for this state of possession. Bottom is certain that he can act any role, whether lion, woman, Hercules, a lover or a tyrant, with the competence of a master conjurer. And his confidence is borne out in 'real life' when he becomes Titania's lover, and plays his part with a dignity and grace surpassing anything the ruling classes in the play can muster.[18] Theseus, as we have seen, has a history of violence he cannot easily shake off – it is replayed in the tyrannical ultimatum he imposes on Hermia. The fairy royal couple squabble over trifles. But Bottom as the Fairy Queen's favourite never strikes a false note. He is modest, denying both his own wisdom and his beauty; generous, in his wish that all 'honest neighbours' might be friends (3.1.138–40); courteous, greeting with affection three fairy servants whose names ally them with small, useful things, condiments (Mustardseed), sticking plasters (Cobweb), and pulses (Peaseblossom) (3.1.171–88). And when he is deposed from his brief eminence, he shows no regret: only a profound wonder at the strangeness of his midsummer vision (4.1.203–17). The source of his monarchic grace is identified after he has ceased to be a mock-monarch: in the warmth with which his friends talk about him during his absence, in the epithets they give him ('O sweet bully Bottom!' (4.2.19)), and in his joyful greeting to them when he rejoins them against all odds: 'Where are these lads? Where are these hearts?' (4.2.25). Clearly Bottom has a gift for inspiring love. Titania's love for him may be a travesty forced on her by enchantment, but Bottom is a worthy object for it; his friends all love him, and he acts the lover, both in the forest and in the court, with utter persuasiveness. He is a fitting role-model for all classes in the play, from menials to immortals.

At the same time, the theatre-haters would have identified this humble paragon or paramour as the demonic heart of the play, the proof of its hellish origins. His brief interval of power as a grotesque Fairy King illustrates comedy's capacity for insubordination – for wilfully destabilizing the social hierarchy and making mock of legitimate authority. After all, having a moon-goddess fall in love with an ass was a risky plot device in a kingdom ruled by an unmarried Queen who identified herself with Diana. And the fact that the commoner Bottom acquires his royal status through magic only goes to show how ready players and playwrights are to ally themselves with the devil: as *Doctor Faustus* and Greene's *Friar Bacon and Friar Bungay* show us, magic was widely seen as the devil's handiwork, and for theatre-haters the magic of the playhouse was no exception. Bottom's self-confidence could be held to illustrate the overweening arrogance of low-born players, a topic that Robert Greene, in the so-called 'penitent pamphlets' he wrote at the end of his career, elaborated at length.[19] And the constant slippage of the tragedy of *Pyramus and Thisbe* into obscenities – as Thisbe first kisses the wall's 'stones' or testicles and then its 'hole' or anus (5.1.188, 199) – goes to show how far the drama has degenerated from its ancient glory, how crude the modern brand of comedy is, how distant plays are from what they claim to be. Robin Goodfellow is the spirit responsible for Bottom's transmutation, and in the seventeenth century a book of his exploits was published whose title page depicts him as a devil dancing in a conjurer's circle, gripping a phallus in one hand and a broom in the other.[20] For theatre-haters this frontispiece could have served as an illustration for Shakespeare's play as a whole, whose plot moves in a circle from Athens back to Athens again, and whose proximity to hell is confirmed by its many references to things infernal.

Except that these references are for the most part designed to distinguish *A Midsummer Night's Dream* from the works of the devil. The first fairy we meet in the play, who meets Robin Goodfellow or Puck at the beginning of the second Act, offers a description of him that might be devilish: how he loves to terrorize village girls and 'Mislead night-wanderers, laughing at their harm' (2.1.34–9). But this is quickly undercut by Puck's continuation of her account, a comic sequel that reduces him to the size of a crab-apple bobbing against an old woman's lips to make her spill her ale, or a joint-stool slipping from under the bum of an over-serious aunt (2.1.47–54). Such antics hardly deserve to be labelled demonic, and their effect is wholesome: on seeing them 'the whole quire hold their hips and loffe [i.e. laugh] / And waxen in their mirth, and neeze, and swear / A merrier hour was never wasted there' (2.1.55–7). Later, Oberon and Puck together conspire to work malicious magic on Titania, designed to make her fall in love with a beast – 'lion, bear, or wolf, or bull' (2.1.180) – and thus conjuring up the monstrous prospect of bestiality, a practice associated with early modern witches. But again the monster she falls in love with cuts these threatened nightmares down to size: it is the amiable Bottom, whose

ROBIN
GOOD-FELLOW,
HIS MAD PRANKES AND
MERRY IESTS.

Full of honeſt Mirth, and is a fit Medicine
for Melancholy.

Printed at *London* by *Thomas Cotes,* and are to be ſold by
Francis Grove, at his ſhop on Snow-hill, neere the
Sarazens-head.   1639.

FIGURE 7   Title-page illustration to *Robin Good-fellow, his Mad Prankes and
Merry Jests* (1639), showing a decidedly demonic version of Robin Goodfellow or
Puck.

ass's head makes no fundamental difference to his identity (he already had a figurative 'ass-head' of his own before he obtained a real one (3.1.110), and the worst effect his change has on him is to make him itchy).   Demonic possibilities are often invoked in the forest; when Oberon, for instance, orders Robin to cover the stars with 'drooping fog, as black as Acheron' and then plunge the lovers into 'death-counterfeiting sleep' (3.2.357–64), or when Robin later in the same scene warns his fairy lord that the dawn is approaching, when 'Damned spirits' are forced to return to their wormy beds, doomed forever to 'consort with black-brow'd night' (3.2.382–7). But in each case the play refrains at the last minute from allying its own particular brand of magic with the work of the devil.

Responding to Puck's mention of damned spirits Oberon says, 'But we are spirits of another sort', and launches into a disquisition on his love of light, recalling the sport he has made with the goddess of the dawn and the pleasure he takes in watching the sea transformed into 'yellow gold' by the morning sunshine (3.2.388–93). He may be 'king of shadows' (3.2.347), but some shadows are inoffensive (actors, for example, are associated with 'shadows' in Puck's epilogue to the play (5.1.417), as they are in the plays of John Lyly).[21] And some forms of offence, even, may do more good than harm. The drama unfolded in the forest is no more damaging than the 'fierce vexation of a dream' (4.1.68) – capable of terrifying the dreamer, but also of bringing much-needed refreshment to exhausted minds.

Theseus and Hippolyta sum up the situation at the beginning of Act 5. For Theseus, the minds of lunatics, lovers and poets are closely related, and all are equally preoccupied with visions that have no grounding in material reality. The lunatic 'sees more devils than vast hell can hold' (5.1.9); and in saying this Theseus implicitly pokes fun at those who demonize the stage. The lover is incapable of telling beauty from ugliness owing to the influence of his infatuated mind on his outward vision. The poet, meanwhile, has the most roving eye of all, although the objects of his contemplation are not hellish, like the lunatic's: he looks 'from heaven to earth, from earth to heaven' (5.1.13), but does not take his inspiration from the underworld. For Theseus, the poet or playwright 'gives to airy nothing / A local habitation and a name' (5.1.16–17), fleshing out unfocused human emotions, whether joy or fear, by embodying them in some imagined human form that has no real presence. For Hippolyta, though, the 'poetic' story told by the lovers 'grows to something of great constancy; / But howsoever, strange and admirable' (5.1.26–7). Something substantial grows from their flight of nocturnal fancy; something that manifests itself in their collective behaviour ('their minds transfigur'd so together' (5.1.24)), an effect that could never have been produced by 'airy nothing'. Their adventures taught them how to live and speak in harmony, weaning them away from petty and unnecessary antagonisms. And an equally substantial lesson in living together, in the mutual respect and geniality that makes men and women sociable, is imported by the nocturnal shadow or dream that is the play of Pyramus and Thisbe.

Like Bottom's role in Shakespeare's play, the play performed by the mechanicals at court violates decorum: it is a tragedy performed by clowns. The master of ceremonies Philostrate therefore has no time for it as drama. He proposes, however, that it might possibly be enjoyed in the spirit of sadistic pleasure that has broken out from time to time since the play began: 'it is nothing', he says, 'nothing in the world; / Unless you can find sport in their intents, / Extremely stretch'd and conn'd with cruel pain / To do you service' (5.1.78–81). For him, the agony of learning lines is a suitable form of torture to be inflicted on the base-born actors for their misplaced desire to entertain the court; and his suggestion that this pain might give Theseus pleasure betrays his readiness to exploit violence in defence of his own class interests. Theseus, however, has no intention on his wedding-night of taking pleasure in *real* pain as he has in the past. Instead he gives Philostrate some instructions in the art of being a good audience, of 'reading' as much into the silences and hesitations of an incompetent performer as can be gained from 'the rattling tongue / Of saucy and audacious eloquence' (5.1.102–3). The key to this technique of warmly constructive reading, Theseus says, is *love* – the kind of love that binds Bottom to his craftsmen colleagues: 'Love, therefore, and tongue-tied simplicity / In least speak most, to my capacity' (5.1.104–5). *A Midsummer Night's Dream* is a romantic comedy that celebrates the love that binds communities rather than individuals; and this is what rescues it from becoming the sort of tragedy that occurs when love becomes too specific, too exclusive. It is not for nothing that the play ends with a *multiple* marriage.

The response of Theseus and his courtiers to the craftsmen's performance is rooted in this communal love. It is entirely different in tone from the derisory responses of Navarre and his courtiers to the play of the Worthies in *Love's Labour's Lost*. Where the Frenchmen aimed to destroy the humble actors' efforts to create an illusion, the Athenian courtiers seek to reinforce the spectacle they witness, commending the wall's 'wit' (5.1.165), ennobling the lion by calling it 'a very gentle beast' (5.1.224), cheering on the actors in the most exciting moments ('Well roared, Lion! Well run, Thisbe! Well shone, Moon!' (5.1.259–61)) and encouraging each other 'in courtesy' and 'in all reason' to sit through the more tedious parts of the performance (5.1.248). Theseus describes this process of active 'reading' on the part of spectators as 'amending', a word that becomes increasingly important as the play draws to an end. He famously says of the clowns' tragedy that 'The best in this kind are but shadows; and the worst are no worse, if imagination *amend* them' (5.1.209–10); and here amending seems to be a technique of supplying what is absent, perfecting an unsatisfactory illusion by freely giving over your imagination, as spectator, to the dramatic project in hand. The Chorus in *Henry V* asks his audience to engage in the same vigorous practice when he urges them to 'Piece out our imperfections with your thoughts' (Prologue, 23). And the same process of imaginative participation, of the neighbourly or friendly collusion between audience and actors which enables the two communities effectively to share each other's minds, is urged by Puck on the audience of *A Midsummer Night's Dream* in the comedy's epilogue.

If the play has given offence, says Puck, 'Think but this, and all is mended' (5.1.418): that what has been performed has no more substance than a dream, and that the actors' next performance will 'mend' or improve on this one (5.1.423). In this epilogue, reprehenders of the comedy are branded as possessed of the 'serpent's tongue' (5.1.427), identifying them with the snake that has cropped up so often as an image in the course of the play, symbol of disloyalty, double-dealing, sexual violence. Hermia transmutes Lysander's infidelity into the vision of a snake devouring her heart (2.2.144–9), and she later brands the still more faithless Demetrius a double-tongued 'serpent' (3.2.71–3). Lysander in turn shakes Hermia off, with acute hypocrisy, as a tempting 'serpent', emblem of man's seduction into sin (3.2.261). We might ourselves be tempted at this mid-point of the action to see the rich garden of Shakespeare's verse as another Eden, containing its serpent in the form of the lawless fairies, who spread infidelity like a weed through the love-affairs of ordinary men and women. But if we succumbed to this temptation we would be mistaken. 'Spotted snakes with double tongue' are denied entrance to Titania's floral bedchamber (2.2.9), and Oberon sees snakes as no more threatening than sheep, whose cast-off skins make garments for his fairy subjects (2.1.255–6). The real serpents, as Puck suggests, are those who import the venom of their prejudices into the playhouse, making trouble where they might make, as he promises to do, 'amends'. The play closes with a symbolic extending of hands from actor-playwright to audience, as the goblin mischief-maker tells his hearers: 'Give me your hands, if we be friends, / And Robin shall restore amends' (5.1.431–2). Here 'Give me your hands' clearly means 'applaud', but it also implies the clasping of hands to seal a bargain, a contract for future cooperation founded on sincere affection and mutual trust. This is the state we are enjoined to cultivate in the theatre by this most loving of comedies; but it is a state that does not preclude fear, danger and misunderstanding. Rather, it is made stronger by surviving them.

FASHION AND FATALITY IN
MUCH ADO ABOUT NOTHING

A Midsummer Night's Dream takes place in a mythical dimension similar to that inhabited by Shakespeare's narrative poem, *Venus and Adonis*.[22] It is set in long-ago Athens when the moody pagan gods still reign supreme, when man-eating beasts prowl the forest just beyond the city walls, when heroes like Theseus and his kinsman Hercules still ground their reputation on barbaric feats of strength, and when relationships between men and women are not yet far removed from the aggressive sexual habits of wild animals. It can be seen, then, as another of Shakespeare's comic manifestos, a declaration both of comedy's prehistoric origins and of its civilizing function in his own era, which is itself less 'civil' than it claims to be. Athens was the cradle of the classical civilization on which the whole of early modern intellectual and imaginative culture claimed to base itself; and Athens in this play is a place of harsh laws and ungovernable passions, where lunacy is a stronger influence than philosophy. The comic experience of the forest is necessary to make this mythical Athens worth living in; and the well-being of the city depends on a collaboration between its inhabitants which is symbolized by the collaboration between aristocrats, craftsmen and immortals to stage the exhilarating comic spectacle of the play's last scene.

Shakespeare's next comedy of love and death, *Much Ado about Nothing*, takes place in a contemporary setting. In it the now long-established laws of courtly civility are themselves the root of aggression, and the notion of collaboration between classes, and even between genders, seems at first to have been quite lost. Like *Pyramus and Thisbe* as described by Philostrate, the play is about 'nothing'; but it is also about how 'nothing' can be blown up into something of substance, with potentially fatal results for those who get caught in the blast.[23] In the Messina where this play is set, the imagination is claimed by the male aristocracy as its exclusive province; noblemen can make something of nothing with as much ease as a poet can conjure up the illusion of life on a stage. And in the very first scene it is clear how much damage can be caused by this kind of imaginative exclusiveness.

Much Ado takes place in the aftermath of war, courtship coming as a pleasant interval in the lives of aristocratic men between bouts of fighting. And the culture of war disastrously extends itself into the culture of conversation between men in peacetime, and above all between men and women. The war just ended is an oddly light one, more reminiscent of a sport than a power-struggle, in which nobody – or rather, nobody of any importance – has died. Asked in the first scene how many were killed in the action, a messenger replies 'But few of any sort, and none of name' (1.1.7); and this introduces us to a world where the consequences of violence are visited only on the weak. Don John, whose insurrection against his brother is the cause of the war, is forgiven and brought back into polite society as if nothing has happened. And the slaughter of war at once becomes a topic for jesting. The 'merry war' between Beatrice and Benedick supplants the real war between Don Pedro and Don John (1.1.59); and it is not long before the princes get tired of acting as mere auditors of other people's witty performances and start getting involved themselves in the intrigues of peace. As a result of this princely interference the 'merry war' turns sour, and starts to have effects as devastating (for some) as armed conflict.

The first skirmish of the 'merry war' takes place in the first scene, when Beatrice tells the messenger who brings tidings of Don Pedro's military victory that she has promised to make a meal of all the men whom Benedick has killed in combat. This, her first sequence of jokes, proves deeply unsettling for the messenger. Her offer depends on the assumption that Benedick has killed nobody, despite the messenger's assertion that he is a 'good soldier' who has 'done good service' (1.1.51, 46). And the sheer confidence with which she upholds this assumption exposes a gaping absence at the core of the culture of court compliment. The implication is that the messenger's entire report about the recent battle cannot be trusted, issuing as it does from the desire to please his paymasters. Conscious that Beatrice is questioning his credentials as a reporter, the messenger keeps trying to restore Benedick's reputation in the face of her repeated attacks on it; but with each new compliment Beatrice renders Benedick less heroic and more risible. She supposes that his 'good service' in the war must refer to his formidable powers as a trencherman (1.1.48–50), that he is a 'good soldier' only in his sedulous attention to women (1.1.52–3), and that the virtues he is 'stuffed' with are as worthless as the stuffing of a fashionably puffed-up suit of clothes (11.56–7). In the process, she cuts the whole of the war from which he has returned down to size, exposing it as a mere display of masculinity, a pretext for unfounded compliment. Her 'merry war' with Benedick is a war with men, who measure masculinity by a man's readiness to kill but who fail to make the connection between the language of combat and its material consequences: the pain it inflicts, the flesh it divides, the blood it draws.

Beatrice seems determined to teach Benedick, at least, about the damage that can be done with words. The metaphors used by both parties to describe Beatrice's wit are violent ones, implying the hurt she has done with her well-aimed sallies. In the first scene she tells Leonato that in her last verbal 'conflict' with Benedick 'four of his five wits' were incurably maimed, leaving him with only one, like an ex-soldier who has lost most of his limbs and been reduced to beggary (1.1.62–8). When they meet later in the scene Benedick tells Beatrice to stick by her declared hostility to marriage so that 'some gentleman or other shall scape a predestinate scratched face' (1.1.129–30), and she responds by metaphorically scratching Benedick's: 'Scratching could not make it worse, and 'twere such a face as yours were' (1.1.131–2). Her other attacks on him are yet more devastating, aiming as they do at the heart of his trustworthiness, his reputation for keeping his word. He is always making new friends, she claims in the first scene, draining them of their money and then dropping them, just as the plague feeds on, wastes and abandons the human body (1.1.68–86). When she later dances with Benedick at a masque she tells him that he is the 'Prince's jester' whose 'only . . . gift is in devising impossible slanders' (2.1.129–30). Benedick reacts to this last assault with what sounds like genuine shock. He tells Don Pedro that she has launched 'jest upon jest' against him like 'a whole army shooting at me', that 'She speaks poniards, and every word stabs', that 'if her breath were as terrible as her terminations . . . she would infect to the North Star', and that as long as she is alive men would go to hell gladly to avoid her, since 'all disquiet, horror, and per-turbation follows her' (2.1.230–45). Benedick may have returned unscathed from the war with Don John's forces, but Beatrice has taught him to feel something akin to the effects of war – and its after-effects of disease – as they were felt by its nameless victims.

It is hardly surprising if the protagonists of this 'merry war' declare their enmity for that ultimate test of verbal trustworthiness, marriage. Benedick will not marry, he asserts, because he distrusts women; for him, a wedding is a kind of death, and if ever he succumbs to the love that leads to it he invites his male friends to 'hang me in a bottle like a cat and shoot at me' (1.1.242–3). Beatrice will not marry because she has no time for the patriarchal order. She is disgusted by the notion that women should take the husbands men provide for them, or that wives should submit to men who are their equals or inferiors: 'Would it not grieve a woman to be over-mastered with a piece of valiant dust, to make an account of her life to a clod of wayward marl?' (2.1.55–7). For her, death will come as a comic vindication of her refusal to be entrapped by matrimony: when she arrives at the gates of hell she will be redirected to heaven, since hell is 'no place for ... maids' (2.1.39–42). Both Benedick and Beatrice construct their scintillating edifices of wit as a means of avoiding matrimonial entrapment, where words can do them lasting harm, as opposed to the severe but fleeting agonies they put each other through in their skirmishes.

Yet oddly enough, their brilliant verbal combat is built on foundations of trust – despite Benedick's protestations that women cannot be trusted. They are trusted by the other characters in the play: both to their faces and behind their backs, nobody voices any doubts about their integrity. Benedick is praised by Don Pedro as 'of a noble strain, of approved valour, and confirmed honesty' (2.1.358–9); while the same prince describes Beatrice as a 'pleasant-spirited lady' (2.1.322), and later adds that 'out of all suspicion, she is virtuous' (2.3.157–8). The latter phrase is uttered in Benedick's hearing, as part of a scheme to trick her erstwhile enemy into loving her; but there is every reason to suppose Don Pedro means it. After all, he offers early in the play to marry Beatrice ('Will you have me, lady?' (2.1.307)); and he later claims that if she had loved him 'I would have daffed all other respects and made her half myself' (2.3.166–7). Don Pedro's admiration for Leonato's witty niece arises from a conviction that her merry words spring spontaneously from a merry heart, the inverse of the misanthropic melancholy felt by the brother with whom he was at war.

If Benedick and Beatrice are trusted, they are also trusting: they have a clear notion about whose word is to be believed. Benedick is convinced that Beatrice loves him because he hears it from her old uncle Leonato: the 'white-bearded fellow speaks it', he observes (2.3.119), and adds that 'they have the truth of this from Hero', Leonato's young niece (2.3.213–14). For Benedick, old age and youthful innocence are the paradigms of honesty, and the signs of good faith are to be read in the face, bearded or smooth, as much as in words. For Beatrice, on the other hand, it is Hero alone who stands for truth. She never once thinks of questioning what she hears Hero say about Benedick, any more than she entertains for a moment the possibility that Hero may be guilty of the crime of which Claudio later accuses her: 'O, on my soul', she cries with religious fervour, 'my cousin is belied' (4.1.145). For all their love of devising impossible slanders, and for all their light-heartedness (Beatrice wakes herself from unhappy dreams with peals of laughter), Benedick and Beatrice think they know the difference between what seems to be and what is; and this is what sets them apart from the other upper-class characters in this comedy.

The male aristocrats in Messina inhabit a world reminiscent of Navarre in *Love's Labour's Lost*, where words are as light and changeable as air, and as little allied to things of substance. Having finished the serious business of war – although as we have seen they do not take war too seriously – Don Pedro and Claudio commit themselves to the arts of peace as if to an interesting new game, a stimulating new outlet for their relentless male competitiveness. For them these arts consist in extravagant wordplay rather than the dreary business of government; and as amateur players in this tricky verbal medium, they quickly find themselves adrift in unfamiliar waters. This is because unlike Beatrice, their wordplay has no roots in mutual trust. Claudio, especially, seems to lose faith in Don Pedro's honesty with startling ease; and neither he nor Don Pedro notice the absurdity of trusting their former enemy Don John rather than the hitherto blameless Hero. In the peacetime world of wit they are lost without co-ordinates: constantly slipping between lightness and seriousness without good cause, ensnaring themselves with tricks of their own devising, causing terrible damage to Hero with their cruel words one minute, laughing at her elderly father for resenting it the next. If their war was fought without any sense of proportion, their peace is oddly out of proportion too, so that their laughter – like their anger – seems always capable of getting damagingly out of control.

Above all, the noblemen do not know how to read the signs that appear on the surface of things – the expressions on a person's face, the words they speak, the clothes they wear – as an index to what is going on underneath. Leonato introduces us to the difficulty of such readings in the very first scene. When he hears that Claudio's uncle wept with joy to hear of his nephew's triumphant return from battle, Leonato says: 'there are no faces truer than those that are so washed' (1.1.26–7). Tears of joy are an accurate measure of the weeper's feelings; but conversely, it is implied that some faces are *not* true, and that reading them is not always so simple. When Don Pedro asks Leonato if Hero is his daughter he replies with fragile heartiness, 'Her mother hath many times told me so' (1.1.101), and Benedick takes this to mean that Leonato may once have doubted the mother's honesty. Don Pedro at once removes the sting from Benedick's jest by saying that 'the lady fathers herself' (1.1.105–6) – in other words, Hero *looks* like her father Leonato; but the signs are ominous. Husbands may doubt their wives; the feelings of a father for his son need not be taken for granted; any sign may be misread, and the tone of any witty comment may be mistaken. When Beatrice chaffs the messenger in the first scene, Leonato tells him 'You must not, sir, mistake my niece' (1.1.58): clearly the messenger is not sure she is joking. Soon afterwards Claudio asks Benedick what he thinks of Hero, and it is some time before Benedick realizes that Claudio may have a serious purpose in making these inquiries: 'But speak you this with a sad brow', he asks, 'or do you play the flouting Jack?' (1.1.174–5). When Don Pedro congratulates Claudio on his new love for Hero, 'for the lady is very well worthy', Claudio is again unsure of his tone: 'You speak this to fetch me in, my lord', and the Prince is forced to reassure him that 'I speak my thought' (1.1.209–12). In this atmosphere of paranoid uncertainty – lightly uttered though it is, and fenced in by banter – it is hardly surprising if Claudio quickly grows suspicious of the Prince when he bestows his attentions on Hero. The two friends have agreed that Don Pedro will woo Hero on Claudio's behalf; but when Claudio hears from Don John that the Prince has been wooing her for himself, he believes it at once. The petty paranoias that have surfaced in the play's dialogue so far transform themselves at this moment into a deep distrust of friendship, of princes, of dialogue itself: 'Let every eye negotiate for itself', Claudio concludes, 'And trust no agent; for beauty is a witch / Against whose charms faith melteth into blood' (2.1.169–71). Claudio claims it is women's beauty that dissolves the trust that should govern male friend-ship; but from what we have seen so far in this play, trust between men has always been based on the flimsiest of foundations.

This is borne out by the many representations of eavesdropping in this comedy. In Shakespeare's earlier plays, eavesdropping was the best way of gaining access to a person's secret thoughts. Berowne gets the upper hand of his fellow courtiers in *Love's Labour's Lost* when he overhears their love-complaints in the daytime; Romeo discovers Juliet's love for him when he overhears her soliloquizing at night. In *Much Ado*, by contrast, eavesdropping is always unreliable. Conversations overheard get misunderstood, or carefully stage-managed to deceive the hidden listener, or exploited to damage the conversationalists. The first act of eavesdropping occurs when Antonio's servant overhears Claudio and Don Pedro talking about Hero, and mistakenly assumes that it is the Prince who intends to marry her. Soon afterwards we learn that the same conversation has been overheard by Don John's follower Borachio, who interprets the situation correctly; but Borachio plans to use what he has heard to damage the Prince's friendship with the Count. Don John then puts Claudio in the position of eavesdropper, pretending not to recognize him in his festive mask as he maliciously misinforms him of Don Pedro's courtship of Hero. By the time the three major eavesdropping scenes of the play take place in the second, third and fourth acts, we have been made thoroughly suspicious of the eavesdropping process. The play's title sums up this ambivalence.[24] In early modern English, 'nothing' sounds much like 'noting', which means noticing, listening carefully, paying close attention – as in Claudio's question to Benedick, 'didst thou note the daughter of Signior Leonato?' (1.1.155–6). Eavesdroppers note what they hear, of course; but it is likely too that they will hear *nothing* that has any bearing on the truth. Noting may also mean making music: the kind of 'notes' produced by the singer Balthazar in the eavesdropping scene staged for Benedick by Don Pedro (2.3.53–6), where Don Pedro produces his own ravishing verbal performance to make Benedick think Beatrice loves him. Such quasi-musical playing on people's emotions could of course be damaging when practised for the wrong reasons. And there is a fourth meaning of 'nothing' that gets tangled up with this darker aspect of eavesdropping. 'Nothing' in certain contexts could mean a woman's vagina;[25] and the contexts in which it acquired this meaning often involved misogynistic banter among men. In the third of the major eavesdropping scenes in the play – the scene where Don John fakes Hero's infidelity – misogyny takes centre stage, and men's wit becomes in fact what it has always been in potential: a sadistic power-game, a torturer's music-making, as the nobles exploit Hero's body as their instrument, making free both with the 'nothing' of her genitals and the 'nothing', the total lack of proof, on which her condemnation is based.

Hero has, however, been a willing instrument of men since the play began. Her resemblance to her father marks her as his possession, and her obedience to him is never questioned – at least, until Don John sets her up. When her Uncle Antonio tells her 'I trust you will be ruled by your father' (2.1.46–7), he, her father and Hero herself think Don Pedro plans to woo her; yet as soon as Claudio emerges as her suitor she takes him to her heart without a murmur. She assents readily to Don Pedro's plot to deceive Benedick and Beatrice; and plays a central role in all three of the major eavesdropping scenes, despite the fact that she is only present in one. Hero is, in fact, the ideal woman of the Renaissance male: beautiful, obedient, mostly silent, and willing to be moulded into whatever shape men care to make of her. Her name confirms this, being the name of the first woman lover to have been celebrated in verse by a man. Hero is the heroine of a tragic poem by Musaeus, *Hero and Leander*, thought by early modern scholars to predate all other poems and updated for an Elizabethan readership by Marlowe.[26] But Shakespeare's Hero is a character on stage, not the subject of a poem: her behaviour is a performance, a dramatic embodiment of men's desires; and this is what makes her so vulnerable to being enlisted as an embodiment of men's fears, their paranoia that women, like professional actors, may have desires of their own that do not conform with those they profess in public. She can be dressed in garments of men's choosing – can be seen, indeed, as less substantial than the clothes she wears – and it is for her puppeteers, the noblemen who control her, to decide what lies beneath her sumptuous outer surface.

At first, the men in the play assume that Hero's youthful outward appearance provides an accurate index to the simple honesty of her mind. When Leonato and Don Pedro arrange for Benedick to overhear them discussing Beatrice, it is Hero they use to confirm their claim that she is in love: 'my daughter tells us all', says Leonato, and later, 'my daughter says so ... it is very true' (2.3.132–51). The eavesdropper

Benedick concludes that 'they have the truth of this from Hero' (2.3.213–14), because nothing that emerges from Hero could possibly be fabricated. In the next scene, Hero conspires with her waiting-woman Ursula to lay the 'false sweet bait' for Beatrice (3.1.33); yet here too, despite her willingness to indulge in amateur theatricals, she presents herself as the advocate of honest 'simplicity' in contrast with the excesses of wit. Hero tells Ursula that Beatrice overvalues her own verbal ingenuity, and that she can sportingly transform the best qualities in men into the worst of blemishes: she 'never gives to truth and virtue that / Which simpleness and merit purchaseth' (3.1.69–70). Beatrice, in other words, cannot see the value of plain honesty like Benedick's; and Hero pretends to have decided that she must dissuade Benedick from loving such a mocker: 'I'll devise some honest slanders / To stain my cousin with: one doth not know / How much an ill word may empoison liking' (3.1.84–6). She speaks with the simplicity of one who is convinced of the excellence of her own motives: her words are not ill ones, and she is not poisoning Beatrice's liking but cultivating it (all the eavesdropping scenes up to this point have taken place in Leonato's orchard, where fruit is cultivated for the delectation of the aristocratic palate). Beatrice is convinced, both of Benedick's affection for her and of the 'simpleness' of the woman who reports it: 'I / Believe it', she says, 'better than reportingly' (3.1.115–16).

At the same time, Hero in this scene identifies the quality in wit that will be her downfall: its propensity for noting things in people that are not there. Hero's celebration of 'simpleness' *is*, after all, a performance, and so could be taken as a sign of her capacity for deviousness, for making things look as they are not. And she herself notes that Beatrice can 'spell' any gentleman 'backward' (3.1.61), turn virtues into vices with a slip of the tongue; so that witty men, too, may be equally capable of inverting a person's character, of poisoning liking with an 'ill word'. The honesty of witty slanders depends on the motives of those who devise them; and the next eavesdropping scene involving Hero is set up by a man who describes himself as 'a plain-dealing villain' (1.3.29–30). Don John is a man like Shylock with no sense of humour – or rather, not one that he shares with the rest of the play's community. 'I must be sad when I have cause', he tells his follower Conrade, 'and smile at no man's jests ... laugh when I am merry, and claw no man in his humour' (1.3.13–17). Like Shylock, Don John plays his jokes in the interests of revenge, as an extension of his rebellion against his brother Don Pedro. And he finds a willing audience – disturbingly ready to have his liking poisoned – in Count Claudio; a young man whose limitations Don John seems to understand all too easily.

What Don John recognizes in Count Claudio is the supreme instance of the inability of noblemen in Shakespeare's Messina to penetrate the surface of things: a peculiarity that manifests itself in the Count's fixation on fashion, his excessive interest in clothes.[27] Claudio's 'love' for Hero is a fabricated affair, prompted by a sense that the appropriate *time* has come for loving, the moment when everyone who is anyone will be doing it, so that he had better do it too if he is not to feel excluded. As he tells Don Pedro, he liked Hero before he went to war, and now that he has earned a vacation, as it were, he can afford to do something practical about his liking (1.1.279–88). Before wooing her, however, he is careful to ascertain her market value by appeals to other men. He asks Benedick if he shares his assessment of this commodity ('Can the world buy such a jewel?' (1.1.173)), and checks with Don Pedro to make sure that she is her father's only child and therefore the heir to his fortune (1.1.277–8); her value is nothing if her beauty and wealth are not judged by the male community exactly as Claudio judges them. Claudio is clearly a slave to male fashion, and he marks his conversion to love with a thoroughly conventional change of dress. 'I have known', says Benedick, 'when he would have walked ten mile afoot to see a good armour, and now will he lie ten nights awake carving the fashion of a new doublet' (2.3.15–18). For Claudio, clothes are as satisfactory an indication of the state of a person's heart as either conversation or long acquaintance; so that when he sees Hero's clothes at night staging an assignation with Don John's follower Borachio, he has no doubt at all that Hero (and her heart) must be inside them.

Claudio has no doubt, too, about his own ability to 'fashion' other people's hearts as easily as his own – to cut them according to any pattern he chooses, like an expert tailor. He shares this confidence with his fellow noblemen. As Don Pedro plots to bring Benedick and Beatrice together he declares, 'I would fain have it a match, and I doubt not but to fashion it' (2.1.346–7); and Don John is equally certain that he can make Hero into anything he wants. When Claudio asks if she is disloyal, Don John replies, 'The word is too good to paint out her wickedness. I could say she were worse; think you of a worse title, and I will fit her to it' (3.2.100–2). It is not surprising, then, if when Don John's servant Borachio looks back on the scene he has just acted out with Margaret – impersonating Hero so as to incriminate her – he sees it as an illustration of the sudden changes in contemporary style, as if he and his master have accomplished something spectacular in the field of *haute couture*. 'What a deformed thief this fashion is', he says, 'how giddily a turns about all the hot bloods between fourteen and five-and-thirty' (3.3.127–9). Borachio's term 'fashion' becomes more ominous when in the following scene we see Hero trying on a gown of 'a most rare fashion' in advance of her wedding (3.4.13–14). Don Pedro had earlier compared Claudio's bride-to-be to a child's new coat, which must be worn as soon as the child is given it (3.2.5–7). She may be formed or deformed at the whim of the men who claim ownership of her, with no more compunction than if she had been made of cloth; and when they tire of her she may be discarded like an outmoded garment. From the moment Claudio sees her it seems inevitable that this disposal will happen at one time or another.

When it comes, though, Hero's rejection occurs with astonishing ferocity. The scene is rendered more shocking by the fact that it is sprung like a nasty practical joke, an extension of the peacetime merriment in which the noblemen have indulged throughout the play. Worse still, this is the first verbal exchange we have heard between Claudio and Hero; and as evidence of Claudio's attitude to verbal exchanges with women it is not encouraging. The Count subjects Hero's body to a rhetorical assault that transforms it into a cloak designed to hide her secret sexual agenda:

> Behold how like a maid she blushes here!
> O, what authority and show of truth
> Can cunning sin cover itself withal!
> Comes not that blood as modest evidence
> To witness simple virtue? Would you not swear,

> All you that see her, that she were a maid,
> By these exterior shows? But she is none:
> She knows the heat of a luxurious bed:
> Her blush is guiltiness, not modesty.
>
> (4.1.32–40)

Intoxicated by his own wit, Claudio here 'spells' Hero 'backwards', to use Hero's phrase. The blush that is the sign of her 'simple virtue' becomes the mark of her sexual sophistication; the evidence of her modesty becomes proof positive of her guilt; and her language, too, is recruited to ratify his preconceived opinion of her. Soon afterwards Claudio asks her to answer one question to confirm or deny her guilt, and demands that she answer it 'if you are a maid' (4.1.84). Yet when Hero answers as instructed, telling him truthfully that she met no man the night before, Don Pedro crows, 'Why, then you are no maiden' (4.1.86), and proceeds to narrate the story of what he and Claudio thought they saw under cover of darkness. Neither the language of the body nor that of the tongue can shake their conviction of their own judgement. As inveterate punsters they can turn any one set of signs into its opposite, flipping phrases back and forth with the agility of professional clowns, as Claudio demonstrates when he sums Hero up as a walking paradox ('Thou pure impiety and impious purity' (4.1.103)), then extends his view of her to embrace all women:

> For thee I'll lock up all the gates of love,
> And on my eyelids shall conjecture hang,
> To turn all beauty into thoughts of harm,
> And never shall it more be gracious.
>
> (4.1.104–7)

Wit has become the chief witness in a kangaroo court, where what is seen is shaped by conjecture and prejudice determines the outcome of every trial. We are suddenly back in the territory of *The Merchant of Venice*, where the weapons of comedy reinforce the tyrannous will of those in power instead of facilitating the rebellion of the powerless, as the theatre-haters claimed it did.

What gives the wit of the powerful its potency in Messina is the priv-ileging of words over matter, the radical detachment of signifier from signified. When Leonato reacts in horror to the accusation of Hero ('Are these things spoken, or do I but dream?') Don John replies with devast-ating confidence, 'Sir, they are spoken, and these things are true', as though a prince's word is all that is needed to establish truth (4.1.65–6). Later, Don John compounds the sense that words have become detached from any substance as he berates his brother for try-ing to articulate Hero's infidelities. 'Fie, fie!' he says, 'they are not to be named . . . There is not chastity enough in language / Without offence to utter them' (4.1.94–7). Language has been used to conjure up Hero's guilt, yet language will not do to flesh it out. Far more seriously than the messenger's compliments to Benedick in the opening scene, a lack is here exposed at the heart of the aristocratic discourse privileged in Shakespeare's Messina.

This lack is accentuated by the sheer speed with which things of importance are decided or dismissed in the play. When the long-winded Constable Dogberry approaches Leonato before the wedding scene with information the audience knows is vital – information pertaining to Hero's innocence – Hero's father replies, 'I am now in great haste, as it may appear unto you', and leaves him to interrogate his prisoners him-self (3.5.47). Leonato's impatience here is pardonable; but it prefigures the less pardonable impatience of Don Pedro when he meets the grief-stricken Leonato after demolishing his daughter's reputation – after killing her, in fact, so far as Don Pedro is aware. 'We have some haste, Leonato', he claims (5.1.47), and tries to hurry away from the old man as if embarrassed by the violence of his emotion. The situation is not unlike that in Thomas Kyd's great tragedy of the 1580s, *The Spanish Tragedy*, where an elderly court official whose son has been murdered finds it impossible to get his case heard by the king. The official, Hieronimo, vents his frustration at his own inability to get justice for the murder in terms that closely resemble Leonato's empty threats against Hero's accusers, uttered as the grief-stricken father tries to convince himself that he has the power to take revenge against Don Pedro, his Prince:

> Time hath not yet so dried this blood of mine,
> Nor age so eat up my invention ...
> But they shall find, awak'd in such a kind,
> Both strength of limb and policy of mind ...
> To quit me of them throughly.
>
> $(4.1.192–9)^{28}$

Hieronimo eventually found one man who would listen sympathetically to the outpourings of grief for his dead son: another elderly father who had lost his own son under similar circumstances and found no means of getting justice for his murder. In him Hieronimo traces 'the lively image of my grief', and he adopts the old mourner as his companion until such time as he can achieve retribution.[29] Leonato searches vainly for an equally congenial companion in his sorrow: 'let no comforter delight mine ear / But such a one whose wrongs do suit with mine' (5.1.6–7); and when he cannot find one, he vents his frustration in an angry confrontation with Claudio and the Prince, defused of its tragic potential by their resolute refusal to take it seriously. By the time Shakespeare wrote *Much Ado*, *The Spanish Tragedy* was seen by many playwrights as risibly old-fashioned, and Hieronimo's antics as amusing; additions written for the play after Kyd's death stress the horrific comedy of the old man's madness.[30] Leonato and his brother Antonio are funny as they strive to goad Claudio into a fight, using the language of street insult appropriate to younger men – their insults recall Mercutio's taunting of Tybalt. But the frustration of these old men at their own impotence also recalls the tragic context of Kyd's work, and reminds us that Don Pedro and Don John are Spanish Princes, foreign rulers of the Sicilian port of Messina and scions of a nation whose name had become synonymous with tyranny in the minds of many Elizabethans.[31] When Don Pedro tells Leonato 'I will not hear you', his words have a disturbing political resonance, and there is real menace in Leonato's response: 'I will be heard' (5.1.107–8).

Don Pedro's tyranny at this point might be called the tyranny of the light or comic. The 'haste' he is in when he meets Leonato has nothing to do with serious business: he is merely eager to find Benedick, whose jokes, he hopes, will dispel the mild depression from which he has been

suffering since Hero's 'death' (5.1.123–5). In fact, the lightness or shallowness of Messina's ruling classes is both what nearly turns their story
to deadly earnest and what protects it from following *Romeo and Juliet*
into darkness and death. The revenger Hieronimo in Kyd's play was
determined to transform the glib world of the Spanish court into the
setting for tragedy. As he organizes the dramatic performance in which
his vengeance will be bloodily exacted, he is challenged by one of his
courtly enemies over his choice of genre for the play ('Hieronimo,
methinks a comedy were better'), and responds with a declaration that
tragedies are the fit mode for the ruling class, since they deal with
'matter, and not common things'.[32] In Shakespeare's Messina, by contrast, comedy is the mode that best suits the court, and the performance
put on by Hero's friends is only superficially tragic. The 'death of Hero'
does not really happen, unlike the deaths in the tragedy staged by
Hieronimo, and like any feat of legerdemain it may be reversed in an
instant. It derives its power not from its reproduction of tyrannical violence but from the dexterity with which it snatches the comic initiative
away from the princes' hands.

Comedy abets tyranny when it is monopolized by the powerful; what
saves Messina is the restoration of the comic to the people to whom it
traditionally belongs, the classes below the level of the aristocracy. This
process of restoration is initiated by the comic Constable Dogberry and
his watch; a collection of 'shallow fools', as Borachio calls them, who
blunderingly bring to light what the deeper 'wisdom' of the ruling
classes failed to uncover (5.1.224–6). Dogberry is so eager to protect his
watch from corruption that he enjoins them to 'take no note' of criminals (3.3.28), and to spend their nights in peaceful inactivity, sedu-
lously avoiding contact with drunks, thieves and other troublemakers
in order to preserve their collective integrity. At the same time, the
watch is specifically designated 'the Prince's watch' (3.3.6); and in
Dogberry's opinion, this makes them as responsible for the surveillance
of the Prince as it does for spying on lesser miscreants. 'If you meet the
Prince in the night', he says, 'you may stay him' – so long as the Prince
is willing (3.3.71–9). Like other humble law-men in Shakespeare's
plays – Constable Elbow in *Measure for Measure*, Constable Dull –
Dogberry is a hopeless malapropist, but he has a clear sense of his own

responsibility and 'place', which the aristocracy has not, and his invol-
untary inversions compensate for the malicious 'spelling backward' of
Don Pedro and Don John. The watch's eavesdropping is the only one in
the play that is not the result of a royal plot. Instead it is the chance
overhearing by 'good men and true' of evidence that implicates royalty,
and when they bring Borachio and Conrade before the Prince the
charges they level against them are as applicable to Don Pedro as to the
retainers of Don John. 'Marry, sir', says Dogberry, 'they have committed
false report, moreover they have spoken untruths, secondarily they are
slanders, sixth and lastly they have belied a lady, thirdly they have veri-
fied unjust things, and to conclude, they are lying knaves'
(5.1.208–12). It does not matter what order these indictments are
uttered in, since they are all identical, and all signal Don Pedro's failure
to permit truth to triumph over falsehood in his royal demesnes. It is
Dogberry's revelation that the Prince has 'belied a lady', in fact, that
'Runs . . . like iron' through Don Pedro's blood (5.1.236–7), and obvi-
ates the necessity for Benedick to run his iron through Claudio, at the
behest of Beatrice, in the final act.

Another transference of comic initiative from the princes' hands
occurs at the end of the abortive wedding scene, when Friar Francis
plays a kind of redemptive prank on the noblemen who have humiliated
Hero so cruelly. Like the friars in *Romeo and Juliet* and *Measure for
Measure*, this religious brother sees his primary role as that of bringing
people together – whether as priest or pimp; and like them he is an
intriguingly ambiguous figure. His first reaction to the accusation of
Hero is to assume that Claudio has misread the signs of her modesty:
throughout the scene, he says, he has been 'noting of the lady', and in
doing so

> I have mark'd
> A thousand blushing apparitions
> To start into her face, a thousand innocent shames
> In angel whiteness beat away those blushes,
> And in her eye there hath appear'd a fire
> To burn the errors that these princes hold
> Against her maiden truth.
>
> (4.1.157–63)

The Belman of London:

BRINGING TO LIGHT
THE MOST NOTORIOVS
VILLANIES THAT ARE NOW
Practifed in the Kingdome.

Profitable for Gentlemen, Lawyers, Merchants, Citizens, Farmers, Ma-
flers of houfholds, and all forts of feruants, to marke, and delightfull for
all men to reade.

Lege, Perlege, Relege.

Printed at London for Nathaniel
Butter. 1 6 0 8.

FIGURE 8   Night Watchman, on the title page of Thomas Dekker, *The
Bellman of London* (1608). Dekker's Bellman serves as a satirical commentator
on the state of things in the English capital, rather as Dogberry and his men
comment on the state of things in Messina.

Hero's face is both more complex (with erotic reds and whites at war in its cheeks and an angry fire in its eyes) and more easily read than Claudio's hasty assessment of it suggested; and Friar Francis offers to teach Claudio his more sympathetic art of reading by the same means Friar Laurence used to free Juliet from the unwanted attentions of another Count: by faking her death. Death, he claims, alters men's judgement of what they have lost – changes the remembered appearance of the dead more radically than a new wardrobe changes the look of the living. 'When he shall hear she died upon his words', the Friar claims,

> Th'idea of her life shall sweetly creep
> Into his study of imagination,
> And every lovely organ of her life
> Shall come apparell'd in more precious habit,
> More moving-delicate and full of life,
> Into the eye and prospect of his soul
> Than when she liv'd indeed: then shall he mourn . . .
> And wish he had not so accused her:
> No, though he thought his accusation true.
>
> (4.1.222–32)

It is the final phrase that makes Friar Francis's plot so comically ambiguous. He is concerned less with establishing the truth of Hero's conduct than with changing Claudio's opinion; seducing him, as it were, with his own sensual daydreams about the woman he thinks he has lost. In the Friar's account, death eroticizes Hero – dresses or apparels her organs in 'precious habit' as if she had been professionally made over – and thus restores her to sexual life in the young man's imagination, whether or not 'he thought his accusation true'. The Friar's prank operates, in fact, on the same superficial level as the minds of the noblemen who slandered Hero, where the secondary meaning of the verb 'to die' in Elizabethan English – to achieve orgasm – takes precedence over its gloomier primary meaning.[33] It is for this reason, perhaps, that the practical joke proves so effective; it relies not on a wholesale transformation of the culture of Messina but on a shift of power within that culture, a redressing of the balance between ruler and subject that renders tyranny inoperable.

The transference of the comic initiative from the Prince and Claudio to their social inferiors accelerates in the scenes that follow the abortive wedding. First Leonato and his brother Antonio unexpectedly accost them, replacing the discourse of court compliment with laughable, if uncomfortably accurate, insults: Antonio calls them 'Scambling, out-facing, fashion-monging boys, / That lie, and cog, and flout, deprave, and slander ... And this is all' (5.1.94–99). Then Benedick refuses to play the fool for their pleasure: 'You have among you killed a sweet and innocent lady', he tells them, and they are startled to conclude that 'He is in earnest' (5.1.186–90). Finally the bumbling Dogberry surprises them with the results of the watch's eavesdropping, including a full confession from Don John's accomplice Borachio, at the end of which Hero's image is restored to its former glory. 'Sweet Hero', Claudio says, 'now thy image doth appear / In the rare semblance that I lov'd it first' (5.1.243–4). Claudio is still fixated on externals (it is her image that concerns him, not her inward qualities); but from this moment he and Don Pedro are prepared to place themselves under any 'heavy weight' of penance Leonato cares to impose on them (5.1.269).

Leonato's response is first to make the Prince and Count confess their errors to their ordinary subjects: 'Possess the people in Messina here / How innocent she died' (5.1.273–4), and then to make Claudio marry a substitute Hero, a woman he has never set eyes on, as a sign of his humility. Claudio consents readily, cracking jokes about adultery as he approaches the altar, and reacting with complacent delight when he finds his verbal assassination of Hero improbably undone by her re-appearance. In this play the ruling classes of Messina skip lightly away from the consequences of their actions, a process symbolically enacted in the dance with which it closes. Even Don John, who fled before his plot against Claudio was discovered, is chastised for his second act of treason not by the official organs of the law but by Benedick, who prom-ises to 'devise ... brave punishments for him' as part of his own and Claudio's wedding entertainment (5.4.126–7). But all this would have been impossible if the powerful men in the comedy had not been dis-empowered, exposed as the most absurd manifestation of the nothing about which much is made, and forced to take part in the concluding dance on equal terms with the men and women whose lives they had all but ruined. 'Man', says Benedick, 'is a giddy thing' (5.4.106–7), and in this play as in *Love's Labour's Lost* it is specifically aristocratic men who have been forced to confront their giddiness.

Giddiness has different effects depending on who succumbs to it, just as jokes have a different impact depending on who cracks them and the context in which they are cracked. At the end of *Much Ado about Nothing* nearly everyone left on stage is related: Claudio has become Beatrice's cousin by marriage, Hero has become Antonio's heir as well as Leonato's, Benedick has become Claudio's kinsman in the eyes of the law (at the beginning of the play he was only his *sworn* brother). The Spaniard Don Pedro, on the other hand, is unrelated to any of these in-laws-to-be, and Benedick thinks he looks sad ('get thee a wife, get thee a wife', he cries (5.4.121)). And in the final lines we are reminded of his nearest relative: the morose Don John, traitor and rebel. The divorce of royalty from the rest of the nobility – its relative detachment from the sense of communal fusion that closes the comedy – is what renders its giddiness and lightness potentially deadly, linked as they are to the lightning of royal retribution and the two-edged sword of arbitrary power. Laughter in the presence of princes is always a risky business, especially when it is the princes who are doing the laughing.

Chapter Four

THE PLURAL BODIES OF
SHAKESPEARE'S BOYS

THE TRUE DELIGHTS OF *AS YOU LIKE IT*

In *Much Ado about Nothing*, Hero is cut to measure by men, tailored to suit their fancies like an expensive piece of cloth. From one point of view, it is a suit of Hero's clothes that Claudio marries at the end of the play rather than the unknown woman inside it. Beatrice escapes Hero's fate – if she finally does so – by waging an energetic war of words that bears witness to her recalcitrance, her refusal to be spoken for by anyone but herself. In *As You Like It* and *Twelfth Night*, by contrast, women tailor *their own* bodies to protect them from the predatory fantasies of men, and use their customized masculine garments to learn what they can about the bodies, minds and habits of their usual wearers.[1] In the process they discover something that could have been inferred from nearly all of Shakespeare's comedies since *The Two Gentlemen of Verona*: that social and sexual conventions are little more than sartorial fantasies, capable of being remodelled, reworked or radically reconceived at the desire of the community that constructs them. This discovery is a potentially revolutionary one, transforming the human body into a miniature stage within which an almost infinite range of roles may be imagined. More disturbingly, it exposes the extent to which both genders consent to their own entrapment within ridiculously narrow parameters. Both plays, I shall argue, provide a specifically theatrical escape-route from this entrapment.

As You Like It begins in a universe crafted by a cynic: a universe where any cruelty that is imaginable may be practised and any impulse of spite may be acted upon, where the powerful are without exception corrupt and the weak without exception exploited. Violence once again seems endemic in relations between men, who hatch murderous plots and break each other's ribs and necks with the casual cruelty of huntsmen. Paranoia, too, is endemic in the rich and powerful, who imagine everyone to be conspiring against them, and whose paranoid imaginations generate genuine acts of resistance: the 'mutiny' to which Orlando is provoked by his bullying elder brother Oliver (1.1.22); the flight of Celia and Rosalind to 'liberty' in response to the tyranny of Celia's father (1.3.135). Language itself is the weapon of the strong, used by Oliver to rail on Orlando, to insult his old servant Adam, and to persuade the wrestler Charles that Orlando deserves to die. Orlando, meanwhile, is denied access to the resources of language by Oliver's neglect of his education; and the tyrant Duke Frederick, too, effectively deprives his subjects of speech by ignoring or misreading whatever they have to say. When Rosalind protests her innocence of the charge of treason he brings against her, the Duke replies: 'Thus do all traitors. / If their purgation did consist in words, / They are as innocent as grace itself' (1.3.49–51); and when Celia tries to defend her he tells her: 'open not thy lips' (1.3.79). The Duke's best-intentioned subjects find themselves wordless at crucial moments: when Orlando first meets Rosalind he cannot articulate his feelings ('What passion hangs these weights upon my tongue?' (1.2.247)), and Rosalind, equally smitten, has 'Not one [word] to throw at a dog' (1.3.3). This universe is ripe for the sort of satirical assault that Thomas Lodge thought was the proper business of comedy, an imaginative dismantling that clears the way for better times to come.

There are indeed hints of these better times in the opening act, allusions to alternative modes of living that point in the direction the comedy will take us. We hear of a deposed and banished brother of the Duke, who lives like 'Robin Hood of England' with 'many merry men' in the Forest of Arden, where they reconstruct the 'golden world' of classical myth (1.1.111–15). One of the Duke's courtiers looks forward to the moment when this ideal existence will entirely supplant the tyranny of now: 'Hereafter, in a better world than this', he tells Orlando, 'I shall desire more love and knowledge of you' (1.2.274–5). And appropriately enough, love or desire manifests itself in the first act as the most effective form of resistance to tyranny. Despite the Duke's disapproval, his daughter Celia loves Rosalind, the daughter of his banished brother, with such intensity that she would die if they were separated: 'never two ladies loved as they do', Charles enthuses (1.1.108–9). Celia is always urging Rosalind to 'be merry' (1.2.1, 22), as if in an effort to capture the mood of the golden world enjoyed by her banished father in Arden, and it is Celia's conviction 'that thou and I am one' (1.3.94) that encourages the women to flee to Arden together, escaping to the one location where their mutual love can subsist unmolested. When Rosalind puts on her male disguise, then, and sets off on her travels like an itinerant player, it is in the interests of pursuing liberty and protecting love, the most ambitious of motives for a comic performance. If her performance is also tinged with sexual scandal – the name Ganymede was associated with erotic love between men and boys, an activity that the comic theatre was supposed to encourage[2] – then perhaps scandal itself is merely another term for that most evasive and potent of imaginative constructs, freedom. And a semblance of freedom, at least, is something she finds in her guise as Ganymede.

The woods of Arden are like Eden, as their name suggests.[3] The banished Duke Senior tells us that in them he feels free from 'the penalty of Adam, / The seasons' difference' (2.1.5–6); and later Adam himself returns to live there in the shape of Orlando's old retainer of that name, who brings with him the values of a legendary past, 'The constant service of the antique world, / When service sweat for duty, not for meed' (2.3.57–8). As is well known, Adam carried strong egalitarian associations in Elizabethan times: rebels like Jack Cade invoked him as a reminder that nobles and commoners shared a common ancestry, and the utopian gardener in Shakespeare's *Richard II*, who holds that 'All must be even in our government' (3.4.36), is described as 'old Adam's likeness' (3.4.73).[4] The presence of Adam in Arden, then, signals the forest's egalitarian credentials. In Arden, the old retainer no longer needs to sweat as Adam did when he left his fabulous garden: it is his master who fetches him food, like a doe caring for her fawn (2.7.128–9). And instead of Adam having duties or obligations to his master, it is his master Orlando who owes his servant an incalculable debt of gratitude for the five hundred crowns he gave him when he had nothing (2.3.38–68). The roles of master and servant seem, then, to be interchangeable, a property of the 'wild wood' that finds its most startling manifestations at the end of the play, when Adam's former master Oliver falls in love and decides to become a shepherd (5.2.5–12) and Duke Frederick is suddenly converted at the forest's edge from ducal tyranny to a life of solitary religious service (5.4.157–63).

Although masters and servants still exist in Arden, their relationship is one of mutual convenience rather than of domination and submission. Servants switch between employers whenever they want, as the shepherd Corin does when he meets Ganymede, or as Jaques does at the end of the play when he refuses to return to the court with Duke Senior. And servants always have a strong sense of their own dignity. Corin tells Touchstone that the pastoral profession is equal to the courtier's, since 'Those that are good manners at the court are as ridiculous in the country as the behaviour of the country is most mockable at the court' (3.2.43–6). The humble 'hedge-priest' Oliver Martext, whose services are employed and then dismissed by Touchstone, tells the audience that 'Ne'er a fantastical knave of them all shall flout me out of my calling' (3.3.98–9). And at the end of the play a shepherd, Silvius, gives voice to the common experience of love that he and his social superiors share: 'It is to be all made of fantasy . . . All adoration, duty and observance . . . All purity, all trial, all observance' (5.2.92–6). In love, then, everyone is a servant – there is no such thing as mastery, whatever your gender – and the forest is full of lovers. The boy Ganymede sums up the balanced relationship between masters and servants in Arden when Duke Senior asks him 'of what parentage' he is and he answers: 'of as good as he' (3.4.33–4). This is literally true, of course, since Duke Senior is Rosalind's father, and Ganymede is Rosalind in disguise. But the Duke does not know this, and his response to the boy's impertinence is telling: 'he laughed and let me go' (3.4.34–5). Where Duke Frederick hates Orlando and Rosalind on account of their parentage, in Arden heredity is a bit of a joke, something to be lost and won in a moment as the Duke loses and regains his dukedom or the sons of Roland de Boyes lose and regain their respective shares in their father's fortune. If all men are willing to trace their family lines to Adam, any more recent claim to superiority seems easily laughed off.

In this Edenic Arden presided over by a genial laughing Duke, free speech is practised by all, and takes a bewildering variety of forms. Three commentators frequent the forest: a satirist, a fool and an impudent boy; and between them they successfully dismantle the cultural conditions that reinforce tyranny in the play's first act. Hierarchies of all kinds – among genders, ages in a man's life, social functions such as ruling and keeping sheep, or locations such as the country and the court – are wittily taken apart by these three commentators, until by the end of the play when the banished Duke returns to his former dukedom it seems inconceivable that his future government could fail to take account of the radical lessons he has learned in his fruitful exile. In this comedy, to a greater extent than in any other, the comic happy ending brings with it a sense of emancipation from the oppressive associations of conventional marriage and the reassertion of order: its weddings appear to be equal ones, its order libertarian. Its commentators, and the ruler who sanctions them, have ensured that the play concludes 'in true delights' (5.4.196), social as well as sexual.

The first commentator we meet in Arden is the satirist Jaques. Like the other two commentators, the fool and the boy, he is geographically and socially mobile: he has acquired his cynicism in the course of his global wanderings, which means he owes no fealty to any specific social superior, and cannot be defined by any country or profession. He is, he tells us, neither scholar, musician, courtier, soldier, lawyer, lady, nor lover, but possesses 'a melancholy of mine own, compounded of many simples, extracted from many objects, and indeed the sundry contemplations of my travels, in which my often rumination wraps me in a most humorous sadness' (4.1.10–19). Free from obligations and influences, Jaques is ideally placed to practise the art of satire, the fearless and biting form of comic criticism that points up social injustices and inequalities with a view to stamping them out.

At the time of *As You Like It* satire was all the rage in London, whether in verse or on the stage, and had already provoked harsh censorship in both these forms.[5] Ben Jonson and Thomas Nashe were jailed in 1597 for writing a satirical play, *The Isle of Dogs*, and a number of verse satires were burned by order of the Bishop of London in 1599, along with erotic texts by, among others, Christopher Marlowe.[6] Celia may or may not allude to the burning when she tells us in Act 1 that 'since the little wit that fools have was silenced, the little foolery that wisemen have makes a great show' (1.2.85–7). Certainly she implies that Duke Frederick is given to silencing wits, and that in Duke Frederick's world criticism of the powerful must be uttered cautiously, in private: the fool Touchstone is threatened with whipping if he over-steps the mark, and the courtier Le Beau scrupulously refrains from articulating his views on the Duke: 'what he is . . . More suits you to conceive than I to speak of' (1.2.256–7). In the forest, by contrast, social criticism is all-pervasive, as it was in the pastoral tradition from Theocritus to Sidney and Spenser.[7] Frank speech is generated even by inanimate objects; Duke Senior finds 'tongues in trees, books in the run-ning brooks, / Sermons in stones, and good in everything' (2.1.16–17), and chooses to read this omnipresent clamour as a critique of the cor-rupt hierarchy from which he has been expelled. Jaques is his most favoured commentator on his situation as exile, transforming the scene of a deer's death into an elaborate attack on contemporary *mores*, from the selfish extravagance of 'fat and greasy citizens' to the tyranny of Duke Senior himself, who treats the native citizens of the wood – the beasts – more cruelly than his brother treated him (2.1.25–63). Far from being offended by Jaques' bluntness, the banished Duke finds it 'full of matter' (2.1.68), thus lending his endorsement to the satirist's later cele-bration, after meeting the jester Touchstone, of the value of licensed satirical comedy as a means of protecting the equilibrium of a just state.

The professional clown or fool, says Jaques, must have 'liberty' as well as the traditional motley coat (2.7.47). To be a successful jester, the cynic would need 'as large a charter as the wind, / To blow on whom I please' (2.7.48–9), and only on this condition would his wit have the desired therapeutic effect on its recipients: 'Give me leave / To speak my mind, and I will through and through / Cleanse the foul body of th'infected world, / If they will patiently receive my medicine' (2.7.58–61). For Jaques, the potency of comic satire stems in part from the theatrical nature of human life itself: every role a person can play is a performance, and can be modified as readily as a versatile player changes character. His famous meditation on this subject ('All the world's a stage' (2.7.139–66)) is prompted by a particular episode, when the desperate Orlando rushes with drawn sword into the glade where Duke Senior is about to dine and demands food for old Adam. The Duke returns him a 'gentle' answer (2.7.105–6), and the embarrassed Orlando recognizes that he has found civility where he least expected it, among the inhabitants of a wilderness. For many Elizabethans, gentleness meant conduct befitting a lady or a gentleman; it was inextricably bound up with the blood and organs of the aristocratic body, and specifically located in the halls and chambers where that body made its home. But in this scene the word has clearly escaped from its class affiliations and become a way of acting independent of birthright or provenance. Before he has any knowledge of Orlando's rank the Duke tells him to 'sit you down in gentleness, / And take upon command what help we have' (2.7.124–5), while Orlando associates gentle manners with life in a community, where bells 'knoll' men and women to their collective prayers at a church, tears are shed in sympathy for other people's misfortunes, and all comers are welcome at a 'good man's feast' (2.7.113–18). The episode drives home for the Duke the fact that his own sudden shift in social status, from governor to outlaw, is hardly unique: 'This wide and universal theatre / Presents more woeful pageants than the scene / Wherein we play in' (2.7.137–9). The material conditions of a man's life change, and with them the role he plays and the voice he speaks with. Jaques then transforms this momentary perception into an extended disquisition on the multiplicity of roles played by a single person in his or her lifetime. 'One man in his time plays many parts', he says (2.7.142), and the parts he describes merge into one another, shifting between power and powerlessness with each succeeding moment.[8] 'All the world's a stage' articulates the radical instability of social identities, and as such forms the centrepiece of this warily optimistic comedy.

The seven-part life described by Jaques moves in cycles, as time did according to the early modern understanding of history.[9] Helpless infancy occurs twice, at the beginning and end of one's existence; the clothes of one's youth, 'well saved', may be rehabilitated in old age, when a man finds his voice 'Turning again towards childish treble'; while the fourth and fifth ages share an obsession with collecting phrases (the soldier is 'Full of strange oaths', the justice 'Full of wise saws, and modern instances', and both take an immoderate pride in their splendid beards). Orlando, then, and Adam, could well be the same person at different ages, while the Duke with his well-lined belly could be Orlando at a different age again. Even the differences between classes may be experienced within one man's career, as he moves from suffering under coercion as a 'whining schoolboy' to dealing out the law 'with eyes severe' as a judge, from the sudden quick quarrels of the soldier to the utter powerlessness of second childishness. Jaques's great speech cleanses the foul body of the infected world by showing that it is indeed one body, and that Duke Senior's gentleness and Orlando's concern for old Adam are the only appropriate response of one man to the distress of another, who is, after all, effectively himself. The implications of this argument are radical both for the stage, which becomes a potential blueprint for political action, and for Elizabethan society in general, which proves capable of being acted upon at every level. No wonder Jaques's voice has so often been conflated with that of Shakespeare himself.[10]

In the rest of the play, though, it is the second of our commentators, the boy/girl Ganymede/Rosalind, who has the most to tell us about the radical implications of a comic stage performance. For Rosalind, as for all the early modern theorists of laughter, such a performance depends for its effect on careful timing; and time is central to her role as Ganymede. When Ganymede arrives in Arden he finds himself in a spot where time is suspended or wasted, as the theatre-haters said it was in the playhouse. Duke Senior and his company of exiles 'Lose and neglect the creeping hours of time' (2.7.112), and their inactive life encourages contemplation. Touchstone turns 'foolosopher' when he gets there,[11] to Jaques's delight, and ponders the effects of time on his body: 'And so from hour to hour, we ripe, and ripe, / And then from hour to hour, we rot, and rot, / And thereby hangs a tale' (2.7.26–8). People's lives in Arden run to an organic timetable set not by the authority of church and state but by the demands of an ever-changing body; and Ganymede's body, as Rosalind invents it, exemplifies better than anyone else's the tale of the body's changes.

The boy stands at a kind of temporal gateway, an evanescent moment suspended between recognized roles in Elizabethan society.[12]

His age sets him outside the seven ages listed by Jaques, at a midway point between the schoolboy and the lover: he describes his education at the hands of an 'old religious uncle' as if it has hardly finished (3.2.336–43), and undertakes to cure Orlando of love's madness as if he has not yet been infected by it. Thanks to his time of life, then, poised at the entry to adulthood but not yet furnished with the signs of 'ripe' masculinity – a beard and a deep voice – his attitude to time, as to other things, is not yet fixed. It is capricious, changing with his changing situation, thus proving not only that 'Time travels in divers paces with divers persons', as he tells Orlando (3.2.303–4), but that it travels at different paces with the same person, depending on his or her state of mind and body. When Ganymede interrogates his sister about Orlando, for instance, his impatience for answers is such that 'one inch of delay ... is a South Sea of discovery' (3.2.193–4), and he wants simultaneous answers to a dozen questions, so that Celia will have to 'borrow ... Gargantua's mouth' if she is to answer him as he wishes (3.2.222). Yet Ganymede also interrupts the answers he does get: his tongue, as Celia points out, 'curvets unseasonably' like an untrained horse (3.2.241–2). His impatience when Orlando is late seems to mark him out as a lover, for whom 'sighing every minute and groaning every hour [detects] the lazy foot of Time, as well as a clock' (3.2.299–300); yet he is also content to pass the time while waiting for Orlando in the lazy pursuit of watching and acting in the 'play' of Phebe's courtship by Silvius (3.4.56). His time in Orlando's company seems potentially boundless, taken up with a stream of witty answers to Orlando's questions; answers designed to protract the conversation indefinitely, to put off forever the moment when the demands of some outside schedule force them apart. Yet the boy is also sensitive to the moment when extempore wit has run its natural course and desire demands action. When Orlando declares that 'I can live no longer by thinking', Ganymede's response is instantaneous: 'I will weary you then no longer with idle talking' (5.2.51–2). The infinite flexibility of Ganymede's wit, generated by his temporary state of suspended animation – free from the rules that enclose less fortunate beings – exemplifies better than anything else the extent to which time, thought and speech are free in Arden, where Jaques's seven ages of man are no trap but a basic scale on which themes and variations may be playfully improvised, limited only by a boy's imagination.

It is appropriate, then, that Rosalind imagines Ganymede as a native of Arden, born and bred there like 'the cony that you see dwell where she is kindled' (3.2.332–3). Ganymede's origins free him from the constraints of class: his birthplace may be as humble as a shepherd's, but the uncle who raised him was a courtier, so that the boy's accent is 'something finer' than Orlando would have expected of a rustic (3.2.334). Ganymede's origins explain why he finds it so easy to communicate with all classes: he is as comfortable in the company of dukes as of agricultural labourers, and commands the second son of a gentleman, Orlando, with as much confidence as he commands the shepherds Silvius and Phebe. And these origins explain, too, the ease with which he finally accomplishes the transition from shepherd to priest-magician, transforming himself into a young, fair-minded Prospero, whose authority extends by democratic consensus over all the characters in the play, from Touchstone to Duke Senior and his court. It is Rosalind's imagination that wins Ganymede this authority by fancying his origins to be as unfixed as his age, thus opening up sympathetic links between him and every person he encounters. And in doing so she pays homage to the liberating effect of the imagination itself, especially in the theatre.

If Ganymede's age exempts him from the set roles available to men, it also exempts him from the necessity of subscribing to set notions of gender. He is a 'pretty youth' (3.2.328), his complexion manifesting the complex mixture of reds and whites that are valued by men in a woman's cheek. His sparkling repartee resembles a woman's; and the ease with which he acts a female part for Orlando's benefit arises, he claims, from the fact that his emotions are still, like a woman's, under the influence of the ever-changing moon. As a 'moon-ish youth' he can:

> grieve, be effeminate, changeable, longing and liking, proud, fantastical, apish, shallow, inconstant, full of tears, full of smiles, for every passion something and for no passion truly anything, as boys and women are for the most part cattle of this colour. (3.2.399–404)

In this fickle state he is equally attractive to both sexes, and can apply his wit with equal skill to debunking male and female efforts to impose tyrannical limits on desire.

By his very existence, Ganymede mocks both the Petrarchan tradition of idealized, unapproachable femininity and the more widespread myth of masculine toughness, born from the association between manhood and violence with which Shakespeare's plays are so problematically filled. Both of these are gender clichés to which Orlando is addicted. In the first act, Orlando treats the ritualized violence of a wrestling match as a passport into the harsh world of adult masculinity, dominated as it is by the tyrants Oliver and Duke Frederick. In Arden the young man turns to another, gentler but no less problematic model of manhood, the literary lover, 'deifying the name of Rosalind' in verse to an extent that renders any potential relationship with her untenable (3.2.354–5). It is hardly surprising, then, if both Rosalind and Ganymede see masculinity as comic, its monopoly on aggression an arrant piece of nonsense, its construction of relationships with women absurd. Rosalind watches Orlando's wrestling match with voyeuristic glee, ignoring Touchstone's view that 'breaking of ribs' is no sport for ladies (1.2.129–30) (she even half-wishes to join in: 'The little strength that I have', she tells Orlando, 'I would it were with you' (1.2.183–4)). Later, Ganymede hurries with equally voyeuristic pleasure to watch and comment on the cruel 'play' of Silvius and Phebe as it is acted out in the forest; and again he finds himself inadvertently caught up in the action. These two incidents – Rosalind's involvement in the wrestling match (Orlando says afterwards that she has 'overthrown' him (1.2.249)) and the boy Ganymede's supplanting of the girl Phebe as the cruel lover in the romantic comedy he was watching – demonstrate the extent to which masculine and feminine roles are interchangeable, in spite of Orlando's fictions. And Rosalind's transformation into Ganymede offers further proof of this interchangeability, complicating and confusing every sexual stereotype with which she comes into contact.

In making the transition from female to male, Rosalind takes it for granted that her concealment of 'woman's fear' beneath 'a swashing and a martial outside' is common practice among 'mannish cowards' (1.3.115–19), for whom theatrical posturing serves as a substitute for heroic action. Rosalind's construction of Ganymede, in other words, adds another layer of complexity to his/her already complex gender position: a boy actor may conceal a 'female' identity beneath his male appearance even *before* he plays Rosalind, who then plays Ganymede, who then plays Rosalind again. The theatrical nature of conventional masculinity is later confirmed by Orlando's brother Oliver. When Ganymede faints at the sight of Orlando's blood, Oliver tells him 'You lack a man's heart' (4.3.164–5), and dismisses the boy's claim that the faint was a pretence: 'there is too great testimony in your complexion that it was a passion of earnest' (4.3.169–71). For Oliver, clearly, as for Rosalind, a male body may harbour either a 'masculine' or 'feminine' heart; and in spite of his body's weakness Ganymede must learn to perform as his culture expects him to: 'take a good heart', he advises him, 'and counterfeit to be a man' (4.3.173–4). Meanwhile, Ganymede shows himself acutely aware of the other role available to men, the literary lover, as a performance. When Orlando adopts this role in the forest Ganymede rebukes him, first, for not doing it properly (he is too neatly dressed for a lover and too lax in his time-keeping (3.2.360–74, 4.1.37–46)) and then for taking literary conventions too seriously (whatever the poets say, no man has ever died for love (4.1.89–102)). The boy mocks, too the manufactured image of women that corresponds to that of the Petrarchan man. For Ganymede, the defining characteristic of women is not virtue and wisdom, as Orlando thinks, but the more volatile quality of wit, the capacity for rapid improvisation that refuses to be pinned down by someone else's script: 'Make the doors upon a woman's wit, and it will out at the casement; shut that, and 'twill out at the key-hole; stop that, 'twill fly with the smoke out at the chimney' (4.1.154–7). Women experience desire, jealousy, grief and hilarity like men, and are far more adept than men at giving their feelings vent. Try as Orlando may to domesticate his Rosalind, she will always find clever ways to preserve her waywardness – even to the extent of donning a masculine doublet and hose and becoming Ganymede, who can explain the workings of a woman's wit so wittily to her baffled lover.

If Orlando needs to be taught by Ganymede to recognize the hackneyed nature of the literary tradition from which he draws his views on love, other inhabitants of Arden are fully conscious that conventional romantic love is a matter of performance. Touchstone, for instance, burlesques romance in his dialogues with the countrywoman Audrey, freely confessing the 'feigning' nature of the poetry with which he woos her (3.3.18–20), and openly acknowledging his hope that his marriage to her will last only as long as his sexual interest in her continues (3.3.82–6). Celia, too, sees the conventions of literary love as a set of elaborate fictions, and strives to deflate Ganymede's delight in Orlando by dropping caustic remarks about the brittleness of a lover's promises (3.4.28–30). And the shepherdess Phebe dismisses Silvius's love for her as a silly fantasy, fit only to furnish material for a second-rate drama. 'Now counterfeit to swoon', she tells him, 'why now fall down, / Or if thou canst not, O for shame, for shame, / Lie not, to say mine eyes are murderers' (3.5.17–19). At the same time, both Phebe and Celia end up by reaffirming the validity of the literary conventions they mock. Phebe's scorn for Silvius casts her in the familiar role of the cruel mistress of Petrarchan tradition. And when she falls in love with Ganymede – as if in obedience to the famous dictum she quotes from Marlowe's *Hero and Leander*: 'Who ever lov'd that lov'd not at first sight?' (3.5.82)[13] – she subscribes at once to the foolish fiction she had earlier dismissed, that eyes may kill, and writes Ganymede a poem to say that the 'scorn of your bright eyne' will end her life (4.3.40–63). Celia, too, falls in love in an instant, and rushes through the conventional stages of courtship at breakneck speed in her eagerness to reach the consummation of marriage. For all their dismissal of the classical and post-classical literature of desire, only this literature can supply them with a vocabulary to express, at the proper moment, 'how many fathom deep they are in love' (4.1.198).

Ganymede shares both Phebe's scepticism concerning the literary conventions of love and her rapt participation in these conventions. Like Phebe he doubts if men have ever been killed by desire ('men have died from time to time and worms have eaten them, but not for love' (4.1.101–2)); but he later suffers a kind of death when he faints on seeing Orlando's blood, as if to illustrate the hold a fiction may have on a lover's heart (4.3.156ff.). To conceal his true passion Ganymede feigns it to be feigned: 'a body would think this was well counterfeited' (4.3.166–7); and this bit of feigning is of course a complex mixture of truth and falsehood. In this it resembles Ganymede's performance of the role of Rosalind for Orlando's benefit. Orlando takes the performance to be a pure fiction, so that when Ganymede says 'Am not I your Rosalind?' he answers, 'I take some joy to say you are because I would be talking of her' (4.1.84–6). Yet Ganymede *is* Rosalind, in so far as Rosalind is real at all, and Orlando ends by promising to treat him 'with no less religion than if thou wert indeed my Rosalind' (4.1.189–90). Dramatic or literary tradition, then, lends lovers a crude linguistic framework for their desire. It is a provisional framework, constantly being accepted and rejected, embraced and discarded as a relationship develops. And it is a temporary one, like Rosalind's role as Ganymede, which finally proves an unsatisfactory substitute for amorous action, as Ganymede concedes when he tells Orlando, 'Why, then, tomorrow I cannot serve your turn for Rosalind' (5.2.48–9). But even as it is accepted as a sham, this literary-theatrical language liberates a lover's tongue from the awkward silence that grips it when passion grips his or her body. On their first meeting, Rosalind and Orlando found themselves without a word to throw at a dog, silenced by the tyranny of desire as effectively as the tyranny of Duke Frederick silenced his subjects. Once apprenticed to the conventions of literary-dramatic love, however, their tongues are set in motion, so that Orlando forgets that he was ever tongue-tied ('Who could be out [i.e. wordless], being before his beloved mistress?' (4.1.77–8)), and Ganymede discovers a delight in speech as deep as a gourmet's in eating and drinking. Begging Celia to pronounce Orlando's name, the boy cries: 'I would thou couldst stammer, that thou mightst pour this concealed man out of thy mouth, as wine comes out of a narrow-mouthed bottle; either too much at once or none at all' (3.2.195–8). Romantic clichés help lovers to learn the pleasure of talking; and the very fact that non-lovers find the lovers' language so irrational, so light, so absurd, permits the latter to shake off the attentions of unwanted spectators – as Ganymede, Orlando and even Touchstone evade the unwanted commentary of the cynic Jaques. Lovers are as witty and sometimes even as sardonic as satirists, but in the end each breed of commentator dances to a very different tune, and it is the 'dancing measures' of the lover that dominate the close of Act 5 (5.4.191).

FIGURE 9   Pieter Pourbus (1523/4–84), 'An Allegory of True Love'
(c. 1547), one of many early modern representations of love in a wooded
landscape not unlike Arden. Note the fool in the bottom right-hand corner

The shift from the satirist's tune to the lover's is marked in Arden
by the changing nature of the songs with which the forest is filled. The
earlier songs are social commentaries, celebrating the wilderness as an
escape from the ambition and enmity of the court (2.5.1–8, 35–42),
the wind as a trenchant critique of false friendship (2.7.174–93), and
the cuckold's horn as a true emblem of marriage (4.2.10–19). Jaques
listens to these songs with pleasure, even writing a new stanza for one
of them. The last song, by contrast, is presided over by the fool
Touchstone, and is a ditty of 'no great matter' (5.3.40), a hymn to sex
in spring-time and the need to seize 'the present time' with all its beau-
ties before they vanish forever (5.3.15–38). Despite the fact that
Touchstone shares Phebe's and Ganymede's scepticism concerning the
conventions of love (he joins in the multiple wedding service at the end
of the play with the avowed intention 'to swear and to forswear, according as marriage binds and blood breaks' (5.4.55–6)), the fool never
claims, as the sceptic or satirist does, to be exempt from the social practices he mocks.

Duke Senior tells us that Jaques committed many of the sins he
chides in his satires; yet Jaques still proposes to Orlando that the pair of

them sit and 'rail against our mistress the world and all our misery' as if they had no stake in that misery's causes (3.2.273–5). Orlando rejects Jaques's proposal because, he says, 'I will chide no breather in the world but myself, against whom I know most faults' (3.2.276–7); and Touchstone shares Orlando's consciousness both of his faults and of his folly. Where Jaques blames Duke Senior's banished courtiers for the death of the forest's citizens, the deer – despite the fact that he himself joins in the hunt – Touchstone mocks the follies of the ruling classes by acting them out, rudely berating the shepherd Corin for his bad manners, threatening the innocent rustic William with a range of courtly forms of murder, and inveigling the innocent Audrey into a temporary marriage in the time-honoured fashion of the unscrupulous and lustful aristocrat. Yet Touchstone's honesty about his motives is quite literally disarming. Because everyone knows precisely who and what he is, his cod-courtly antics can do no harm to their victims. His consciousness that marriage, pomposity and death-threats are a collection of rites devised to satisfy certain 'desires' that all men have in common (3.3.74), demystifies the mechanisms by which the ruling classes assert their power, and places everyone on the same level as the lovers who seize 'the present time' to assuage their appetite for one another's bodies.

It is Touchstone, the play's third commentator, who provides the 'touchstone' for judging this comedy's many fictions – a touchstone being a lump of rock with which tradesmen tested the purity of gold. In the final act he gives his most revealing account of the way the ruling classes operate, by explaining to Duke Senior the conventions that govern the courtly practice of duelling. A quarrel between courtiers must go through seven stages or 'degrees' if it is to end in a duel to the death (5.4.38ff.). If all these degrees are not gone through, the duel may be avoided and death delayed. Yet even if all the set stages of the quarrel are ascended – all the way to the dreadful seventh degree, the Lie Direct, where one courtier directly accuses another of telling fibs – the duel may still be averted by the deft deployment of a conditional. 'I knew when seven justices could not take up a quarrel', says Touchstone, 'but when the parties were met themselves, one of them thought but of an If, as, "If you said so, then I said so". And they shook hands, and swore brothers. Your If is the only peace-maker: much virtue in If'

(5.4.96–101). By asserting that one's assertions were mere conjectures, statements of possibility rather than of fact, the most rigid of conventions may be circumvented, the most deadly of conclusions turned aside. Touchstone's seven stages of a courtly quarrel serve as a vital refinement on Jaques's seven ages of man. Although Jaques sees each age of a man's life as a new theatrical performance, his players have no choice about the roles they play or the sequence in which they are played: one age follows another in strict succession, and death provides the only exit from the playhouse. The fool, by contrast, is an improviser; he follows no script slavishly. Although he sees the value of a framework, he refuses to be bound by it when it ceases to serve its purpose. Social rituals of all kinds are for him the same: they serve a function, but may be discarded as soon as they cease to work for the good of the community. And this genial 'foolosophy' of conditionals is corroborated by the last two scenes of the play.

These scenes are full of patent fictions, whose conditional nature declares itself by virtue of their sheer implausibility. Oliver and Duke Frederick are converted without warning and without repercussions, as if their former tyrannies had been nothing but a game. Oliver's conversion is effected, moreover, by the most absurd of emblematic devices: he is threatened in his sleep by a serpent and a lioness (4.3.98–156), which gives Orlando the chance to display his 'natural' love for his brother by saving him from these two natural perils. The lioness obeys nature's unwritten convention that it refrain from attacking a sleeping man; Orlando nature's injunction to protect his kinsman, despite the latter's unkindness; and Oliver is left with no option but to obey the same conventions and manifest a 'brother's love' (4.3.144). Few dramatic denouements could be more obviously contrived than this abrupt intervention by 'nature' – a nature that so signally failed to operate in Oliver before this convenient moment. But the incident supplies the perfect illustration of the ease with which one 'if' may be supplanted by another. Orlando's hesitation over whether to save his brother is a moment of choice between two possible modes of existence; and his selection of comic reconcilement instead of tragic revenge releases the barrage of constructive conditionals that closes the play.

Oliver opens the story of his rescue by Orlando with a run of ifs: 'Pray you, if you know ... If that an eye may profit by a tongue ... if you will know of me / What man I am' (4.3.75, 83, 95–6); and the positive response of Ganymede and Celia to each of his conditionals (yes, we know; yes, we are who you think we are; yes, we would like to hear your story) triggers the narrative of his 'conversion' from one mode of being to another. Ganymede's magic in the play's last act is wreathed around with further ifs: believe *if* you please that I can do strange things; *if* you love Rosalind, and *if* you don't object, I can 'set her before your eyes tomorrow'; '*if* you will be married tomorrow, you shall, and to Rosalind *if* you will'; and so on (5.2.58, 61, 65–7, 71–2). And even when Ganymede reappears as Rosalind, his union with Orlando remains dependent on conditionals. '*If* there be truth in sight, you are my daughter', says Duke Senior; '*If* there be truth in sight, you are my Rosalind', adds Orlando; and Hymen concludes, 'Here's eight that must take hands / And join in Hymen's bands, / *If* truth holds true contents' (5.4.116, 117, 126–8). The appearance of the god Hymen at Ganymede's behest is the oddest *if* of all (what universe does he come from and what magic invoked him?). Yet the appearance of this classical god of marriage averts 'confusion' (5.4.123) by involving everyone on stage in a ritual celebration of the imaginative 'bond' or mutual agreement which is matrimony: 'O blessed bond of board and bed. / 'Tis Hymen peoples every town' (5.4.140–1). If Hymen is an extravagant fantasy, then towns have been peopled by fantasy, and fantasy is the motor by which entire civilizations are propelled. Comic theatre, with its dancing measures (in the sense of musical rhythms) and its contempt for measure (in the sense of moderation), is only one of the delightful rites by which societies perpetuate themselves, in spite of their own self-destructive tendencies. And those who oppose this particular rite of theatrical laughter deserve to share in Jaques's self-banishment.

MASTERS AND MISTRESSES IN
TWELFTH NIGHT

Twelfth Night is a mature revision of *The Comedy of Errors*. Like the earlier play, it involves the confusions that arise from the presence of twins in a strange city – although in this case there is just a single set of twins, a boy and a girl. Like the Ephesus of *Errors*, the Illyria of *Twelfth Night* is 'Rough and unhospitable' for strangers (3.3.11), and like Ephesus the town grows progressively darker and more sinister from one scene to the next, with proliferating references to devils, witchcraft, hell, madness and heresy, as the errors that beset its inhabitants multiply and the fears of its visitors grow more intense. Both Ephesus and Illyria are conspicuously concerned with time and money, although Illyria, as the more courtly setting, encourages the accumulation of capital through the 'idle markets' of the leisure industry rather than through trade (3.3.46). In Illyria, Viola earns her living as a Duke's go-between, Feste earns his as a fool at the service of anyone who cares to pay him, while Sir Toby milks Sir Andrew mercilessly for entertainment as well as cash. Time in Illyria is freely available to be squandered, either on lounging among beds of flowers, or on daily rites of mourning, or on drink. Nevertheless, the need for cash is never forgotten by the bulk of Illyria's natives, and time's dominance of the city is repeatedly acknowledged, even if it is rarely measured by the clocks that govern Ephesus.

Above all, both *Errors* and *Twelfth Night* are extended meditations on the nature of comedy, and both testify to Shakespeare's consciousness of the anti-comic sentiment prevalent in some quarters of Elizabethan London. As we have seen, the earlier play incorporates the vexed problem of comic timing into its plot, postulating a range of unsettling consequences for mistimed humour, from a beating to imprisonment and destitution; indeed, a slight mistiming of the final act would have failed to avert an execution. In *Twelfth Night*, too, comic excess has serious repercussions. The victim of a practical joke finds himself imprisoned as a madman possessed by demons (a condition treated with chains and whips) and accused of heresy (a crime punishable by burning). And when the heroine Viola dons a comic disguise as a boy she unleashes a sequence of events that might well have ended in her summary execution at the hands of the man she loves. Shame, pain, disgrace and death are the effects of comic mistiming in both these plays, as the theatre-haters said they were, and *Twelfth Night* abounds in further echoes of Elizabethan anti-comic diatribes. Viola herself at one point describes her masculine camouflage in misogynistic terms that might have been drawn from one of the anti-theatrical pamphlets: 'Disguise, I see thou art a wickedness, / Wherein the pregnant enemy does much' – the 'pregnant enemy' being the devil (2.2.27–8). Later, after bantering with Feste the clown, she ponders the tact required by a professional comedian if he is to avoid getting into trouble for his witticisms: 'He must observe their mood on whom he jests, / The quality of persons, and the time ... This is a practice / As full of labour as a wise man's art' (3.1.62–6). Feste personifies, in fact, the delicate balance that must be struck by the comic performer in an age hostile to humour. His career as a jester is jeopardized by time – both in the form of age (he is an ageing clown whose comic technique is on the verge of being outmoded) and in the form of his own failure to insert himself into his chief employer's schedule. At the beginning of the play he is out of favour with that employer, Lady Olivia, because of a prolonged period of absence without leave; and she points out to him how 'your fooling grows old, and people dislike it' (1.5.107–8). The penalty for Feste's failure to retain his lady's favour would be redundancy, a fate 'as good as a hanging to you', as his fellow servant Maria suggests (1.5.17–18). And for the rest of the play he is engaged in a comic struggle to the death with the chief of Lady Olivia's servants, the steward Malvolio, who would be as happy to see him hanged as made redundant.

Malvolio is the principal source of the play's anti-comic vocabulary, protesting at his mistress's indulgence of Feste, and interrupting the midnight revels of the fool and his companions with a rebuke that is as old as the hostility to laughter itself: 'Have you no wit, manners, nor honesty, but to gabble like tinkers at this time of night? ... Is there no respect of place, persons, nor time in you?' (2.3.78–91). When Malvolio is imprisoned in the fourth act, after being tricked by Feste's friends into behaving like a fool himself, his punishment could be seen as comedy's symbolic revenge on its puritanical enemies (he is even described at one point as 'a kind of Puritan' (2.3.138)).[14] But the nature of his punishment – he likens the prison to hell, and Feste taunts him like 'the old Vice' (4.2.123), the comic devil of early Elizabethan drama – suggests that his disapproval of comedy may have some substance to it. It is Feste who points out to the Duke in Act 2 that 'pleasure will be paid, one time or another' (2.4.70–1), and Malvolio's repayment with excessive interest for his hostility to humour is only one of a series of inappropriate repayments for debt – or non-payments – that punctuate the play. Viola's employer Duke Orsino, for instance, lacks 'recompense' (she says) for his love of Lady Olivia (1.5.279);[15] Antonio's love for Sebastian receives a poor 'recompense' in Sebastian's seeming failure to help him financially when he most needs it. Viola's faithful service to Duke Orsino is poorly recompensed with his decision in Act 5 to kill her, just as Malvolio's service to Olivia is poorly recompensed by his imprisonment on her orders.[16] Finally, Lady Olivia's love for Viola, which leads her to demean herself to the extent of marrying her (as she thinks), is poorly recompensed by Viola's refusal to acknowledge the marriage; whereas Sir Toby's marriage to the servant Maria 'recompenses' her fully for the ingenuity of her machinations against Malvolio (5.1.357). Every time Feste makes a joke he expects payment for it; but the system of service and reward in which he participates would seem from most of these examples to be badly flawed. Within this play, comedy faithfully reproduces the inequalities and injustices of the society it serves, before finally and unexpectedly undoing them. No wonder, then, if laughter-loathers like Malvolio found its operations offensive.

The most alarming element in this system of mismatched reward and punishment is the opportunities it gives for extravagant acts of revenge.[17] From one point of view, comic repartee is the art of verbal vengeance – a way of getting back at someone instantaneously for an insult; and this form of laughing rhetorical revenge is enthusiastically practised in Illyria. The Malvolio/Feste rivalry is a humorous revenge plot that gets out of hand; and it begins with Feste's failure to find a rapid-fire response to Malvolio in Act 1, when the steward tells Olivia that the jester was recently 'put down' by an 'ordinary fool, that has no more brain than a stone' (1.5.81–3). When Feste does not respond to his insult Malvolio pounces at once to demean him: 'Look you now, he's out of his guard already: unless you laugh and minister occasion to him, he is gagged' (1.5.83–5). Malvolio mocks the reliance of comic performers on the community that surrounds them: they require a sympathetic audience to create a context for ('minister occasion to') their jokes if these are not to fall flat, whereas by implication men like Malvolio are self-reliant, capable of maintaining their dignity without any outside help at all. Feste's response is to collaborate with a community of jokers – Sir Toby, Maria, Fabian – in a conspiracy to show Malvolio how completely he depends on others, especially his employer Olivia. In the play's last scene the fool points out the connection between what the conspirators have done to the steward and the original insult given in Act 1: 'But do you remember, "Madam, why laugh you at such a barren rascal, and you smile not, he's gagged"? And thus the whirligig of time brings in his revenges' (5.1.367–9). Feste's co-conspirator Fabian tells Olivia that this comic retaliation was an act of 'sportful malice' that deserves a light response (5.1.358): it should 'rather pluck on laughter than revenge', and should generate no future consequences that might 'Taint the condition of this present hour' (5.1.359, 350). Malvolio, however, disagrees. As soon as Feste has finished taunting him in the last scene the steward announces his own intended retaliation ('I'll be reveng'd on the whole pack of you' (5.1.370)) and quits the stage in high dudgeon, leaving certain essential elements of the play's plot unresolved. And Malvolio's sense of injury recalls other injurious acts that spawned threats of revenge elsewhere in the play: Illyria's intended revenge on Antonio, for instance, for his maritime exploits against the Illyrian state; or the revenge to be exacted from Viola/Cesario by the terrible fighter 'Sir Andrew Aguecheek' as Sir Toby reinvents him ('Of what nature the wrongs are thou hast done him, I know not', Sir Toby tells Cesario, 'but thy intercepter, full of despite, bloody as the hunter, attends thee at the orchard-end', awaiting 'satisfaction . . . by pangs of death and sepulchre' (3.4.219–39)). The play allows, then, for the possibility that Malvolio's revenge on the rest of the cast may raise the process of insult and retaliation to a new, bloody level, precipitating it into a tragic mode that has been hovering at the edge of the action since the opening scene.

The comic plot that generates all these acts of revenge involves many different kinds of disguise. Viola's disguise as the boy Cesario plunges her into an aristocratic milieu where concealment is ubiquitous: from the veil that hides Olivia's identity when Cesario first meets her, to the disguised handwriting Maria uses to trick Malvolio into thinking he has received a love-letter from his mistress, to the disguised voice Feste uses when he impersonates a priest in Malvolio's prison cell. Such disguises illuminate the ease with which the social hierarchy may be infiltrated or overthrown. The disguised Viola could be anyone from anywhere, the veiled Olivia could be one of her own servants, Feste's changes of voice both elevate him to the status of a cleric and debase him to the level of a madman (he reads Malvolio's letter aloud in a 'mad voice' in the final scene). Women and clowns are the masters of disguise in this play, as they are in so many of Shakespeare's comedies; and women in particular, as the subjects of male fantasies, seem conscious of the extent to which changes of clothes and language can reshape a person's identity.

Men, on the other hand, regard their identity as inviolable, even as they seek to change their social role, as Malvolio does. Malvolio is tricked by Maria into donning yellow stockings and cross garters to please his mistress, while smiling his face 'into more lines than is in the new map with the augmentation of the Indies' (3.2.76–8); but the joke here is that he is wholly unable to match his mind to his appearance, as a good impersonator should do. In the same way, Antonio is unable or unwilling to disguise his identity as an enemy of the Illyrian state, or Sir Andrew Aguecheek to perform the role of ruffian in which he is coached by Sir Toby. Men who are not professional comic performers have too much invested in the social hierarchy to imagine destabilizing it, however briefly, by becoming what they are not. When Maria tells Sir Toby that he must 'confine' himself 'within the modest limits of order', Sir Toby replies: 'I'll confine myself no finer than I am. These clothes are good enough to drink in, and so be these boots too: and they be not, let them hang themselves in their own straps' (1.3.8–13). The fat knight's contempt for fine clothes helps to mark him out as 'consanguineous' – a privileged relation of the mistress of the house (2.3.77). For women, on the other hand, disguise is an escape from powerlessness, and who they are is determined largely by externals: above all, by their garments, of which their faces are merely an extension. When Viola reveals her female identity at the end of the play, she seems unwilling to prove it by any other means than by regaining her female clothes from the ship's captain who has been looking after them. In the story from which the play was taken she proves it by showing another woman her breasts – something Shakespeare could have contrived offstage if he had wanted to.[18] In *Twelfth Night* women are conscious that men judge a woman by what they see of her, and what they see is determined by certain conventions, of which clothes, rather than a woman's body or words, are the most widely accepted sign.

The witty women of *Twelfth Night* play freely with these conventions for their own benefit. Robert Greene lists the female virtues in one of his romances: ideally, women should be 'beawtiful, as favored by nature in their exteriour liniaments. Wise, as graced with a divine influence, sober and silent, as portending a temperate and unfained chastity.'[19] Olivia plays the part of a chaste, silent woman as a means of avoiding the unwelcome attentions of Orsino, Duke of Illyria. Since she has sworn to marry no man 'above her degree, neither in estate, years, nor wit' (1.3.107), she chooses to pose as a virginal recluse at the beginning of the play, mourning the death of her brother in solitude for seven years – time enough, one would have thought, to deter even an obsessive admirer like the Duke. She drops the role as soon as she falls in love. Viola, too, invokes the idea of the chaste and silent woman after she has disguised herself as the boy Cesario. Cesario enters the service of Duke Orsino, then becomes infatuated with him; and at one point the disguised page tells his master the story of a wordless woman as a means of hinting at his own desire for the Duke. Cesario had a sister, he explains, who fell in love, but never vented her feelings, with tragic results:

> she never told her love,
> But let concealment like a worm i'th'bud
> Feed on her damask cheek: she pin'd in thought,
> And with a green and yellow melancholy
> She sat like Patience on a monument,
> Smiling at grief.
>
> (2.4.111–16)

The 'history' or story of this girl, Cesario explains, is nothing but a 'blank' (2.4.110–11), since she was constrained by the restrictive nature of the ideal she imitated to waste away without taking part in any narrative. Olivia and Viola, by contrast, are well aware that this ideal is only one of the many fantasies that throng the play. Their confidence that time will resolve their difficulties – Olivia's imposition of a

deadline on her mourning, Viola's famous observation, when she learns
that Olivia loves her, that 'time . . . must untangle this, not I' (2.2.40) –
springs perhaps from the fact that they have written themselves into a
very different narrative than the blank history of Cesario's sister.
Elizabethan fiction on the page and on stage – not least the work of
Greene – was rich in alternative plots involving women, and most
women in Shakespeare's comedies are thoroughly familiar with these
plots, choosing between them at will as occasion demands.

The men in *Twelfth Night* have their own fantastic versions of the
ideal woman, still more absurd than Greene's, which have little or nothing to do with the 'real' women of flesh and blood we see on stage. (The
exception is Sir Toby, who has little patience for the ideal invoked by his
niece Olivia, and who admires the boldness and wit of her maid Maria.)
The greatest fantasist of them all is the most powerful figure in the play,
Duke Orsino. In the first scene, Orsino sees Olivia's mourning for her
brother as a guarantee of her future devotion to the Duke, at some fan-
cied time when she will accept him as her lover:

> O, she that hath a heart of that fine frame
> To pay this debt of love but to a brother,
> How will she love, when the rich golden shaft
> Hath kill'd the flock of all affections else
> That live in her; when liver, brain, and heart,
> These sovereign thrones, are all supplied, and fill'd
> Her sweet perfections with one self king!

> (1.1.33–9)

Clearly the Duke has no interest in Olivia's actual thoughts and feelings;
his celebrated opening speech is all about his own experience of desire,
and Olivia is not even mentioned in it. Instead he is obsessed with a
vision of the absolute monarchic control he will wield over the Countess
when he has won her 'liver, brain, and heart', transforming her body
into an animate receptacle for his own image. In this he resembles
Olivia's steward Malvolio, whose fantasies of marrying his mistress
focus exclusively on the pleasure he will take in ruling her household while Olivia lies asleep in post-coital exhaustion (2.5.43ff.).
Malvolio's desire to replace his lowly post as servant with the position of

servant-lover to Olivia, and his wish to convert her from his mistress (a female master) to his mistress (the woman with whom he sleeps), expose the male-centred agenda behind the terms 'servant' and 'mistress' as deployed in medieval and early modern love-poetry; no wonder Olivia is so insistent on telling Cesario that he is no servant of hers: 'Y'are servant to the Count Orsino, youth' (3.1.101). The heterosexual fantasies of Shakespeare's men consistently consign women to the margins of things; so we should hardly be surprised that it is a woman, Viola – disguised as the boy Cesario, and sent by Orsino to woo Olivia for him – who delivers the most convincing courtship speech in the play. Asked by Olivia what he would do if he were her lover, Cesario replies that he would set up camp at her gate and fix the world's attention on her by repeatedly calling her name (1.5.263–9). This famous picture of determined wooing may be just another far-fetched fantasy, but at least it is one with *both* Olivia *and* her suitor at the heart of it.

Orsino's view of women is both generalized and inconsistent. In one conversation with Cesario, he begins by saying that men are more fickle than women ('Our fancies are more giddy and unfirm, / More longing, wavering, sooner lost and worn / Than women's are' (2.4.33–5)), and ends by claiming what seems to be the opposite: that women are incapable of loving with equal force or 'retention' to men:

> There is no woman's sides
> Can bide the beating of so strong a passion
> As love doth give my heart; no woman's heart
> So big, to hold so much: they lack retention.
> Alas, their love may be call'd appetite,
> No motion of the liver, but the palate,
> That suffers surfeit, cloyment, and revolt;
> But mine is all as hungry as the sea,
> And can digest as much. Make no compare
> Between that love a woman can bear me
> And that I owe Olivia.

(2.4.94–104)

Orsino clearly bases this view of women on himself; it serves only to confirm his narcissism. He started the play, after all, by describing his own love as an 'appetite' capable of devouring endless quantities (of sex or of women? He does not say) without being satisfied (1.1.1–15). In that opening speech, too, his appetite suffered 'cloyment, and revolt' after he had listened to romantic music for too long; and this 'cloyment' anticipates, one presumes, the devaluation Olivia would suffer in his eyes if once she gave him unrestricted access to her body. Orsino's view of women suggests, in fact, that there is little hope of his achieving a satisfactory relationship with any woman at all. It is in response to his fantastic account of women's inability to love that Viola/Cesario tells him the story of his/her imaginary sister who sat 'like Patience on a monument, / Smiling at grief' (2.4.115–16). The sister's very private selflessness is as extreme as Orsino's very public self-obsession, and as incapable of procuring mutual satisfaction for both sexes. Clearly, interaction between the genders depends on the discovery of a new, non-conventional way for them to see one another: a way to which the boy/girl Viola/Cesario offers a beguiling key.

In the meantime, however, Viola's disguise gives her the unwelcome opportunity to learn at first hand about men's fantasies of ideal manhood. In *Twelfth Night* as in so many of Shakespeare's plays men define their masculinity through violence, and this crude means of self-definition subjects non-violent men to considerable pain. Sir Toby's need for revenge on Malvolio is the reaction of a frustrated male to a situation where he cannot vent his hostility on a privileged servant by the time-honoured method of a beating. Instead he swears to '*fool* him black and blue' (2.5.10), and Malvolio's refusal to herd with more aggressive men like Sir Toby and Fabian (who delight in the bloody sport of bear-baiting (2.5.7–8)) leaves him peculiarly vulnerable to such painful fooling. At the same time, Sir Toby restores his sense of pride in his own masculinity by baiting his companion Sir Andrew Aguecheek: exposing him as a comic pastiche of a man's man, subjecting him both to terror and to threatened and actual violence, and in the process identifying Sir Toby as the definitive brutal male. Maria puts her finger on Sir Andrew's nature when she tells us, 'he's a great quarreller; and but that he hath the gift of a coward to allay the gust he hath in quarrelling, 'tis thought among the prudent he would quickly have the gift of a grave' (1.3.30–3). One of the pranks planned by Sir Toby is to display Sir Andrew's lack of manhood by pitting him in battle against an equally 'unmanly' foe, the boy Cesario. This prank, like the trick played on Malvolio, turns sour, when Sir Andrew finds himself confronted first by the 'Notable pirate' Antonio (5.1.66) and later by Viola's brother Sebastian, both of whom are thoroughly 'manly' in their willingness to dish out violence. Sir Andrew ends the play with a broken head, and although Sir Toby too gets his head broken as a reward for his aggression, the fat knight ruthlessly crushes Sir Andrew's suggestion that the two of them should have their wounds treated together. 'Will you help?' he exclaims, 'An ass-head, and a coxcomb, and a knave, a thin-faced knave, a gull?' (5.1.202–3). Even in the face of hard evidence – identical wounds – Sir Toby still insists on defining himself as Sir Andrew's opposite, a man rather than a cheese-paring, and does so in this case by verbal rather than by physical aggression.

Before this, Cesario/Viola discovers the terrifying pressure exerted on young men by their elders, either to comply with the masculine ideal themselves, or else to serve as the guarantor of its embodiment in other men. On being told of Sir Andrew's determination to fight him, Cesario says: 'I have heard of some kind of men that put quarrels purposely on others to taste their valour: belike this is a man of that quirk' (3.4.241–4). Sir Toby insists that this is not the case, and that Sir Andrew has a genuine grievance against him; but the knight then belies his own words by telling the boy to strip his phallic sword 'stark naked' (3.4.250). Clearly the abortive combat Sir Toby sets up between the unmanly man Sir Andrew and the womanly boy Cesario is no more than an elaborate comparison of penises. And his own eager participation in the fight that *does* break out – though neither Sir Andrew nor Cesario are involved in it – confirms that the real point of the competition is to prove his own superior manhood by derogating from theirs.

Besides a willingness to resort to violence, the male ideal of masculinity includes a theoretically unwavering – but in practice highly fragile – loyalty to your closest male friends. In *Twelfth Night* as elsewhere in Shakespeare's work this loyalty asserts itself through aggression. Antonio shows his love for Sebastian by twice putting his life at risk: first following him into Illyria despite the fact that he has 'many enemies in Orsino's court' (2.1.43), then substituting himself for the boy in a sword-fight, just as Mercutio substituted himself for Romeo, with fatal consequences, in Shakespeare's earlier tragedy. It would seem that one's loyalty to other men is as much a test of manliness as the intensity of one's passion for combat. When Antonio thinks Sebastian has betrayed him he stops calling him 'sir' and 'young gentleman' and brands him instead an 'idol', a 'blemish', an 'empty trunk' (3.4.364–9), a 'thing', a source of 'witchcraft' (5.1.86, 73) – terms that strip Sebastian of his gender. Conversely, Sir Andrew's lack of manliness fully vindicates Sir Toby in the contempt he shows for his friendship – or so the fat knight believes. When Fabian observes to Sir Toby that Sir Andrew is 'a dear manikin to you', Sir Toby replies that 'I have been dear to him, lad, some two thousand strong, or so', converting friendship into exploitation with a flippant pun (3.2.52–4). Sir Toby dupes Sir Andrew of his cash as freely as he tricks him into exposing his cowardice; and in the final scene, as we have seen, he annuls their association in a single vitriolic outburst. By virtue of his physical and intellectual frailty, Sir Andrew is a manikin – a little man or puppet – to be played with and discarded at will by 'manly' men like Sir Toby. Male relationships with men, it would seem, are as fragile and as fraught with fantasies as male relationships with women.

All the same, at its best friendship with other men is the most open, intimate and reciprocal form of relationship available to men in *Twelfth Night*. Antonio's love of Sebastian is as selfless as the love of Cesario's imaginary sister for an unknown man, and a good deal more vocal. And in her male disguise as Cesario, Viola gets closer to Orsino than she could ever have done as a woman. After only three days together the Duke is able to tell his new servant, 'Thou know'st no less but all: I have unclasp'd / To thee the book even of my secret soul' (1.4.13–14). This free disclosure of secrets demonstrates that despite their social disparity, in Orsino's eyes Cesario has become what Elizabethan manuals on male friendship describe, after Cicero, as a 'second self', 'another I', a kind of twin of the Duke's, as closely bound to him as Viola is to her twin brother.[20] That Orsino genuinely sees the boy this way is confirmed by his willingness to employ him as his substitute in the courtship of Olivia. The mutuality of their affection reveals itself most strikingly in

the final act, when Cesario gets the chance to sacrifice himself for his
master just as Antonio sacrificed himself for Sebastian. On learning
that Olivia has fallen for Cesario, Orsino promptly resorts to the usual
outlet for male emotion, violence: 'I'll sacrifice the lamb that I do love',
he declares (5.1.127) – that is, he will kill Cesario to spite Olivia; and
the boy at once professes himself willing to die 'a thousand deaths' to
satisfy Orsino (5.1.30). No woman but Viola in Shakespeare's plays gets
such an opportunity to achieve, as a man, the ultimate consummation
of an Elizabethan man's love for another man, which is to lay down his
life for his friend. And no other character, male or female, goes to her
death more 'jocund, apt, and willingly' than she does here (5.1.129),
following him off stage as eagerly as if to a marriage bed.

   In Elizabethan culture there was theoretically no place for a sexual
relationship between men. The crime of sodomy – which encompassed
a range of forbidden sexual activities – was punishable by death.[21] Yet
there is ample evidence that many of these activities went on, un-
deterred by the draconian measures taken against them. The boy
Cesario's declaration of his willingness to die for Orsino is on one level a
public announcement of his willingness to sleep with him; for the
Elizabethans, the verb 'to die' could mean 'to achieve orgasm'.[22] But in
Shakespeare's Illyria, unlike Elizabethan London, his wish may legitimately be granted; because, of course, Cesario is a woman in drag. His
situation as neither man nor woman, but a hybrid 'monster' composed
of both (2.2.34), exempts him from the restrictions imposed on men
and women, either by law or by the ideal forms of behaviour expected of
either sex.

   The advantages of Cesario/Viola's double gender become obvious
soon after Orsino threatens to kill him. Olivia intervenes to save the
boy's life, announcing that she has married him, so that he is now
under the protection of the Illyrian law. At once the Duke turns on
Cesario with a verbal attack that seems hardly less unbalanced than his
earlier threat to murder him: 'O thou dissembling cub' (5.1.161). But
dissembling is not really the issue here; it is disloyalty. Orsino thinks the
boy has betrayed his trust in him, thus breaking their bond of mutual
friendship, which like marriage may be described as 'A contract of eternal bond of love' (5.1.153). The misunderstanding is resolved when

Sebastian turns up and Cesario/Viola reveals her 'true' sex, thus finally unclasping to Orsino the 'book' of her 'secret soul'. At this point the Duke discovers that Viola has been dissembling not her love for him but her gender; and *this* kind of deceit he seems to find wholly admirable. He marries her, he says, in recompense for 'your service done ... So much against the mettle of your sex' (5.1.314–15) – as if it is her ability *not* to be the silent passive woman he has so far imagined for himself that most delights him about her. In token of this delight, he continues to call her 'Cesario' long after he has learned her identity (5.1.377), thus preserving our sense of the relationship as a love affair between men as well as between a man and a woman. And it is in male clothing that Viola leaves the stage with Orsino to begin married life at the end of the play. Her clothes seem to promise that their marriage will be an egalitarian one, based not on mastery and control – as are men's fantasies about women – but on mutual confidence and respect, like the Elizabethan ideal of same-sex friendship. When Orsino discharges Cesario from his service ('Your master quits you' (5.1.314)), he installs Viola as 'Your master's mistress', his 'fancy's queen' (5.1.319, 380) – phrases that may be taken to imply that power will be shared more or less equally between them after marriage. ('Master' and 'mistress' are terms used throughout the play for men and women in positions of authority; Feste, for instance, tells Viola 'I would be sorry, sir, but the fool should be as oft with your master as with my mistress' (3.1.40–3).) In view of the ideals of femininity that have prevailed up to this point, it is hard to imagine Orsino saying these things with such conviction to a woman dressed in ordinary clothes.

Cesario also liberates Olivia from the condition of stasis to which her stance as the chaste, silent woman of male myth has consigned her. If it is true, as Sir Toby says, that Olivia has sworn 'she'll not match above her degree, neither in estate, years, nor wit' (1.3.106–7), and that as the Captain claims she has 'abjur'd the company / And sight of men' (1.2.40–1), then the unmanly boy releases her from a sexual impasse. Because he is no man, she can admit him to her presence; while at the same time because he *is* a man – in the sense of a servant, the opposite of a 'master' – his status is below hers, thus making him available as a potential partner for her. In addition to his youth, his refusal of conventional 'manliness' dissociates him from the gender she has abjured. When Olivia tells him she loves him, she expects, she says, to be 'baited' for her confession (3.1.120), since the gentlemen in her household, Toby and Fabian, have a passion for that most barbarous of Elizabethan sports, the baiting of bears. Instead Cesario pities her; and from this moment Olivia sees something sympathetically 'feminine' about him. She imagines, for instance, that in challenging the boy to a sword-fight Sir Toby has 'started one poor heart of mine, in thee' (4.1.59) – that is, scared Cesario, who possesses Olivia's female heart, as much as he has scared Olivia. And she assumes it is 'female' fear that deters the boy from acknowledging their marriage in the final act.

By his violation of gender conventions, Cesario encourages Olivia in her efforts to circumvent the power-relations imposed on her by patriarchy. 'Would thou'dst be rul'd by me', she tells him (4.1.64), and Cesario – or rather the wonder-struck Sebastian, whom she has mistaken for Cesario – willingly concurs. Sebastian thus commits himself to a marriage where the wife, not the husband, is master, a reversal of roles to which he later seems to subscribe when he describes himself to Olivia as 'a maid' (5.1.257) – meaning a virgin, but the word has traditionally been applied to young girls – as well as a man. For Olivia, however, this unequal marriage elevates the boy's status to the level of a Duke. 'Fear not', she tells him, 'take thy fortunes up, / Be that thou know'st thou art, and then thou art / As great as that thou fear'st' – meaning Orsino (5.1.145–7). Olivia is only a Countess, but in keeping control of her destiny with Cesario's help she has proved herself and her spouse to be 'As great as' Illyria's ruler. And she reaffirms her greatness when she invites the Duke to 'crown' her alliance with him (they have become siblings by marrying siblings) by celebrating both his and her nuptials 'Here at my house, and at my proper cost' (5.1.311–12). Like Portia in *The Merchant of Venice*, her control over her household seems to have been strengthened rather than weakened by her acquisition of a husband.

It could be argued, then, that in this play 'master' and 'mistress' are terms of *equal* authority, and that their equivalence extends itself by the final act to power relations between the genders. This is hardly surprising, of course, when we consider that the mistresses in all of

Shakespeare's plays are in fact masters: boy actors like the youth imagined by Oscar Wilde to have been the dedicatee of Shakespeare's sonnets, Master W.H.[23] When Orsino calls Viola 'Your master's mistress', he
recalls the most explicitly homoerotic poem written by Shakespeare,
sonnet 20. The poem celebrates the beauty of a boy loved by the son-
neteer, whose face combines the best qualities conventionally assigned
to both sexes: 'A woman's face with nature's own hand painted / Hast
thou, the master mistress of my passion' (1–2). This suggests, among
other things, that Shakespeare could imagine a space where the 'masculine' and the 'feminine' are fused, and that for him the mind and body
of an adolescent boy could be one such space. Hence the attractiveness
of Wilde's proposition that the boy addressed in Shakespeare's sonnets
could have been an actor. Since women were not allowed to perform
on the Elizabethan public stage, boy actors took the female roles in
plays, and in doing so drew attention to the possibility that gender itself
might be a matter of performance. As the theatre-haters pointed out,
men could be, or could become, effeminate, and the boy actor's craft
showed just how easy it was to accomplish this particular feat of
gender-bending. Rosalind in *As You Like It* and Viola in *Twelfth Night*
foreground the boys' theatrical accomplishment. Rosalind changes
from boy's to girl's clothes at the end of the play, then speaks the
epilogue as a cross-dressed boy ('If I were a woman', she tells the men in
the audience, 'I would kiss as many of you as had beards that pleased
me' (5.4.212–13)); while Viola resolutely *refrains* from changing her
clothes when she announces that she is a girl. And each of these
boy/girls becomes in his/her different way the master/mistress of the
play in the final act: Rosalind as she magically unites all the main characters under the aegis of Hymen, Viola as she takes her place – still
dressed as a boy-servant – as the transvestite 'queen' of an Illyrian
Duke. In these plays, to be an effeminate boy or a masculine woman is
to be powerful, liberating dukedoms from a range of self-imposed tyrannies and replacing them with more liberal modes of government.

   Like the master/mistress of the sonnets, Rosalind/Ganymede and
Viola/Cesario are bodies in transit through time, refusing stasis. Duke
Orsino comments on the relationship between time and the fusion of
gender attributes as manifested in the effeminate boy Cesario:

For they shall yet belie thy happy years
That say thou art a man; Diana's lip
Is not more smooth and rubious: thy small pipe
Is as the maiden's organ, shrill and sound,
And all is semblative a woman's part.

(1.4.30–4)

Malvolio notes it, too, when he says that Cesario stands at a cusp between two stages of male development: 'Not yet old enough for a man, nor young enough for a boy ... 'Tis with him in standing water, between boy and man ... One would think his mother's milk were scarce out of him' (1.5.153–8). As Malvolio observes, a boy is closer to his mother than most grown men are. And at the end of the play this particular boy is revealed to be a woman, whose performance as the opposite gender has fooled everyone. What Viola's achievement as an actor suggests – however improbably – is that nobody need be fixed or trapped in a single mode of being. The comedy begins in stalemate, with Orsino as well as Olivia locked in the behaviour prescribed by their culture for lovers of their class and gender, and with no immediate prospect of escape from their entrapment. When Viola first resolves to enter Orsino's service she plans to present herself to him as a eunuch (1.2.56) – a boy whose sexual development has been artificially arrested by castration, a suitable servant for a man in a state of terminal sexual frustration. But Orsino's and Malvolio's descriptions of Cesario indicate their recognition that he is no eunuch, but an adolescent in the process of growing to sexual maturity, whose mere presence serves as an awakening call to desire for the transfixed characters in the play. Neither male nor female, neither man nor boy, and in the end neither servant, mistress nor master, he is a kind of riddle, a pun or *double entendre* in human form, testifying to the power of comedy as a means of disrupting settled notions and complicating illusory certainties.

The play as a whole is a paean to change, as its full title suggests. The phrase *Twelfth Night* pays homage to a crucial moment of transition in the Elizabethan calendar: the last day of the Christmas festivities, when the celebrations are at their most hilarious as they draw to a close, and

FIGURE 10   Caravaggio (1573–1610), 'Amor vincit omnia' (*c.* 1601–2).
Caravaggio's cheerful Cupid sports a pair of eagle's wings as if in homage to
Ganymede, who was carried to heaven by a lascivious eagle. Like Shakespeare
in his comedies, Caravaggio seems to link love with slightly menacing laughter.

when anyone can be 'What You Will'. *Twelfth Night* extends this moment of transition over many days, and Viola is its presiding spirit, embodying the transitions that are always in process in the human body and mind. At various points in the play, the changes undergone by Viola and her companions look set to be terrible ones, bringing entrapment and death instead of the new life promised by Viola's youth. Melancholy intervenes on many occasions, especially in the songs of the ageing clown Feste, which testify to the sorrow that terminates so many transactions between men and women, and to the onset of old age and death as the necessary counter-weight for the onset of sexual maturity. Even the end of the play is suffused with melancholy, as Malvolio runs off threatening to trigger a new, more violent dramatic action ('I'll be revenged on the whole pack of you') and Feste sings his final song alone on stage. But the action as a whole takes place in what Orsino calls a 'golden time' (5.1.374), a time of hope and laughter like the festival of Christmas. And it is a continuation of this golden time that is predicted in the final scene, when three sets of couples prepare to make a 'solemn combination ... Of our dear souls' (5.1.375–6). The play's unsettling emphasis on time, change and confusion ensures that these final weddings are by no means a tame return to the 'normality' of Elizabethan England, as critics have so often described them. Instead, the play makes it possible to believe that there is no such thing as a stable normality where gender is concerned, either in Elizabethan times or in our own.

COMEDY FOR A NEW REIGN

It seems fitting to end this book with *Measure for Measure*, which has one of Shakespeare's most outrageous comic endings. In it, the conventional happy-ever-after marriage is replaced with a spontaneous mismatch between an ascetic ruler and a postulant nun, the product of a world where conversation is contamination, and where the exchange of words, like the exchange of bodily fluids in a sexual act, exposes their users to possibly lethal infection.[1] Yet the ending of *Measure for Measure* also signals a new beginning: a way of writing designed for a new era. On one level, its awkward closing union enacts the awkward union between England and Scotland that took place in 1603; like the marriage of Vincentio and Isabella, an unexpected bringing-together of two ill-suited partners.[2] And the comedy that engineers this union may be seen as staking the playwright's claim to address both partners, reconciling their differences without concealing them.

If *Measure for Measure* declares Shakespeare's comic agenda for the Jacobean period, it is a breathtakingly audacious one. Written in the early days of a new king (James I of England) who was also an old one (James VI of Scotland), it takes as its male lead a duke who has reigned for years but who wishes to begin afresh, reviving old laws that have long lain dormant and testing the integrity of his ministers by investing them with new powers. Old and new clash in the play, as it revisits comic territory already covered by Shakespeare – notably in *Love's Labour's Lost* and *The Merchant of Venice* – and subjects it to sometimes shocking transformations. Like these earlier comedies it recklessly meddles with affairs of state and of the law-courts; but it adds to these an irreverent interference with the business of the church, and a presiding monarch – Duke Vincentio of Vienna – who has many of the characteristics of the new King of England at the time it was performed. His distaste for public ostentation, his lack of interest in women, his penchant for disguise, his bookishness, his fascination with the concept of the absolute – all these were known attributes of King James.[3] And when the Duke unexpectedly turns into the chief comic plotter of the play, who plays tricks on his own chief ministers with the help of two women, a rash of friars and a prison warden, the comic world seems to have been well and truly stood on its head. Majesty has been permanently compromised by its association with the comic lower orders, and comedy has established itself not so much as a mediator between a monarch and his or her people – the role it played in the court comedies of John Lyly – but as a kind of pimp between them, a saucy professional go-between whose business is imaginatively to get them into bed with one another. It would hardly seem possible for Shakespeare to embrace more openly and scandalously the paranoid fantasies of the anti-theatrical lobby.

For the theatre-haters, comedies performed in playhouses – many of which were built in the suburbs of London alongside the brothels – operated hand in glove with the pimps and madams of the illicit sex industry.[4] As if to confirm this prejudice, *Measure for Measure* is filled with metaphors of sexual procurement; but unlike the theatre-haters, Shakespeare finds pimping and prostitution in every form of social intercourse, not just the theatrical.[5] Indeed, he discovers it in the mechanics of conversation itself, investing words with unintended *double entendres* at the very moment when they are uttered with the most passionate seriousness. This is a profoundly unsettling discovery, which metaphorically forces puritans, moralists and self-appointed censors into complicity with the criminal underworld they condemn.

Yet for all its preoccupation with prostitution, along with defamation and treachery, this play offers one of the most hopeful analyses of the powers of comic conversation in Shakespeare's works. In it, the cross-contamination that occurs as a result of any verbal exchange serves as a means of demonstrating the ties of kinship that bind the whole of humanity together – that make it impossible finally to sever any one branch of the human family from any other branch, no matter how far socially, morally or even historically distant the two may seem.[6] From its opening the play examines the extent to which men and women are capable of being imaginatively substituted for one another, and finds their capacity to 'become' one another to be more or less infinite. Imaginative sympathy is, after all, the prerequisite for both drama and dialogue; and while the theatre-haters may fear and loathe drama's capacity to inspire imaginative sympathy in its audience, *Measure for Measure* implies that such sympathy lies at the heart of any social transaction – indeed, of society itself. The play begins with characters putting a distance between themselves and others, and ends by precipitating them unexpectedly into one another's places, mixing them together like the ingredients of an exotic stew. The marriage between Duke and nun that closes it may be a botched affair, but it is only one in a range of surprising alliances that get forged in the course of the comedy, alliances that end by uniting a Viennese urban community which had seemed utterly fragmented when the play began.

Measure for Measure opens with the act of substitution responsible for all the substitutions that follow. Duke Vincentio of Vienna appoints his minister Angelo as his deputy while he is away on state business; 'In our remove, be thou at full ourself', he tells him (1.1.43), implying that he has handed over to Angelo not only his robes of office but his body too: 'we have ... drest him with our love, / And given his deputation all the organs / Of our own power' (1.1.17–21). But despite the Duke's reassurances, neither Angelo nor his fellow magistrate Escalus seems sure of the precise extent of their privileges and duties. 'A power I have', says Escalus, 'but of what strength and nature / I am not yet instructed', and Angelo agrees: ''Tis so with me' (1.1.79–81). Their scruples arise from their awareness of the vast distance between their usual status and the Duke's, which the Duke seems blithely to disregard, as if he finds it as difficult to imagine himself into their position as they do to imagine themselves into his. At the beginning of the play, then, there is a fundamental lack of communication between Duke and subjects. And this is only confirmed by the fact that the Duke thinks it unnecessary to discuss with his deputies the nature of the government with which he entrusts them. To speak of such things, he insists,

'Would seem in me t'affect speech and discourse' (1.1.4), since he is sure Escalus already knows what he needs for the business of government. With Angelo, too, he sees no reason to expatiate on the duties of the powerful – he cuts himself short when he begins to do so ('But I do bend my speech / To one that can my part in him advertise' (1.1.40–1)). At the end of the first scene the ministers are left to engage in 'free speech' with one another (1.1.77), since they have singularly failed to obtain it with their ruler. One is reminded of the lack of open communication that vitiated the reign of the King of Spain in *The Spanish Tragedy* – a lack which in that play led to a massacre.

At the same time, Duke Vincentio is keen to know his subjects' minds. The second time we meet him, he is again changing places with someone else; this time a Franciscan friar, whose habit the Duke borrows in the interests of visiting both Angelo and his people to see how his first act of substitution is getting on. In this disguise he aims to gain access to his subjects' inmost thoughts through the sacrament of confession. But in doing so he also finds himself increasingly in collusion with them; implicated in their crimes, sharing the consequences of their inability to restrain their desires, plotting with them to evade the legal consequences of their actions. When he first puts on the friar's garments he says that he aims to use them to spy on his deputies – to see 'If power change purpose, what our seemers be' (1.3.54). But his investigation involves a transformation into a particularly sanctimonious form of 'seeming', so that even before it begins he has made himself into one of the subjects he intends to spy on. He has begun the process of imaginatively taking their place, of seeing their side of things. Such is the transformative power of speaking and listening, of conversation, of verbal exchange – the sharing of diverse perspectives that, of all arts, the theatre most effectively shows in action.[7]

The Duke's second act of substitution – his disguise as a man of God – leads inexorably to the more and more elaborate substitutive acts that make up the rest of the comic action. It subjects him to the necessity of finding a substitute for Isabella when Angelo seeks to sleep with her; then of finding a substitute for her brother Claudio's head when Angelo orders his death; then of finding a substitute for Barnardine's when the condemned murderer refuses to be beheaded in Claudio's place; and finally of substituting himself for judge, witness, plaintiff, prosecutor and counsel for the defence in the trial of Angelo and others that he stages at the end of the play. These successive acts of substitution bring the disguised monarch closer and closer to his subjects, from the highest and most respectable to the lowest and most despised. For a man who declared in the first scene that he did not like 'to stage me' to his people's eyes (1.1.68), he proves by the end an astonishingly adept apprentice in the arts of stagecraft, showing himself not only a skilful actor in a range of roles but an ambitious director, who takes it on himself single-handedly to orchestrate one of the most bewilderingly complex of Shakespeare's final acts. And for a man who declares in the play's third scene that he has an abiding respect for 'decorum' – the scrupulous preservation of social distinctions – he has shown himself prepared to perform actions wholly unfitting for a conventional monarch.

He is not alone, of course, in his transformation. The Duke is only one of the three absolutists who dominate the opening of the play. Absolutists commit themselves wholly to their chosen course, their elected vocation, admitting of no compromise in their behaviour, no collaborator in their enterprises; and the Duke reveals his absolutism repeatedly in the first half of the play. He tells the friar from whom he borrows his robes that he has given over to Angelo 'My absolute power and place here in Vienna' (1.3.13), a statement that implies his disdain for any partner in the business of government: he will wield it alone or hand it over entire to a deputy. Later, when he takes it on himself to instruct Claudio in how to deal with his sentence of execution, he tells him not to be half-hearted in his attitude – not to cling to the hope that his sentence may be revoked – but to 'Be absolute for death' (3.1.5), the mortal moment when the helpless cravings and fears of life will be stilled for ever.

The Duke shares his singleness of mind with his deputy Angelo, a man who seems to be in total command of his senses – who 'scarce confesses / That his blood flows; or that his appetite / Is more to bread than stone', as the Duke unkindly puts it (1.3.51–3). And the two men are matched by the woman who enters soon after these words: Isabella, sister to the condemned man Claudio, who wishes to abjure forever the company of men in the interests of preserving her integrity. But all three of these absolutists quickly learn that the comic world into which they have strayed allows of no rigidity or reclusiveness: everyone, no matter how dignified or aloof, eventually gets drawn into its web of wordplay. And more directly even than the Duke, Angelo and Isabella find that it is the simple act of conversation that ensnares them, forcing them out of their self-imposed seclusion from the rest of Viennese society, and plunging them into a labyrinth of plot and counter-plot where the recurring necessity for improvisation overthrows all their efforts to cultivate stability.

Isabella's first appearance in the play involves her in a thwarted attempt to free herself forever from the complications of dialogue – above all, of dialogue with members of the opposite sex. She seeks admission into the austere community of the Sisters of Saint Clare, whose vows forbid them from talking directly to men; and far from being shocked by the rigour of this rule, Isabella professes herself to be disappointed that it is not more rigorous. If her and the sisters' suspicion of communication between the sexes seems excessive, the same scene shows it to be well-founded. Her brother's friend the 'fantastic' Lucio enters, whom we have witnessed in an earlier scene making jokes about venereal disease with his drinking-companions – jokes that effectively spread the disease about, as Lucio finds ingenious ways to imply that one of his friends has contracted syphilis (1.2.36–9). He salutes Isabella with an elaborate reference to her sexual inexperience and desirability ('Hail virgin, if you be – as those cheek-roses / Proclaim you are no less' (1.4.16–17)); and goes on to tell her that his usual habit when talking to virgins is 'to jest, / Tongue far from heart' (1.4.32–3), presumably in the interest of converting them from their virginal status. For Lucio, conversation with women is normally inseparable from the processes of wooing and making love; and although he tells her that in her case he makes an exception ('I hold you as a thing enskied and sainted … And to be talk'd with in sincerity' (1.4.34–6)), he brings news that will soon plunge her into the most compromising of verbal exchanges. Her brother has been condemned to death by Angelo for his infringement of a long-forgotten law forbidding sex outside marriage, and Lucio has come to ask her to employ her rhetorical gifts to save him. By the end of the scene her efforts to detach herself from the world have collapsed in ruins. She is a sister, not yet a member of a sisterhood, and must therefore honour her obligations to her brother, not her religious community. Moreover, she is the 'cousin' – if only by adoption – of the woman with whom her brother committed fornication (1.4.45–8). She is linked, then, against her will both to her brother's lewd friend Lucio and to the sexual act that brought him to her. No wonder that her next conversation involves her in yet more drastic linkages with the vice she most abhors, the extra-marital act of sex.

This is in part because in the scene where she begs Angelo to spare her brother's life Lucio takes it on himself to act as her pimp, telling her twice 'You are too cold' (2.2.45, 56), urging her to 'touch' Angelo and crying out, as the deputy seems to relent, 'He's coming: I perceive't' (2.2.70, 126). But Isabella's efforts to make Angelo see things her way are also in part responsible for Angelo's erotic attraction to her. In order to speak to Angelo at all Isabella is forced to compromise, finding herself 'At war 'twixt will and will not' (2.2.33); and it is for compromise on Angelo's part that she pleads, asking him to put himself in Claudio's position – the position of a man who has known and succumbed to desire. 'If he had been as you, and you as he', she says, swapping the position of judge and prisoner, 'You would have slipp'd like him, but he like you, / Would not have been so stern' (2.2.64–6). She then wishes she could be like Angelo ('I would to heaven I had your potency, / And you were Isabel' (2.2.67–8)) and reminds him of his own need for mercy, as a sinner ('How would you be / If He, which is the top of judgement, should / But judge you as you are?' (2.2.75–7)), before once again urging him to substitute himself imaginatively for Claudio: 'Go to your bosom, / Knock there, and ask your heart what it doth know / That's like my brother's fault' (2.2.137–9). It is at this point that Angelo finds his 'sense' – both reason and the senses – being aroused by her good 'sense' or reasoning: 'She speaks, and 'tis such sense / That my sense breeds with it' (2.2.141–2). Her speech, that is, impregnates his mind as Claudio impregnated his fiancée Juliet in the act that condemned him to death. Unlike Juliet, however, Angelo finds himself corrupted rather than fertilized by his contact with the other sex. Her virtue excites him: that is, her intelligence and eloquence as well as her chastity; and he discovers for the first time that there is a link between virtue and vice – that they are as intimately connected as any other seeming opposites in a world that is constantly in dialogue. As Isabella suspected, dialogue or conversation involves a breakdown of a person's integrity – their self-imposed isolation from the richly mixed community of which they are a part – which can end by collapsing their sense of moral order beyond recovery. And her first encounter with Angelo is only the beginning of this process.

Their second interview involves a change of position: this time Angelo seeks to coerce Isabella into seeing things from his point of view, with difficulty encouraging her to imagine a scenario where she can save her brother's life only at the cost of an act she considers mortal to her soul – sleeping with Angelo. In doing this Angelo changes the 'language' he speaks, subduing logic and justice to the imperatives of desire and gradually making it clear to Isabella that he has shifted his position radically from the one he took at their first meeting. As it dawns on her that he means what he says ('My words express my purpose', Angelo tells her (2.4.147)), Isabella begs him to 'speak the former language' (2.4.139); but his language has been too far contaminated by desire ever to return to the formal logic of their first meeting. And ironically enough, the cause of this alteration was her own unwilling compromise of her initial hard-line position on the matter of her brother's sexual misconduct, her attempts to find a means of pleading for him without implicating herself in his 'crime'. Isabella's compromise for the sake of 'good' led to Angelo's corruption, where her goodness became the stimulus to his evil. Seismic shifts have taken place in the course of one interview, shifts that have shattering implications for the entire state over which Angelo currently reigns. Angelo believes that he can make her compromise further for the sake of her brother; and Isabella suddenly finds her most entrenched convictions under assault from the highest power in the land. The irony of the situation would be comic if it were not so unsettling.

In addition, Isabella finds herself rendered voiceless by this second interview – forced into the position of the most famous classical rape victim Philomela, whose tongue was cut out by King Tereus after he raped her.[8] She tells Angelo that she will tell the world 'with an outstretch'd throat' about his intolerable proposal (2.4.152), and he answers that all her eloquence will be ineffectual:

> Who will believe thee, Isabel? ...
> My vouch against you, and my place i'th'state,
> Will so your accusation overweigh,
> That you shall stifle in your own report,
> And smell of calumny.
>
> (2.4.153–8)

Isabella's political weight cannot be measured against Angelo's; he will crush her if she dares to speak in public. Conversation between her and him, in other words, is at an end. There can be no further compromises on his part because there is no way she can persuade him to take her part, to put himself in her position, except on his own abominable terms. Angelo, in fact, is refusing further dialogue (as Shylock did in Act 3, scene 3 of *The Merchant of Venice*), and threatening to turn this play into a tragedy, the genre where compromises cannot be reached and death is the only refuge from tyranny.

At this stage, Isabella's one hope is that she has a mutual under-standing with her closest relative, Claudio: a unity of values that means he will agree to die before he allows her to undergo rape for his sake. At one stage in her second interview with Angelo she tells him she would be willing to die for Claudio – that she would strip herself for death as gladly 'as to a bed / That longing have been sick for, ere I'd yield / My body up to shame' (2.4.102–4). In saying so she acknowledges for the first time that her own body, too, might become sick with desire, even if it is a desire for honourable death. Her proximity to her brother increases as she says it; but her choice of a sexual metaphor to express her revulsion at Angelo's proposition also shows that she now sees her-self, in part at least, as Angelo sees her, as a sexual object whose efforts to debate concepts of right and wrong serve only to heighten his pas-sion. And the power of the male bodily appetite to subordinate all other considerations to its needs augurs ill for her chances of convincing her brother to die for her right to keep her own body sexually inviolate.

So too, oddly enough, do the Duke's efforts in the following scene to persuade Claudio to dispense with the perplexities of bodily existence, to resign himself to his imminent execution and 'Be absolute for death' (3.1.5). The reason the Duke gives for such a stance is life's confusion: the impossibility of living rationally, of freeing oneself from fear of what one cannot avoid or desire of what one cannot have. The mind is unable to settle itself in any one condition: it is constantly on the move, undergoing endless 'shifts to strange effects / After the moon' (3.1.24–5). To die, then, is to attain peace: but to resign oneself to die would seem impossible, given the lunatic shiftiness of the human brain. Claudio seems at first to be convinced by the Duke's argument, resolving to find life by 'seeking death' (3.1.43). But as soon as Isabella offers him a new chance to escape death he does just what the Duke ought to have expected – he changes his mind. When she asks him if he dares to die he answers, in words that echo her earlier ones, that if death is inescapable 'I will encounter darkness as a bride / And hug it in my arms' (3.1.83–4). But when he learns that an actual unwanted sexual act on her part will free him from the necessity of this metaphorical unwanted sexual encounter, he seizes on the possibility with passion ('Sweet sister, let me live' (3.1.132)), invoking as his justification a vision of an afterlife as physically and mentally tormented as the most loathsome life on earth: 'Ay, but to die, and go we know not where ... or to be worse than worst / Of those that lawless and incertain thought / Imagine howling, – 'tis too horrible' (3.1.117–27). Even the state of death, the most absolute condition available to men and women because, in the Duke's view, it is an entry into featureless oblivion, may all too easily become infected by the fears that govern life; pain, violence, despair may all be projected into it, making it as impure as every other object of the human imagination.

Isabella's response to what she sees as Claudio's betrayal demonstrates the extent to which she has moved from her desired condition of absolute purity and become imaginatively complicit with his sexual profligacy. She accuses him of incest for proposing to 'take life / From thine own sister's shame'; accuses her mother of having committed adultery to engender him, since 'such a warped slip of wilderness' could never have issued from her father's blood (3.1.138–42); and ends by branding him a libertine, one for whom sexual law-breaking is a way of life so that 'Mercy to thee would prove itself a bawd', a pimp dedicated to

furthering Claudio's profligate career (3.1.149). This is language a
hundred and eighty degrees removed from the chaste language she used
in her initial tentative pleas on her brother's behalf. Finding her words
repeatedly misinterpreted, read as incitements to lust first by Angelo and
then by her own sibling, she begins to see the world as a brothel and to
allow her own speech to mimic that of the brothel's inmates.

In this play, then, goodness is never absolute: it cannot be severed or
set apart from evil. The Duke explains as much in his friar's disguise
when he enters after overhearing Isabella's attack on her brother. The
divine hand that made her 'fair', he tells her, 'hath made you good'; yet
at the same time 'The goodness that is cheap in beauty makes beauty
brief in goodness' – presumably because beauty gives incentives to vice
– unless the beautiful good woman is protected by a third quality,
'grace', which keeps the soul beautiful whatever happens to the body
(3.1.179–82). The Duke's celebration of grace would seem, at first, to
suggest that here is a form of goodness that retains its absolute purity
under even the most trying circumstances, the most contaminating
contexts; indeed, this is how the word comes to be used in Shakespeare's
late plays.[9] But he introduces the concept just at the point when he is
about to disclose a plan to protect her from Angelo's lusts by means that
involve yet more sexual and moral compromises, and to expose Isabella
and himself to the charge of complicity with the arts of pimping and
prostitution. It is in this scene that the Duke proposes that he should
arrange for another woman to sleep with Angelo in Isabella's place,
assuring her that 'the doubleness of the benefit defends the deceit from
reproof' (3.1.256–7). Like her brother, Isabella seizes on this opportunity to save herself by sacrificing someone else; and she declares her
assent to the Duke's proposal in a metaphor of pregnancy that links this
assent to Claudio's impregnation of Julia: 'I trust', she says, that this
plan 'will grow to a most prosperous perfection' (3.1.259). This from a
woman who at the beginning of the interview insisted that she 'had
rather my brother die by the law, than my son should be unlawfully
born' (3.1.188–90). If the Duke's plan offers an instance of the workings of 'grace', then grace is a quality that is deeply entangled in the
corrupt workings of the sublunary world as represented by
Shakespearean Vienna.

The Duke's plan is a comic one – albeit unintentionally so; there is no reason to think he believes it to be comic when he first thinks it up – and it becomes more so as it unfolds. It begins as a piece of classic comic deception, in which a man is tricked into thinking one woman is another; and it ends, in the wonderfully convoluted final scene of the play, as a farce, where deceptions extend themselves to include every character in the play and the Duke as chief playwright and performer very nearly loses control of his own plot. It is through the staging of a comedy, then, that the Duke finds his way out of the dilemma he has created for himself through his detachment from and lack of communication with his subjects. It is through comedy that Isabella is made to re-engage in dialogue with the society she sought to escape, and through comedy that Angelo is rescued from the condition of being either angel or devil, and made human again – that is, an embodiment of both. Above all, comedy is identified in the second half of this play as a vehicle for freedom of speech, and a potential model for the role of free speech in a nation state. The Duke's comic plan finds a way to give Isabella a voice, in spite of Angelo's attempt to silence her. And in doing this it teaches the Duke that he, too, is part of a dialogue, and that an engagement in open verbal exchange with his subjects is the only way he can establish a just kingdom.

This discovery is gradual: as gradual as his discovery that he is orchestrating a comedy. At first, after telling Isabella of his plan to substitute Mariana for herself in Angelo's bed, he is inclined to go on talking like an absolutist. Meeting the pimp Pompey on his way to prison he urges him to think about the moral implications of his trade: 'Canst thou believe thy living is a life, / So stinkingly depending?' (3.2.25–6). This injunction demonstrates Vincentio's utter failure to recognize his own 'stinking dependence' on a plan to procure Mariana for Angelo. His participation in the crime he berates in Pompey is something that Lucio, by contrast, takes for granted. Vincentio encounters Lucio soon after his first encounter with Pompey, and Lucio at once begins to talk with comic freedom about the Duke he does not know he is addressing. For Lucio, the Duke's leniency towards the sexual misdemeanours of his subjects springs from a consciousness of his own promiscuity: 'He had some feeling of the sport ... and that instructed him to mercy'

(3.2.114–15). While conscious of the danger of rash speech about a monarch (Lucio will not say why the Duke has left Vienna, since ''tis a secret must be locked within the teeth and the lips' (3.2.129–30)), Lucio's ebullience makes it impossible for him to restrain himself from speaking, despite the Friar-Duke's promise that he will report Lucio's words to the Duke himself (3.2.152). And ironically, it is Lucio's conviction of Vincentio's secret vices that makes him 'love him' and yearn for his return to take the place of the frosty Angelo (3.2.143). So the comic Lucio teaches the Duke that authoritarian censorship of language is useless ('What king so strong / Can tie the gall up in the slanderous tongue?', Vincentio ponders (3.2.180–1)) – at the very moment when the Duke himself is working, through a comic stratagem, to enable Isabella to speak openly about Angelo without being accused of slander. But at this stage the Duke takes himself too seriously to see the funny side of Lucio's lesson. Even at the end of the play, when he is forgiving the would-be rapist and murderer Angelo with cheerful abandon, the Duke finds it difficult not to reward Lucio's calumnies with death – he forgives him only at the last minute. The Duke's problem is that like Angelo and Isabella he lacks a sense of humour;[10] and it is the business of the play to teach it him – or perhaps more accurately (since Vincentio never quite succeeds in mastering the art of laughter), to teach the new King James of humour's value to a monarch.

As the play goes on, the Duke finds himself – despite himself – increasingly drawn into the toils of merriment, increasingly forced into the position of having sympathy with all people which is characteristic of the most genial forms of comedy. In his next scene, he goes to great lengths to retain his absolute confidence in his own good judgement in the face of mounting evidence against it. Angelo has slept with Isabella (or so he thinks) but instead of sending a pardon to Claudio, as the Duke predicted, he sends a message urging the prison provost to make haste with his execution and give him proof of it in the shape of Claudio's head. The Duke hardly seems shaken by Angelo's treachery: like the wily slave in a Roman comedy he has a genius for improvisation, and at once devises a stratagem to remedy the situation. Let another man, a convicted felon, be executed in Claudio's place, and let the felon's head – suitably disguised – be sent to Angelo as proof that his orders have been obeyed. But this stratagem has one thing wrong with it: it is not a comic way to bring about a comic ending, since it involves an execution, the casual termination of a man's life. The Duke leaves the stage perfectly satisfied that he has resolved his dilemma, telling the sceptical prison provost that he shall soon find his scruples about this new plot 'absolutely' removed (4.2.207).

However, when he actually encounters the criminal who is to be executed, the Duke finds his conviction of his own absolute rightness badly shaken once again. Barnardine refuses to agree to the timing of his death, insists on having 'more time to prepare me' (4.3.54), and rejects every effort to persuade him otherwise. To execute him in this state of mind, the Duke sees, would be 'damnable' (4.3.69) – both for Barnardine and for the authorities who knowingly send him to his damnation. The joke is on the Duke: for when Barnardine was first brought in, the executioner used the Duke-Friar's presence to show that the man's impending execution was *not* a joke: 'Look you, sir, here comes your ghostly father. Do we jest now, think you?' (4.3.48–9). But Barnardine's recalcitrance makes a mockery of the threatened decapitation, and the Duke finds himself comically reliant on the substitution of a second head for Barnardine's, which was itself intended as a substitute for the head of Claudio. Fortunately, the provost tells him, another criminal has died in the prison of natural causes, and his head may be sent to Angelo for Claudio's. The Duke takes this stroke of good luck as divine intervention: 'O, 'tis an accident that heaven provides' (4.3.77). To the Duke's audience it looks more like a disturbingly funny demonstration that one head is as good as another – that any one man may be readily substituted for any other without difficulty, since the differences between them are purely accidental.

At the end of this scene the Duke once again attempts to wrestle the play back to his preferred mode of seriousness. Controversially, he decides not to tell Isabella that her brother's life has been spared, and instead to goad her to greater bitterness against Angelo by convincing her that the Duke's substitute has succeeded in having her brother put to death. Isabella's laments, which evoke Hecuba's response to the murder of her son Polydorus ('O, I will to him and pluck out his eyes!' (4.3.120)),[11] bring the play closer than it has yet come to the tragic

genre; but it is held off from tragedy by the Duke's continuing conviction that he can sort things out through the rigorous truthfulness of his
own speech: 'Mark what I say, which you shall find / By every syllable a
faithful verity ... Command these fretting waters from your eyes / With
a light heart; trust not my holy order, / If I pervert your course'
(4.3.126–49). The Duke's awkward balancing act between the heaviness of grief he induces in Isabella and the lightness of heart he urges
her to cultivate exposes his ineptitude as a theatrical director; and he
soon finds his control over the mood of the scene challenged by the
reappearance of the irrepressibly light-hearted Lucio, who insists on
accompanying the Duke from the scene while regaling him with 'pretty
tales' about himself (4.3.164). As Lucio puts it, 'I am a kind of burr, I
shall stick' (4.3.176); and his sticking to the Duke suggests how difficult
it will be for that governor to shake off Lucio's libellous account of him
as 'the old fantastical duke of dark corners' (4.3.156–7). Barnardine
and Lucio comically resist the Duke's control over the comedy he is part
of; they are recalcitrantly inconvenient figures, whose presence compli-
cates what should be a neat plot and suggests that comedy is under the
control of other authorities than that of a monarch.

The play's last scene confirms the Duke's precarious hold over the
judicial drama he plans to stage. Throughout it he is frantically busy,
talking incessantly in his efforts to marshal the large cast of characters
he has assembled, issuing a stream of new instructions while oversee-
ing the enactment of instructions he gave certain members of the cast
– in particular, Isabella, Mariana and Friar Peter – before the scene
began. At one point he dashes off stage in a miniature re-enactment of
his removal from his Dukedom at the beginning of the play, leaving the
scene in the charge of his deputy Angelo and his assistant Escalus –
only to return a few lines later in his friar's disguise, goad the
bystanders into tearing off his hood, and proceed to pass judgement on
everyone in the assembly, including himself. But for all his efforts, there
is a sense throughout the scene that events are always on the verge of
getting out of hand. For one thing, the scene has been introduced with
a reminder of the power authority has to bind the tongue of the weak,
in violation of all justice. In a soliloquy Angelo confesses to the audience his guilt at the rape of Isabella and the murder of her brother,

while at the same time articulating his conviction that these misdeeds will never come to light:

> But that her tender shame
> Will not proclaim against her maiden loss,
> How might she tongue me! Yet reason dares her no,
> For my authority bears so credent bulk
> That no particular scandal once can touch,
> But it confounds the breather.

(4..4.24–9)

This certainty that authority will suppress all speech that threatens its stability is borne out time and again in the final scene. First the Duke himself interrupts Isabella's attempts to accuse Angelo with a call for her imprisonment: 'To prison with her! Shall we thus permit / A blasting and a scandalous breath to fall / On him so near us?' (5.1.124–6). Then Angelo takes up the same theme, accusing Isabella and Mariana of being 'instruments of some more mightier member / That sets them on', and proposing to 'find this practice out' – to loosen their tongues still further, presumably by torture (5.1.236–8). Finally, the Duke himself in friar's disguise speaks with rash directness against the Duke in the Duke's own court ('The Duke's unjust' (5.1.298)), and is promptly savaged by both Escalus and Angelo for 'Slander to th' state' and condemned in his turn to torture (5.1.309–20). Each of these interventions is presumably plotted by the Duke as a means of exposing the corruption of the legal system presided over by Angelo in his absence, where only crimes that do not implicate Angelo's government are permitted to be spoken about. But the Duke's plot degenerates into rough-and-tumble when the Provost and Lucio are ordered by Escalus to lay hands on the Duke himself, an action Lucio supplements with a stream of insults that an early modern audience might have found profoundly shocking when levelled at a ruler, even in disguise. And Lucio himself remains a comic loose cannon throughout the scene, the embodiment of the dilemma over 'lightness' to which his name – derived from the Italian and Latin words for light – draws attention.[12]

In early modern England, 'light' stands both for easy virtue – as in Lucio's phrase 'women are light at midnight' (5.1.278) – and for the light of truth, which it is the law-court's business to seek out. Isabella and Mariana aim to expose the truth of Angelo's crimes, to bring them to light, as it were: as Mariana puts it, when accusing Angelo of breach of promise to her, 'As there comes light from heaven, and words from breath, / As there is sense in truth, and truth in virtue, / I am affianc'd this man's wife, as strongly / As words could make up vows' (5.1.224–7). Words, however, are accepted or rejected by the authorities as it suits them; and the light of truth can draw accusations of sexual lightness on its champions. Angelo glibly turns the sexual tables on Mariana, pitting his word against hers in the full confidence that the court will find for him. He broke off their engagement, he tells the court, chiefly because 'her reputation was disvalu'd / In levity' – that is, she was said to have slept around (5.1.220–1). Lucio, with his malicious and mistimed jokes in the court of law, does no more than articulate the malicious spirit that informs the law's operation in the Viennese state. The law both aims to bring truth to light and apportions 'levity' or sexual lightness to men and women arbitrarily, as it suits the judges. Only the Duke's *deus ex machina* emergence from his friar's garb leads to sexual lightness being properly attributed to the 'lightest' character in the play – the playboy Lucio.

Yet for all his dishonesty – his false accusations of the Friar-Duke and the women – Lucio is also, in this final scene, an agent of truth. He is the man who pulls off the friar's hood and exposes the Duke, thereby effectively 'making' him, as the Duke observes ('Thou art the first knave that e'er mad'st a duke' (5.1.353)). And this action confirms the extent to which the Duke and Lucio have become mixed up with one another.[13] The Duke as ruler is responsible for the state of affairs that allows Lucio to flourish in his kingdom, and Lucio is responsible for revealing to the Duke the current condition of his country. Levity or lightness is an attribute of comedy as well as of sexual offenders, and the insights offered by this particular comedy work two ways: it has as much to say to rulers, that is, as it has to subjects. And comedy's triumph over the ruler's efforts to control it are embodied in this final scene by the 'light' women Isabella and Mariana as well as by Lucio.

At first the women are Duke Vincentio's tools: Mariana tells Isabella to 'Be rul'd by him' (4.6.4), and through much of Act 5 the postulant nun seems to obey, despite the increasingly painful positions into which she is forced. First accused of madness, then of libel, she is finally condemned to prison and torture before being summoned again for interrogation by Escalus, who plans to 'go darkly to work with her' (5.1.277) to discover who put her up to her calumnies – a phrase Lucio interprets as yet another threat of rape ('That's the way; for women are light at midnight' (5.1.278)). Meanwhile, the pain of her brother's death – needlessly inflicted on her by the Duke, who knows he is alive – is protracted to the last possible moment, when the Duke chooses to unveil his face in open court. The Duke's motive for concealing Claudio's survival from Angelo is clear enough; but his concealment of it from Isabella must spring either from a desire to test her, to torment her as her judges threaten to do, or to render her uttered grievances against Angelo more convincing. Any of these possibilities means that the Duke's motive was to work her like a puppet; but his power over her is by no means absolute. Reverting to his absolutist instincts, the Duke declares Angelo to have forfeited his life by killing Claudio against his word: such treachery, he says, deserves to be punished with an identical fate, as if by mathematical necessity: 'An Angelo for Claudio; death for death ... Like doth quit like, and Measure still for Measure' (5.1.406–8). But the play's title need not be interpreted as an endorsement of Old Testament vindictiveness:[14] and it is the women who see its more humane application. 'Measure for Measure' could mean that one thing lost may be replaced by another of equal value, or that one human being is more or less equivalent to another, no matter what their respective faults or stations. Mariana chooses to take the phrase as an encouragement to defend Angelo, to whom the Duke has given her in marriage before ordering his execution. 'I crave no other, nor no better man', she cries (5.1.423), unconvinced, perhaps, that any man will prove much better; and she urges Isabella to plead with her for Angelo's life – to put her body at Mariana's service, just as Mariana earlier put her body at Isabella's. 'Lend me your knees', she begs her, 'and ... I'll lend you all my life to do you service' (5.1.427–9).

Eventually Isabella obeys, not only to the extent of kneeling in supplication for Angelo – which is all Mariana asks of her – but even speaking out for him, lending him her voice. In pleading for Angelo Isabella compares him to Claudio (5.1.445–50), just as when pleading for Claudio to Angelo she asked the substitute to compare himself with her brother. Where at the beginning of the play she sought to separate herself from the world of men, at the end she voluntarily links herself and her family (her brother Claudio) with Angelo and his (since Mariana is now Angelo's wife); there could hardly be a more acrobatic volte-face. And her generous act of self-substitution is, it seems, what triggers the Duke's desire to link himself with her. As he unveils the living Claudio, Vincentio declares his intention to become Claudio's relative by marrying Isabella: 'Give me your hand', he tells her, 'and say you will be mine. / He is my brother too' (5.1.489–90). And in thus linking himself to Claudio, who has been linked to Angelo through Isabella's speech, the Duke associates himself once and for all with his deputy. He has been taught, by Isabella's example, that he has no more right to condemn Angelo than he has to exonerate himself from the crimes of his substitute. In orchestrating a situation where powerless women may exchange words with powerful men, the Duke has – perhaps to his own surprise – manoeuvred himself into the position where he can choose to share his life with someone else, despite his initial declaration of his preference for solitude. He has been socialized, and learned that his power and wealth is not his alone: if Isabella accepts his offer of marriage they will belong equally to her, at least according to the terms of the marriage contract.

When the Duke tells Isabella in his final speech that he has a proposal for her which, if accepted, will mean 'What's mine is yours, and what is yours is mine' (5.1.533), he might be summarizing the comic conclusion of the play. Nothing in a given society, the play suggests – whether a possession, a social position, a sexual relationship, or a crime – is any man or woman's exclusive property. Instead it depends for its very existence on a complex web of other things, deriving identity from the (primarily verbal) interaction between people of both sexes and every station – no matter how rigorously we try to dissociate it from its context. The key to this philosophy of interplay or interdependence in *Measure for Measure* is Pompey Bum. His name declares his affinity with the heroes of the classical Roman past (Pompey the Great appears among the Worthies in *Love's Labour's Lost*) as well as with the human fundament, the bum or bottom.[15] His profession is that of a pimp, one who brings people together, just as his name brings together the heroic and the ridiculous: and we have already seen how much pimping as an activity has in common with the actions of the high-born characters in the play. And his entire function in the play is to make it impossible for the authorities in Vienna to segregate themselves from the sexual crimes they wish to extirpate.

On his first entry, Pompey announces the authorities' intention to tear down all the brothels in the suburbs of Vienna; but in the same breath he points out that they have left the inner-city brothels standing 'for seed' (1.2.99), as if with the intention of allowing a rich crop of new brothels to spring up in due time to replace the dismantled ones. For the pimp, then, the authorities have done no more with the whore-houses than a farmer does with his crops in order to make a profit from them. Later, when Pompey is arrested for some sexual misdemeanour involving Constable Elbow's wife, he defends himself by entering into an elaborate description of a dish of prunes – as if to show the impossibility of separating a crime from its context, of distinguishing vice from the situation that produces it (2.1.87–112). In the same scene he succeeds in exposing the criminality of the constable who charges him, who may have committed the crime – extra-marital intercourse – for which Claudio is condemned to death, and who has certainly engaged in corrupt practices to retain his position as constable. A few scenes later, Pompey is officially inducted into the service of the state, becoming the executioner's assistant who is responsible for carrying out the sentences imposed on criminals by the judges who frown on his former profession. In the prison he finds an executioner called Abhorson – the abhorrent son of a whore – and all his old customers from the brothel. Clearly, then, the apparatuses of state control are closely bound up with the criminalized sexual underworld. The trajectory of Pompey's career confirms this; and it is he who gives the most lucid exposition of the extent of their mutual involvement. If extra-marital sex is to be criminalized, he argues, and punished with beheading, in ten years the authorities will be 'glad to give out a commission for more heads' (2.1.235–6). And this, of course, is just what happens: in his efforts to prevent the needless decapitation of a generally law-abiding citizen – to prevent Claudio's beheading from being on *his* head – the Duke is reduced to the necessity of seeking out a succession of new heads to take the place of Claudio's. Comic mercifulness of the kind advocated by Portia in *The Merchant of Venice* is the only honest position to take in a world where the heads of individuals are so difficult to tell apart.

What distinguishes the criminal from the justice in Vienna is timing. Claudio's arrest came as a result of the poor timing of his sex with Juliet; if he had slept with her *after* his marriage day he would have been safe; if he had committed fornication with her at another period in the Duke's reign his misdemeanour would have been overlooked. The distinction between Claudio and Angelo, too, is a matter of time: as Escalus puts it, in his youth Angelo would surely have committed Claudio's fault himself 'Had time coher'd with place, or place with wishing' (2.1.11). The final act of the play is all about delicate timing: from Friar Peter's declaration to Isabella, 'Now is your time: speak loud, and kneel before him' (5.1.20), to the Duke's deferral to a 'fitter time' of his proposal to her (5.1.490). Even class is a matter of timing on the grand scale: in the classical past the Pompey family was 'Great', where in the present age they find themselves at the rear end of the social order. The timing of Shakespeare's daring conversation in this play with his monarch James I is crucial also. His declaration here that both comedy and justice are a matter of good timing, and that comedy can teach justice a thing or two about the way it should operate, is timed to catch the King at the beginning of his reign, before the anti-theatrical lobby has had a chance to prejudice him forever against the comic medium in which Shakespeare is working. The Duke's proposed marriage with Isabella conceals another, more hesitant proposal of marriage between the comic playwright and the new English monarchy: a marriage that will supplant Shakespeare's long service to the Virgin Queen Elizabeth I, just as Isabella's will divorce her from the chaste religious life she was about to embrace when the play began. But the play is also an astonishingly honest admission that the proposed marriage will be a difficult and perhaps a tempestuous one, in which the husband-monarch's authority will never go unquestioned. Only time, it implies, will tell if the marriage will be happy. Hence Isabella's silence at the end of the play. When we leave her, she has not accepted the Duke's proposal; she has not even formally heard it. The nature of her speech to come depends on the King's response to the Duke's performance in *Measure for Measure*. At the end of the play, then, when dialogue ceases, the real dialogue between stage, court and people is only just beginning. For its first audience, the prospect of its continuation into the brave new world of Stuart England must have been thrilling and troubling in equal measure.[16]

NOTES

INTRODUCTION

1. *Samuel Johnson on Shakespeare*, ed. H.R. Woudhuysen (Harmondsworth, 1989), p. 127.
2. *Samuel Johnson on Shakespeare*, ed. Woudhuysen, p. 125.
3. On genre in Shakespeare's time see: Rosalie Colie, *The Resources of Kind: Genre Theory in the Renaissance*, ed. Barbara K. Lewalski (Berkeley, 1973); Lawrence Danson, *Shakespeare's Dramatic Genres*, Oxford Shakespeare Topics (Oxford, 2000); Madeline Doran, *Endeavors of Art: A Study of Form in Elizabethan Drama* (Madison, 1954).
4. See, for instance, *The First Part of the Contention of the Two Famous Houses of York and Lancaster* (*The Second Part of Henry VI*); *The True Tragedy of Richard Duke of York and the Good King Henry the Sixth* (*The Third Part of Henry VI*); *The Comical History of the Merchant of Venice, or Otherwise Called the Jew of Venice*; *The History of Troilus and Cressida*; *The Life of Timon of Athens*.
5. See the discussion of the different names given to Shakespeare's comedies in *Shakespeare's Comedies*, ed. Emma Smith, Blackwell Guides to Criticism (Oxford, 2004), pp. 29–35.
6. See the epilogues of *Henry V* (which abruptly reminds us of the tragedies that followed on from Henry's death, 'Which oft our stage hath shown'), and *Troilus and Cressida* (in which the pimp Pandarus bequeaths the audience his 'diseases').
7. George Puttenham, *The Art of English Poesy* (1589), p. 25.
8. Sir Philip Sidney, *An Apology for Poetry*, ed. Geoffrey Shepherd, revised R.W. Maslen (Manchester and New York, 2002), p. 98, lines 34–8.
9. *The Mirror for Magistrates*, ed. Lily B. Campbell (New York, 1960), pp. 346–59. The story of Collingborne is discussed by Andrew Hadfield in *Literature, Politics and National Identity: Reformation to Renaissance* (Cambridge, 1994), pp. 102–7.
10. Puttenham, *Art of English Poesy*, p. 26.
11. Puttenham, *Arte of English Poesy*, p. 25.
12. For hostility to laughter in the Middle Ages see Jean Verdon, *Rire au Moyen Âge* (Paris, 2001).
13. Horace, *Of the Art of Poetry*, trans. Ben Jonson, in Ben Jonson, *The Complete Poems*, ed. George Parfitt (Harmondsworth, 1988), p. 362, line 321.

14. Horace, *Art of Poetry*, trans. Jonson, pp. 322–3, lines 319–64.

15. Horace, *Art of Poetry*, trans. Jonson, p. 323, lines 367–70.

16. Horace, *Art of Poetry*, trans. Jonson, p. 354, line 12, and pp. 370–1, lines 643–80.

17. Horace, *Epistles* 2.1, lines 139–55, in *Satires, Epistles and Ars Poetica*, trans. H. Rushton Fairclough, Loeb Classical Library (London and Cambridge, Mass., 1966), pp. 408–9.

18. Horace, *Epistles* 2.1, lines 55ff., p. 409ff.

19. The essay on drama is now thought to be by the fourth-century grammarian Evanthius, but was assigned to Donatus for many centuries. See *Medieval Literary Criticism: Translations and Interpretations*, ed. O.B. Hardison, Jr., *et al.* (New York, 1974), p. 39.

20. *Medieval Literary Criticism*, ed. Hardison, p. 43.

21. *Medieval Literary Criticism*, ed. Hardison, p. 43.

22. William Webbe, *A Discourse of English Poetry*, in *Elizabethan Critical Essays*, ed. G. Gregory Smith, 2 vols (London, 1904), vol. 1, p. 236, lines 1–8.

23. Webbe, *A Discourse of English Poetry*, p. 236, lines 21–3.

24. Webbe, *A Discourse of English Poetry*, p. 236, line 33–p. 237, line 1.

25. See Jonas Barish, *The Anti-theatrical Prejudice* (Berkeley, 1981), and Laura Levine, *Men in Women's Clothing: Anti-theatricality, 1579–1642* (Cambridge and New York, 1994). A selection of pro- and anti-theatrical texts can be found in E.K. Chambers, *The Elizabethan Stage*, 4 vols (Oxford, 1923), vol. 4, Appendix C.

26. I have discussed Gosson elsewhere. See my *Elizabethan Fictions: Espionage, Counter-espionage and the Duplicity of Fiction in Early Elizabethan Prose Narratives* (Oxford, 1997), pp. 51–67; and Sidney, *Apology for Poetry*, ed. Shepherd, rev. Maslen, Introduction.

27. *Markets of Bawdrie: The Dramatic Criticism of Stephen Gosson*, ed. Arthur F. Kinney (Salzburg, 1974), p. 69. All references to Gosson's work are to this edition.

28. For the staging of Gosson's plays, see *Markets of Bawdrie*, ed. Kinney, p. 146; *The Play of Plays* is discussed on pp. 181–91; and the play by Robert Wilson, *The Three Ladies of London* (published 1584), on pp. 165–6 (and see Kinney's note). The jig is 'Tarlton's Jigge of a horse loade of Fooles', in *Tarlton's Jests, and News out of Purgatory*, ed. James Orchard Halliwell (London, 1844), pp. xx–xxvi. The jig may, however, be a fake; see Charles Read Baskervill, *The Elizabethan Jig and Related Song Drama* (Chicago, 1929), pp. 103–4.

29. On the Vice see F.H. Mares, 'The Origin of the Figure called the Vice', *Huntington Library Quarterly*, vol. 22, no. 1 (1958), pp. 11–29. Marie Axton (*Three Tudor Interludes* (Cambridge, 1982), p. 32) hypothesizes that the Vice wore a mask.

30. The fullest account of the five-act structure as understood and used in the

sixteenth century is T.W. Baldwin, *Shakspere's Five-act Structure* (Urbana, 1947).

31. Gosson's attack on Italian books is discussed in my *Elizabethan Fictions*, Introduction and ch. 1.

32. Sidney, *Apology for Poetry*, ed. Shepherd, rev. Maslen, p. 96, lines 13–29; *Coriolanus*, 1.1.85–152.

33. Probably for this reason none of the surviving copies of this text has a title page, and it is known by several titles. See *Elizabethan Critical Essays*, ed. Smith, vol. 1, p. 61. All references to Lodge's *Defence* are to this edition.

34. *Medieval Literary Criticism*, ed. Hardison, p. 45.

35. I discuss his later career in 'Lodge's *Glaucus and Scilla* and the Conditions of Catholic Authorship in Elizabethan England', in the e-journal *EnterText*, vol. 3, no. 1 (Spring 2003), *Renaissance Renegotiations*, ed. William Leahy and Nina Taunton, pp. 59–100.

36. For Shakespeare's education see T.W. Baldwin, *William Shakspere's Small Latine and Less Greeke*, 2 vols (Urbana, 1944–50), and Neil Rhodes, *Shakespeare and the Origins of English* (Oxford, 2004), ch. 2. For the place of rhetoric in Shakespeare's thought see Jane Donawerth, *Shakespeare and the Sixteenth-century Study of Language* (Urbana, 1984); Richard A. Lanham, *Motives of Eloquence: Literary Rhetoric in the Renaissance* (New Haven and London, 1976); Russ McDonald, *Shakespeare and the Arts of Language* (Oxford, 2001); and Marion Trousdale, *Shakespeare and the Rhetoricians* (London, 1982).

37. Cicero, *De oratore*, trans. E.W. Sutton and H. Rackham, 2 vols (London and Cambridge, Mass., 1942), vol. 1, 2.54.

38. Quintilian, *Institutio oratoria*, trans. H.E. Butler, 4 vols (London and New York, 1921), vol. 2, 6.3.2–5.

39. Quintilian, *Institutio oratoria*, 6.3.6 and 6.3.13.

40. Quintilian, *Institutio oratoria*, 6.3.65 and 6.3.5.

41. Quintilian, *Institutio oratoria*, 6.3.35.

42. *Twelfth Night*, 2.3.90–1.

43. Cicero, *De oratore*, 2.56.229

44. Baldassare Castiglione, *The Book of the Courtier*, trans. Thomas Hoby, Everyman's Library (London, 1974), p. 142.

45. Castiglione, *The Book of the Courtier*, p. 156.

46. Castiglione, *The Book of the Courtier*, p. 134.

47. Castiglione, *The Book of the Courtier*, p. 137.

48. Castiglione, *The Book of the Courtier*, p. 138

49. Cicero, *De oratore*, 2.58.237.

50. Cicero, *De oratore*, 2.54.218; Quintilian, *Institutio oratoria*, 6.3.39ff. and 6.3.45ff.

51. Thomas Wilson, *The Art of Rhetoric* (1560), ed. Thomas J. Derrick (New York

and London, 1982), p. 275, lines 20–4. Wilson's section on laughter (pp. 274–315) is the most extensive account of humour and rhetoric written in sixteenth-century England.

52. Laurent Joubert, *Treatise on Laughter* (*Traité du ris*, 1560), trans. Gregory David de Rocher (Alabama, 1980), p. 24. Michael D. Bristol discusses Joubert's book in *Carnival and Theater: Plebeian Culture and the Structure of Authority in Renaissance England* (New York and London, 1985), pp. 133–7.

53. I discuss Lyly's *Euphues* books at length in *Elizabethan Fictions*, chs. 5 and 6.

54. *Complete Works of John Lyly*, ed. R.W. Bond, 3 vols (Oxford, 1902), vol. 1, p. 186.

55. Lyly, *Works*, vol. 2, p. 60.

56. Reprinted in *Shakespeare Jest-Books*, ed. W. Carew Hazlitt, 3 vols. (London, 1864), vol. 1, 131–62.

57. Cicero, *De oratore*, 2.54.219.

58. Quintilian, *Institutio oratoria*, 6.3.13.

59. Wilson, *Art of Rhetoric*, p. 275, lines 8–18.

60. Women in jest-books are explored by Pamela Allan Brown in *Better a Shrew than a Sheep: Women, Drama, and the Culture of Jest in Early Modern England* (Ithaca and London, 2003).

61. Kiernan Ryan, *Shakespeare*, 3rd edn (Basingstoke, 2002), p. 124.

62. The association between clowning and seasonal festivities has been much discussed; I shall not be making much of it in this book, because I am concerned with laughter that occurs *out* of season. See Mikhail Bakhtin, *Rabelais and his World*, trans. H. Islowsky (Bloomington, 1984); C.L. Barber, *Shakespeare's Festive Comedy: A Study of Dramatic Form and its Relation to Social Custom* (Princeton, 1959); Sandra Billington, *A Social History of the Fool* (Brighton, 1984); Bristol, *Carnival and Theater*; and François Laroque, *Shakespeare's Festive World: Elizabethan Seasonal Entertainment and the Professional Stage* (Cambridge, 1991).

63. The most important of these was Erasmus's *Adagia*. I discuss another collection, William Baldwin's *A Treatise of Moral Philosophy* (1547), in 'William Baldwin and the Politics of Pseudo-Philosophy in Tudor Prose Fiction', *Studies in Philology*, vol. 97, no. 1 (Winter 2000), pp. 29–60.

64. Joubert, *Treatise on Laughter*, pp. 126–8.

65. For an account of the biographical jest-book see Margaret Schlauch, *Antecedents of the English Novel 1400–1600* (Warsaw and London, 1963), pp. 90–9.

66. *Merry Tales ... made by Master Skelton* and *Scoggin's Jests* were probably written by the physician Andrew Borde (or Boorde) in the early 1540s; both can be found in *Shakespeare Jest-Books*, ed. Hazlitt, vol. 2. See my 'The Afterlife of Andrew Borde', *Studies in Philology*, vol. 100, no. 4 (Fall 2003), pp. 463–92. For Falstaff's scrap with Scoggin see *2 Henry IV*, 3.2.26–8.

67. The classic study of the fool remains that of Enid Welsford, *The Fool: His Social and Literary History* (London, 1935). See also Billington, *A Social History of the Fool*.

68. *Shakespeare Jest-Books*, ed. Hazlitt, vol. 2, pp. 68 and 74.

69. See Virginia Stern, *Gabriel Harvey: His Life, Marginalia and Library* (Oxford, 1979), p. 49.

70. *Tarlton's Jests and News out of Purgatory*, ed. Halliwell, p. xi, fn. 4.

71. *Tarlton's Jests and News out of Purgatory*, ed. Halliwell, p. 13.

72. *Twelfth Night*, 3.1.39–40. For Tarlton's career and influence see Robert Weimann, *Shakespeare and the Popular Tradition in the Theater: Studies in the Social Dimension of Dramatic Form and Function*, ed. Robert Schwartz (Baltimore and London, 1978), pp. 185–92.

73. *Tarltons' Jests and News out of Purgatory*, p. 55.

74. *Tarlton's Jests and News out of Purgatory*, p. 56

75. *Tarlton's Jests and News out of Purgatory*, p. 57.

76. *Tarlton's Jests and News out of Purgatory*, p. xxxiii.

77. *Tarlton's Jests and News out of Purgatory*, p. xxxiv, fn. 2.

78. *Kind-Heart's Dream*, sig. E3v.

79. *Kind-Heart's Dream*, sig. E4r.

80. For Shakespeare's acquaintance with Lyly see Leah Scragg, *The Metamorphosis of Gallathea: A Study in Creative Adaptation* (Washington, DC, 1982). For his use of jest-books see Ian Munro, 'Shakespeare's Jestbook: Wit, Print, Performance', *ELH*, vol. 71, no. 1 (Spring 2004), pp. 89–113.

81. See Anthony Munday *et al.*, *Sir Thomas More*, ed. Vittorio Gabrieli and Giorgio Melchiori (Manchester and New York, 1990), Introduction.

82. For this material see Stuart Gillespie, *Shakespeare's Books: A Dictionary of Shakespeare's Sources* (London and New Brunswick, 2001). For the native and continental theatrical traditions on which he drew for comedy, see Leo Salingar, *Shakespeare and the Traditions of Comedy* (Cambridge, 1974); and Richard Andrews, 'Shakespeare and Italian Comedy', *Shakespeare and Renaissance Europe*, ed. Andrew Hadfield and Paul Hammond, Arden Critical Companions (London, 2004), pp. 123–49.

83. For these regulations see Janet Clare, *Art Made Tongue-tied by Authority: Elizabethan and Jacobean Dramatic Censorship*, 2nd edn (Manchester, 1999); Richard Dutton, *Mastering the Revels: The Regulation and Censorship of English Renaissance Drama* (Basingstoke, 1991); and Richard Dutton, *Licensing, Censorship and Authorship in Early Modern England: Buggeswords* (Basingstoke, 2000).

84. The novel, *Pandosto: The Triumph of Time* (1588), is reprinted in *An Anthology of Elizabethan Prose Fiction*, ed. Paul Salzman, The World's Classics (Oxford, 1987), pp. 151–204. See p. 204. For Shakespeare's use of it see Lori Humphrey Newcomb, *Reading Popular Romance in Early Modern England* (New York, 2002).

85. Shakespeare's games with genre are brilliantly discussed by Peter Conrad in *The Everyman History of English Literature* (London and Melbourne, 1985), ch. 10. See also Susan Snyder, *The Comic Matrix of Shakespeare's Tragedies* (Princeton, 1979).

86. For convenience's sake I am accepting the chronology of *The Norton Shakespeare*, ed. Stephen Greenblatt *et al.* (New York and London, 1997), since this prints the plays in 'chronological order'. But it needs to be stressed that the dates of early performances of Shakespeare's plays are mostly conjectural.

1: COMIC MANIFESTOS

1. Imitations of Roman New Comedy included Nicholas Udall's *Ralph Roister Doister* (c. 1547–8) and *Jack Juggler* (c. 1553–8); George Gascoigne's *Supposes* (1566); and Lyly's *Mother Bombie* (c. 1590). Moral and political allegories included T. Lupton's *All for Money* (1577) and Nathaniel Woodes's *The Conflict of Conscience* (1581).

2. For gods and transformations, see John Lyly's *Sapho and Phao* (c. 1583), *Gallathea* (c. 1585), and *Love's Metamorphosis* (c. 1588); for romances, George Peele's *The Old Wives' Tale* (c. 1590) and the anonymous *Clyomon and Clamydes* (c. 1570–83) and *Common Conditions* (1576).

3. The history plays include *George a Greene, the Pinner of Wakefield* (c. 1590) and *A Merry Knack to Know a Knave* (1591); social satires include Robert Wilson's *Three Ladies of London* (1581) and *The Cobbler's Prophecy* (1592) and Thomas Lodge and Robert Greene's *A Looking Glass for London and England* (1588).

4. See Charles Read Baskervill, *The Elizabethan Jig and Related Song Drama* (Chicago, 1929).

5. By Thomas Nashe in *Pierce Penniless his Supplication to the Devil* (1592). See Thomas Nashe, *The Unfortunate Traveller and Other Works*, ed. J.B. Steane (Harmondsworth, 1985), p. 116.

6. For Shakespeare's debt to earlier comedies, see Janette Dillon, 'Shakespeare and the Traditions of English Stage Comedy', in *A Companion to Shakespeare's Works, Volume 3: The Comedies*, ed. Richard Dutton and Jean E. Howard (Oxford, 2003), pp. 1–22.

7. See Jonas Barish, *The Anti-theatrical Prejudice* (Berkeley, 1981).

8. I have argued something similar with reference to writers of Elizabethan prose fiction in *Elizabethan Fictions: Espionage, Counter-espionage and the Duplicity of Fiction in Early Elizabethan Prose Narratives* (Oxford, 1997), Introduction.

9. See the dialogue between Honest Recreation and Idleness in John Redford, *Wit and Science* (c. 1531–4), in *Tudor Interludes*, ed. Peter Happé

(Harmondsworth, 1972), pp. 195–7; Nicholas Udall, Prologue to *Ralph Roister Doister* (*c.* 1547–8), in *The Dramatic Writings of Nicholas Udall*, ed. John S. Farmer (Guildford, 1966), pp. 3–4; Richard Edwards, Prologue to *Damon and Pythias* (1564), in Ros King, *The Complete Works of Richard Edwards: Politics, Poetry and Performance in Sixteenth-century England* (Manchester, 2001), pp. 110–12; George Gascoigne, Prologues to *The Supposes* (1566), in *A Hundreth Sundrie Flowres*, ed. G.W. Pigman III (Oxford, 2000), p. 7, and *The Glass of Government* (1575), in *The Complete Works of George Gascoigne*, ed. John W. Cunliffe, 2 vols (Cambridge, 1910), vol. 2, p. 6; and George Whetstone, Dedication to *Promos and Cassandra* (1578), in G. Gregory Smith, *Elizabethan Critical Essays*, 2 vols (Oxford and London, 1904), vol. 1, pp. 58–60.

10. See my Introduction, pp. 8–9.

11. An important recent collection of essays on these plays is *Shakespeare's Sweet Thunder: Essays on the Early Comedies*, ed. Michael J. Collins (Newark and London, 1997).

12. Several of these links are detailed in Leah Scragg, *Shakespeare's Mouldy Tales: Recurrent Plot Motifs in Shakespearian Drama* (London and New York, 1992), pp. 126–9.

13. See especially the version of Proteus developed by Spenser in *The Faerie Queene*, Bk. 3, Canto 8. A.C. Hamilton refers to other versions in his note to stanzas 40–41.4. See Edmund Spenser, *The Faerie Queene*, ed. A.C. Hamilton (Harlow, 1977), p. 381.

14. The Duke describes himself as Proteus's friend at 3.2.45, and Proteus accepts the designation – and implicitly makes the Duke his best friend – when he agrees to persuade Silvia to stop loving his former best friend, Valentine.

15. For the relationship between Proteus and Euphues see G.K. Hunter's analysis of Shakespeare's debt to the work of John Lyly, *John Lyly: The Humanist as Courtier* (London, 1962), ch. 6.

16. She does so in conversation with a friend, Lucetta, whose name means something like 'little light' (recalling the name of the 'light' heroine of Lyly's *Euphues*, Lucilla). The name Lucina in *The Comedy of Errors* suggests a similar meaning. On Shakespeare's games with the various meanings of 'light' later in his career see my Chapter 3 and Afterword.

17. See the notes on lines 5 and 7 of the Induction in *The Norton Shakespeare*.

18. On the relationship between these erotic pictures and the play that follows see Jonathan Bate, *Shakespeare and Ovid* (Oxford, 1993), pp. 118–29.

19. For Hippocratic theories of laughter as interpreted by Joubert and Borde, see my 'The Afterlife of Andrew Borde', *Studies in Philology*, vol. 100, no. 4 (Fall 2003), pp. 463–92.

20. For an analysis of this early modern condition, see Douglas Trevor, *The Poetics of Melancholy in Early Modern England* (Cambridge, 2004), ch. 1.

21. For the use of New Comedy in schools see Robert S. Miola, *Shakespeare and Classical Comedy: The Influence of Plautus and Terence* (Oxford, 1994), ch. 1.

22. In this it resembles English 'italianate' prose fiction of the 1570s, such as Lyly's *Euphues*. See my *Elizabethan Fictions: Espionage, Counter-espionage and the Duplicity of Fiction in Early Elizabethan Prose Narratives* (Oxford, 1997), Introduction etc.

23. The text of *The Taming of a Shrew* is printed in an appendix to Barbara Hodgdon's edition, The Arden Shakespeare (London, 2005).

24. For this jest-book tradition and women's place in it, see Pamela Allen Brown, *Better a Shrew than a Sheep: Women, Drama, and the Culture of Jest in Early Modern England* (Ithaca and London, 2003).

25. See Gosson's postscript to *The School of Abuse*, 'To the Gentlewomen Citizens of London': 'The best counsel that I can give you, is to keepe home, and shun all occasion of ill speech . . . And if you perceive your selves in any danger at your owne doores, either allured by curtesie in the day, or assaulted with Musicke in the night; Close up your eyes, stoppe your eares, tye up your tongues . . .'. *Markets of Bawdrie: The Dramatic Criticism of Stephen Gosson*, ed. Arthur F. Kinney (Salzburg, 1974), pp. 115–18. The resemblance to Shylock's instructions to Jessica, *The Merchant of Venice*, 2.5.28–36, is marked.

26. John Fletcher, *The Woman's Prize* (1611), reprinted in *English Renaissance Drama: A Norton Anthology*, ed. David Bevington *et al.* (New York and London, 2002), pp. 1215–94.

27. Thomas Dekker, *The Gull's Horn-book* (1609), *The Non-dramatic Works of Thomas Dekker*, ed. A.B. Grosart, 5 vols (n.p., 1885), vol. 2, p. 247.

28. See the letter of 3 November 1594 from the Lord Mayor of London to Lord Burghley: 'our apprentices and servants ar by this means [i.e. lascivious plays] corrupted and induced . . . to defraud their Maisters, to maintain their vain and prodigall expenses occasioned by such evill and notorious companie . . . to the great hinderance of the trades and traders inhabiting this Citie . . .'. E.K. Chambers, *The Elizabethan Stage*, 4 vols (Oxford, 1923), vol. 4, p. 317.

29. William Harrison, *The Description of England*, ed. Georges Edelen (Washington, D.C. and New York, 1994), p. 379.

30. Harrison, *The Description of England*, pp. 379–80.

31. Harrison, *The Description of England*, p. 389.

32. E.K. Chambers, *The Elizabethan Stage*, vol. 4, p. 322: letter from the Lord Mayor of London to the Privy Council, 28 July 1597.

33. See Miola, *Shakespeare and Classical Comedy*, ch. 2.

34. Sir Philip Sidney, *An Apology for Poetry*, ed. Geoffrey Shepherd, rev. R.W. Maslen (Manchester, 2002), p. 98, lines 4–7.

35. For the additional definition of 'errors' as 'mistakes of identity' see Miola, *Shakespeare and Classical Comedy*, p. 19.

36. 'We have it termed a "tragical comedy"'; Edwards, *Works*, ed. King, p. 112, line 38 (and see note).

37. Time in *The Comedy of Errors* is brilliantly discussed by Kiernan Ryan in *Shakespeare*, 3rd edn (Basingstoke and New York, 2002), pp. 122–33.

38. See the Prologue to Gascoigne's comedy *The Supposes*: 'understand, this our Suppose is nothing else but a mystaking or imagination of one thing for an other'; Gascoigne, *A Hundreth Sundrie Flowres*, ed. Pigman, p. 7.

39. Such as Charles Whitworth in his edition of *The Comedy of Errors* (Oxford, 2002), and the editors of the Oxford Shakespeare. See the note on this line in *The Norton Shakespeare*.

40. Greene's so-called Cony-catching Pamphlets include *A Notable Discovery of Cozenage* (1591), *The Second Part of Cony-catching* (1591), *The Third and Last Part of Cony-catching* (1592) and *A Disputation between a He Cony-catcher and a She Cony-catcher* (1592).

41. In Greene's *The Defence of Cony-catching* (1592), R.G. – that is, Greene himself – is 'a conny-catcher in his kinde, though not at cards'; *Life and Works of Robert Greene*, ed. A.B. Grosart, 15 vols (London and Aylesbury, 1881–3), vol. 11, p. 47. Later he is accused of having cheated two companies of players by selling the same play to both (pp. 75–6). See Derek Alwes, *Sons and Authors in Elizabethan England* (Newark, 2004), ch. 6.

42. John Milton, *Complete Shorter Poems*, ed. John Carey, 2nd edn (London and New York, 1997), p. 137 line 13.

43. See Thomas Wilson, *The Art of Rhetoric*, ed. Thomas J. Derrick (New York and London, 1982), p. 282: 'some had as leve lose their life, as not bestowe their conceived jest, and oftentimes thei have, as thei desire'.

44. Ephesians 5.22–4: 'Wives, submit yourselves unto your own husbands, as unto the Lord. For the husband is the head of the wife, even as Christ is the head of the church: and he is the saviour of the body. Therefore, as the church is subject unto Christ, so let the wives be to their own husbands in every thing.'

45. See previous note.

46. Harrison, *Description of England*, p. 381.

47. Harrison, *Description of England*, p. 382.

2: COMIC CONVERSATION AND ROUGH JUSTICE

1. Patricia Parker discusses puns in *The Comedy of Errors* in *Shakespeare from the Margins: Language, Culture, Context* (Chicago and London, 1996), ch. 2.

2. Thomas Elyot, *The Book Named the Governor*, ed. S.E. Lehmberg, Everyman's Library (London and New York, 1962), p. 170. For 'simplicity' see my *Elizabethan Fictions: Espionage, Counter-espionage and the Duplicity of Fiction in Early Elizabethan Prose Narratives* (Oxford, 1997), ch. 1.

3. *King Richard III*, 1.1.36–61 and 147–8.

4. George Puttenham, *The Art of English Poesy* (London, 1589), p. 128.

5. Puttenham, *Art of English Poesy*, p. 128.

6. Puttenhem, *Art of English Poesy*, p. 129.

7. Puttenham, *Art of English Poesy*, p. 129.

8. Puttenham, *Art of English Poesy*, p. 129.

9. Puttenham, *The Art of English Poesy*, Bk. 3, chs 23 and 24, pp. 218–49.

10. For an account of situations in which early modern women are represented as judges see Pamela Allen Brown, *Better a Shrew than a Sheep: Women, Drama, and the Culture of Jest in Early Modern England* (Ithaca and London, 2003), ch. 5.

11. See Keir Elam, *Shakespeare's Universe of Discourse: Language-games in the Comedies* (Cambridge, 1984).

12. The earliest example of the phrase 'Twelve good men and true' for a jury given in *OED* is from 1634, though it may well be older. See J.S. Cockburn and Thomas A. Green (eds.), *Twelve Good Men and True: the Criminal Trial Jury in England, 1200–1800* (Princeton, 1988), chs 5 and 6.

13. Ben Jonson, *Three Comedies*, ed. Michael Jamieson (Harmondsworth, 1966), p. 45.

14. For an account of Renaissance understandings of the term 'conversation', see Jenny Richards, *Rhetoric and Courtliness in Early Modern Literature* (Cambridge, 2003), esp. introduction and ch. 1.

15. For its verbal inventiveness see Elam, *Shakespeare's Universe of Discourse*, and William C. Carroll, *The Great Feast of Languages in 'Love's Labour's Lost'* (Princeton, 1976).

16. See Jeff Shulman, 'At the Crossroads of Myth: The Hermeneutics of Hercules from Ovid to Shakespeare', *English Literary History* 50 (1983), pp. 83–105. For Hercules in *Love's Labour's Lost*, see H.R. Woudhuysen's edition, The Arden Shakespeare (Walton-on Thames, 1998), p. 5.

17. Abraham Fraunce, *The Third Part of the Countess of Pembroke's Ivychurch, entitled Amyntas' Dale* (London, 1592), fol. 46v.

18. 'Hercules, painted with his great beard and furious countenance, in woman's attire … breedeth both delight and laughter. For the representing of so strange a power in love procureth delight: and the scornfulness of the action stirreth laughter.' Sir Philip Sidney, *An Apology for Poetry*, ed. Geoffrey Shepherd, rev. R.W. Maslen (Manchester, 2002), p. 112, lines 36–40. For early modern representations of Hercules as a figure of fun see Edgar Wind, 'Hercules and Orpheus: Two Mock-heroic Designs by Dürer', *Journal of the*

Warburg and Courtauld Institutes, vol. 2, no. 3 (January 1939), pp. 206–18.

19. Fraunce, *The Third Part of the Countess of Pembroke's Ivychurch*, fol. 47r.

20. Fraunce, *The Third Part of the Countess of Pembroke's Ivychurch*, fol. 47r.

21. These men – now sometimes known as the University Wits – sometimes expressed contempt for playwrights like Shakespeare who did not have the benefit of a university education. Thomas Nashe, for instance, in his preface to Robert Greene's romance *Menaphon* (1589), refers disparagingly to the ignorant playwrights who 'having no more learning in their skull, than will serve to take up a commoditie; nor Arte in their braine, than was nourished in a serving mans idlenesse, will take upon them to be the ironicall censors of all, when God and Poetrie doth know, they are the simplest of all'. *Life and Works of Robert Greene*, ed. A.B. Grosart, 15 vols (London and Aylesbury, 1881–3), vol. 6, p. 10.

22. The tragedies included Euripides, *The Madness of Hercules*, Sophocles, *Trachiniae*, and Seneca, *Hercules Furens* and *Hercules Oetaeus*.

23. Mercury declares *Amphitruo* to be a tragicomedy in the prologue: 'I shall mix things up: let it be tragicomedy'. Plautus, *Works*, trans. Paul Nixon, Loeb Classical Library, 5 vols (London and New York, 1928), vol. 1, pp. 10–11.

24. See *The Heroical Epistles of the Learned Poet Publius Ovidius Naso*, trans. George Turberville (London, 1569), epistle 9, 'Deianeira to Hercules', fols. 11v–59r.

25. The whole scene in which the king's oathbreaking is revealed is filled with references to treason: e.g. 4.3.172 ('Are we betrayed thus to thy over-view?'); 4.3.173 ('Not you to me, but I betrayed by you'); 4.3.176 ('I am betrayed by keeping company / With men like you'); 4.3.187 ('Some certain treason. What makes treason here?'); 4.3.189 ('The treason and you go in peace away together'); 4.3.191 ('Our person misdoubts it; 'twas treason, he said'); 4.3.209 ('Walk aside the true folk and let the traitors stay').

26. For the association between *Love's Labour's Lost* and Navarre, see Hugh M. Richmond, 'Shakespeare's Navarre', *Huntington Library Quarterly*, 43 (1978–9), pp. 193–216; and *Love's Labour's Lost*, ed. Woudhuysen, pp. 67–70.

27. For the play's date see *Love's Labour's Lost*, ed. Woudhuysen, Introduction.

28. In his treatise on the rich rhetorical style, *De Copia* (1512–34), Erasmus distinguishes *verbum* and *res* ('expression' and 'subject matter') as follows: 'Richness of expression involves synonyms, heterosis or enallage, metaphor, variation in word form, equivalence, and other similar methods of diversifying diction. Richness of subject-matter involves the assembling, explaining, and amplifying of arguments by the use of examples, comparisons, similarities, dissimilarities, opposites, and other like procedures.' *Collected Works of Erasmus: Literary and Educational Writings 2, De Copia / De Ratione Studii*, ed. Craig R. Thompson (Toronto, Buffalo, London, 1978), p. 301.

29. See Jenny Richards, *Rhetoric and Courtliness in Early Modern Literature*, Introduction and ch. 1.

30. *The Civil Conversation of M. Stephen Guazzo*, trans. George Pettie and Bartholomew Young (London, 1581 and 1586), ed. Sir Edward Sullivan, 2 vols (London and New York, 1925).

31. Thomas Wilson, *The Art of Rhetoric* (1560), ed. Thomas J. Derrick (New York and London, 1982), p. 278, line 25.

32. See François Laroque, 'Popular Festivity', in *The Cambridge Companion to Shakespearean Comedy*, ed. Alexander Leggatt (Cambidge 2002), pp. 64–78.

33. Hercules' difficult birth is described in Ovid, *Metamorphoses*, trans. Mary M. Innes (Harmondsworth, 1955), Bk. 9, pp. 210–11.

34. Sir Philip Sidney, *An Apology for Poetry*, p. 112 line 17–p. 113 line 17.

35. See Edward Berry, 'Laughing at "Others"', *The Cambridge Companion to Shakespearean Comedy*, ed. Alexander Leggatt (Cambridge, 2002), pp. 123–38.

36. For Christian attitudes to Jews in Elizabethan culture see James S. Shapiro, *Shakespeare and the Jews* (New York, 1996).

37. The comic aspects of Christianity were explored by Desiderius Erasmus in *The Praise of Folly* (1514), where Christ's sacrifice is represented as a supreme act of folly (whose kinship with laughter is stressed throughout the treatise): 'God hath disposed to save the worlde by foolishnesse'; 'To Folie onely is gevin perdone and forgeveness of trespasses'; 'I saie in my conceite, that Christian Religion seemeth to have a certaine sybship with simplicitee, and devoute foolishnesse, in nothing agreyng with worldly wysedome'. *The Praise of Folly*, trans. Thomas Chaloner (1549), ed. Clarence H. Miller, Early English Text Society (London, New York, Toronto, 1965), p. 120, lines 8–11; p. 117, lines 4–6; and p. 119, lines 9–10.

38. See Chapter 1 above, note 25, on the resemblance between this speech and Stephen Gosson's injunction to the women of London to stay away from theatres and other forms of revelry.

39. For a similar view of Portia, see Coppelia Kahn, 'The Cuckoo's Note: Male Friendship and Cuckoldry in *The Merchant of Venice*', *Shakespeare's Comedies*, ed. Gary Waller (London and New York, 1991), pp. 128–37.

40. The term 'complexion' is used in the sense 'temperament' by Rosalind in *As You Like It* (3.2.191, and see 3.2.178 note in *The Norton Shakespeare*). For an important recent account of race in Shakespeare's time, see Mary Floyd-Wilson, *English Ethnicity and Race in Early Modern Drama* (Cambridge, 2003), especially Part 1. See also Kim F. Hall, *Things of Darkness: Economies of Race and Gender in Early Modern England* (Ithaca and New York, 1995).

41. Ecclesiastes 3.1: 'To every thing there is a season, and a time to every purpose under the heaven.'

42. *Markets of Bawdrie: The Dramatic Criticism of Stephen Gosson*, ed. Arthur F. Kinney (Salzburg, 1974), p. 85.

43. On Shakespeare's tendency to disrupt the comic closure of a 'happy ending' in marriage, see Lisa Hopkins, *The Shakespearean Marriage: Merry Wives and Heavy Husbands* (Basingstoke and London, 1998), ch. 1. On miscegenation in *The Merchant of Venice* see Kim F. Hall, 'Guess Who's Coming to Dinner? Colonization and Miscegenation in *The Merchant of Venice*', *Renaissance Drama*, new series, vol. 23: *Renaissance Drama in an Age of Colonization*, ed. Mary Beth Rose (Evanston, 1992), pp. 87–111.

3: LIGHTNESS, LOVE AND DEATH

1. On the concept of lightness see Italo Calvino, *Six Memos for the Next Millennium* (London, 1996), Memo 1. Ronald Knowles discusses laughter in *Romeo and Juliet* in 'Carnival and Death in *Romeo and Juliet*', *Shakespeare and Carnival: After Bakhtin*, ed. Ronald Knowles, Early Modern Literature in History (Basingstoke and New York, 1998), pp. 36–60. For a rich selection of texts associated with the play see *Romeo and Juliet: Texts and Contexts*, ed. Dympna Callaghan (Boston and New York, 2003). On love, sex and laughter in Shakespeare see Alexander Leggatt, *Shakespeare's Comedy of Love* (London, 1974) and Mary Beth Rose, *The Expense of Spirit: Love and Sexuality in English Renaissance Drama* (Ithaca and London, 1988).

2. The story was available to Shakespeare in two English versions: Arthur Brooke's poem *The Tragical History of Romeus and Juliet* (1562) and William Painter's prose translation of the story by Matteo Bandello, 'The Goodly History of … Romeo and Julietta', from his story collection *The Palace of Pleasure* (1566–7). The former is reprinted in *Narrative and Dramatic Sources of Shakespeare*, ed. Geoffrey Bullough, 8 vols (London and New York, 1957–75), vol. 1, pp. 284–63; the latter in *Elizabethan Love Stories*, ed. T.J.B. Spencer (Harmondsworth, 1968), pp. 51–95.

3. For the competition between violent masculinity and heterosexual desire see Coppelia Kahn, *Man's Estate: Masculinity and Shakespeare* (Berkeley, 1981), pp. 82–103.

4. William Harrison, *The Description of England*, ed. Georges Edelen (Washington, DC and New York, 1994), pp. 237–8.

5. The death of William Bradley at the hands of Thomas Watson is described by Charles Nicholl in *The Reckoning: The Murder of Christopher Marlowe* (London and Basingstoke, 1993), pp. 178–9. Marlowe's death is, of course, the topic of the whole book.

6. See Anne Barton, *Ben Jonson: Dramatist* (Cambridge, 1984), p. 2. For Jonson's claim about the length of his opponent's sword see his *Conversations with William Drummond of Hawthornden*, in *The Complete Poems*, ed. George Parfitt (Harmondsworth, 1988), p. 467, lines 241–5).

7. In *The School of Abuse* Gosson attacks the abuse of fencing together with the abuse of logic: 'the skil of logicians, is exercysed in caveling, the cunning of Fencers applied to quarrelling: they, thinke themselves no Schollers, if they bee not able to finde out a knotte in every rushe; these, no men, if for stirring of a strawe they proove not their valure uppon some bodyes fleshe'. *Markets of Bawdrie: The Dramatic Criticism of Stephen Gosson*, ed. Arthur F. Kinney (Salzburg, 1974), p. 103.

8. For an account of the culture of the sword in early modern England see Charles Edelman, *Brawl Ridiculous: Swordfighting in Shakespeare's Plays* (New York, 1992).

9. William Painter, *The Palace of Pleasure*, ed. Joseph Jacobs, 3 vols (London, 1890), vol. 2, p. 154.

10. *Narrative and Dramatic Sources of Shakespeare*, ed. Bullough, vol. 1, pp. 284–5.

11. Theseus' violent past figures largely in Louis Adrian Montrose's influential essay '"Shaping Fantasies": Figurations of Gender and Power in Elizabethan Culture', *Representing the Renaissance*, ed. Stephen Greenblatt (Berkeley, Los Angeles, London, 1988), pp. 31–64.

12. Helen was carried off by Theseus as a child, and rescued by her twin brothers Castor and Pollux. See Paul Harvey, *The Oxford Companion to Classical Literature* (Oxford and New York, 1937, reprinted 1984), under Dioscuri (i.e. Castor and Pollux), Helen and Theseus.

13. The myth of Endymion was recast as a comedy by John Lyly (*Endymion*, *c*. 1587, reprinted in *Complete Works of John Lyly*, ed. R.W. Bond, 3 vols (Oxford, 1902), vol. 3, pp. 5–80), and as a poem by Michael Drayton (*Endymion and Phoebe*, 1593). For classical versions of the myth see *Complete Works of John Lyly*, ed. Bond, vol. 3, p. 9.

14. See Thomas Vicary, *The Anatomy of the Body of a Man* (1577), ed. F.J. Furnivall and Percy Furnivall, Early English Text Society (London, 1888), p. 33, lines 20–31: 'Also the brayne hath this propertie, that it moveth and followeth the moving of the Moone: for in the waxing of the Moone, the Brayne followeth upwardes: and in the wane of the Moone, the brayne discendeth downwardes, and vanisheth in substaunce of vertue: for then the Brayne shrinketh togeather in it selfe, and is not fully obedient to the Spirit of feeling. And this is proved in menne that be lunatike or madde, and also in men that be epulentike, or having the falling sicknesse, that be most greeved in the beginning of the newe Moone, and in the latter quarter of the Moone.'

15. For Shakespeare's diminution of the fairies see K.M. Briggs, *The Anatomy of Puck: An Examination of Fairy Belief among Shakespeare's Contemporaries and Successors* (London, 1959), pp. 45–6.

16. Gosson's essay is *An Apology of the School of Abuse*, appended to his prose fiction *The Ephemerides of Phialo* (1579) and reprinted in *Markets of Bawdrie*,

ed. Kinney, pp. 121–35. For the attack on poets in Plato's *Republic* see Sir Philip Sidney, *An Apology for Poetry*, ed. Geoffrey Shepherd, rev. R.W. Maslen (Manchester, 2002), p. 107, lines 8–30, and note to lines 8–11.

17. For a reappraisal of the craftsmen's place in the comedy see Annabel Patterson, 'Bottom's Up: Festive Theory', *Shakespeare and the Popular Voice* (Oxford, 1989), ch. 3.

18. This puts him in the position of the 'mock king', a figure familiar to Shakespeare's audience from seasonal festivities, especially at Christmas. See Sandra Billington, *Mock Kings in Medieval Society and Renaissance Drama* (Oxford, 1991).

19. See Robert Greene, *Francesco's Fortunes: or, The Second Part of Greene's Never too Late* (1590), in *Life and Works of Robert Greene*, ed. A.B. Grosart, 15 vols (London and Aylesbury, 1881–83), vol. 8, pp. 129–33. At one point Greene has Cicero attack the comic actor Roscius as follows: 'Why Roscius, art thou proud with Esops Crow, being pranct with the glorie of others feathers? Of thy selfe thou canst say nothing, and if the Cobler hath taught thee to say *Ave Cesar*, disdain not thy tutor, because thou pratest in a King's chamber: what sentence thou utterest on the stage, flowes from the censure of our wittes . . . I graunt your action, though it be a kind of mechanical labour; yet wel done tis worthie of praise: but you worthlesse, if for so small a toy you waxe proud.'

20. *Robin Goodfellow, his Mad Pranks and Merry Jests* (London, 1639).

21. See for example the prologue to *Campaspe*, which describes the play as 'the daunsing of *Agrippa* his shadowes, who in the moment they were seene, were of any shape one woulde conceive'; and the prologue to *The Woman in the Moon*, which describes the play itself as 'the shadow of our Authors dreame'. In the prologue to *Sapho and Phao*, incidentally, the play's royal auditor Elizabeth I is invited to 'imagine your self to be in a deepe dreame', while the epilogue compares the play to the 'daunce of a Farie in a circle'. See *The Complete Works of John Lyly*, ed. R.W. Bond, 3 vols (Oxford, 1902), vol. 2, pp. 316, 372 and 416, and vol. 3, p. 241. For further examples of 'shadows' meaning 'actors', see *OED* 6b.

22. For this setting see my '*Venus and Adonis* and the Death of Orpheus', *The Glasgow Review*, Issue 1 (1993), pp. 67–78.

23. For the play's tragicomic status see Karen Newman, *Shakespeare's Rhetoric of Comic Character: Dramatic Convention in Classical and Renaissance Comedy* (New York and London, 1985), ch. 8.

24. For the multiple meanings of 'nothing' see William Shakespeare, *Much Ado about Nothing*, ed. A.P. Humphreys, The Arden Shakespeare (London and New York, 1981), pp. 4–5.

25. For this meaning of 'nothing' see William Shakespeare, *The Sonnets*, ed. Katherine Duncan-Jones, The Arden Shakespeare (London, 2001), sonnet

12, line 13 note and sonnet 20, line 12 note. See also *Hamlet*, ed. Harold Jenkins, The Arden Shakespeare (London and New York, 1982), 3.2.119 note.

26. See Christopher Marlowe, *The Poems*, ed. Millar MacLure, The Revels Plays (Manchester, 1968), p. xxv. Musaeus' poem was translated by George Chapman in 1616 as *The Divine Poem of Musaeus First of All Books*. Chapman ended his continuation of *Hero and Leander* with the couplet: 'And this true honour from their love-deaths sprung, / They were the first that ever poet sung'. Marlowe, *Poems*, p. 103.

27. For the place of clothes in early modern culture see Ann Rosalind Jones and Peter Stallybrass, *Renaissance Habits: Clothing and the Materials of Memory* (Cambridge, 2000).

28. Compare Hieronimo's famous revenge speech in Thomas Kyd, *The Spanish Tragedy*, ed. J.R. Mulryne, New Mermaids (London and New York, 1985), 3.13.1–44. *Much Ado* seems to be haunted by the ghost of Kyd's play; from the easy dismissal of soldiers killed in battle (*ST* 1.2.108, and see Mulryne's note) to the eavesdropping on Horatio and Bell-Imperia in a garden (2.2); from a line quoted by Don Pedro (*ST* 2.1.3, and see Mulryne's note) to the intervention of an efficient Watch to arrest a villain's henchman (3.3.34ff.).

29. Kyd, *The Spanish Tragedy*, 3.13.162.

30. Anne Barton discusses these additions in *Ben Jonson: Dramatist*, pp. 13–28. Mulryne prints them at the end of his edition of *The Spanish Tragedy*, p. 125ff.

31. Sicily itself was associated with tyranny on account of its ancient ruler Dionysius of Syracuse, who presides over Richard Edwards's *Damon and Pythias* (1566). Kyd's *The Spanish Tragedy* (*c.* 1589) sealed Spain's reputation for tyranny, along with John Lyly's play *Midas* (1589), a satire at the expense of Philip II of Spain.

32. *The Spanish Tragedy*, 4.1.155–61.

33. 'Die: to achieve a sexual orgasm', Eric Partridge, *Shakespeare's Bawdy: A Literary and Psychological Essay and a Comprehensive Glossary* (London, 1955), p. 101.

4: THE PLURAL BODIES OF SHAKESPEARE'S BOYS

1. On cross-dressing, gender and sexuality on the Elizabethan stage, see Laura Levine, *Men in Women's Clothing: Anti-theatricality, 1579–1642* (Cambridge and New York, 1994); Catherine Belsey, 'Disrupting Sexual Difference: Meaning and Gender in the Comedies', *Alternative Shakespeares*, ed. John

Drakakis (London, 1985), pp. 166–90; Barbara Hodgdon, 'Sexual Disguise and the Theatre of Gender', *The Cambridge Companion to Shakespearean Comedy*, ed. Alexander Leggatt (Cambridge, 2002), pp. 179–97; Carol Thomas Neely, 'Lovesickness, Gender, and Subjectivity: *Twelfth Night* and *As You Like It*', *A Feminist Companion to Shakespeare*, ed. Dympna Callaghan (Oxford, 2000), pp. 276–98; and Stephen Orgel, 'Nobody's Perfect: or Why did the English Stage Take Boys for Women?', *South Atlantic Quarterly* 88 (1989), pp. 7–29.

2. On the homoerotic context of the Elizabethan stage see Valerie Traub, *Desire and Anxiety: Circulations of Sexuality in Shakespearean Drama* (London, 1992), pp. 117–44, where she specifically discusses *As You Like It* and *Twelfth Night*. The story of Ganymede's abduction by Jupiter is told in Ovid, *Metamorphoses*, trans. Mary M. Innes (Harmondsworth, 1955), p. 229. The wittiest Elizabethan representation of Ganymede is Marlowe's in *Dido Queen of Carthage*, 1.1; see Simon Shepherd, *Marlowe and the Politics of Elizabethan Theatre* (Hemel Hempstead, 1986), pp. 178–207, and Jonathan Goldberg, *Sodometries: Renaissance Texts, Modern Sexualities* (Stanford, 1992), pp. 125–43.

3. The name of the forest should clearly be pronounced 'Arden' throughout – for which reason I think it a mistake that the editors of the Oxford and Norton Shakespeares spell it 'Ardenne'. For a fine account of Arden as a topographical space see Alison Thorne, *Vision and Rhetoric in Shakespeare: Looking through Language* (Basingstoke and London, 2000), ch. 1.

4. For the egalitarian connotations of Adam and Eve see Andrew McRae, *God Speed the Plough: The Representation of Rural England, 1500–1660* (Cambridge, 1996), p. 112ff.

5. On Elizabethan satire, see Alvin Kernan, *The Cankered Muse: Satire of the English Renaissance* (New Haven, 1959); John Peter, *Complaint and Satire in Early English Literature* (Oxford, 1956); and Raman Selden, *English Verse Satire 1590–1765* (London, 1978).

6. See Richard A. McCabe, 'Elizabethan Satire and the Bishops' Ban of 1599', *Yearbook of English Studies*, 11 (1981), pp. 188–93, and Cliff Forshaw, '"Cease Cease to bawle, thou wasp-stung Satyrist": Writers, Printers and the Bishops' Ban of 1599', *EnterText*, vol. 3, no. 1 (Spring 2003), *Renaissance Renegotiations*, ed. William Leahy and Nina Taunton, pp. 101–31. Forshaw also discusses the censorship of *The Isle of Dogs*. For the censorship of erotic texts see Lynda Boose, 'The 1599 Bishops' Ban, Elizabethan Pornography and the Sexualization of the English Stage', *Enclosure Acts: Sexuality, Property and Culture in Early Modern England* (Ithaca, 1994), pp. 185–200.

7. George Puttenham describes the pastoral tradition as follows: 'the Poets devised the Eglogue ... not of purpose to counterfait or represent the rusticall manner of loves and communication; but under the vaile of homely

persons, and in rude speeches to insinuate and glaunce at greater matters, and such as perchance had not ben safe to have beene disclosed in any other sort'. *The Art of English Poesy* (1589), pp. 30–1. For an overview of the genre see Helen Cooper, *Pastoral: Medieval into Renaissance* (Ipswich, 1977).

8. The classic account of Shakespeare's use of metaphors of the theatre is that of Anne Righter (Anne Barton) in *Shakespeare and the Idea of the Play* (Harmondsworth, 1967).

9. For the cyclical view of history see George Boas, 'Cycles', in *The Dictionary of the History of Ideas: Studies of Selected Pivotal Ideas*, ed. Philip P. Wiener, 5 vols (New York, 1973–4), vol. 1, pp. 621–7. For the cyclical nature of human life see Bruce R. Smith, *Shakespeare and Masculinity*, Oxford Shakespeare Topics (Oxford and New York, 2000), ch. 3.

10. See Anne Button's entry on Jaques in *The Oxford Companion to Shakespeare*, ed. Michael Dobson and Stanley Wells (Oxford, 2001), p. 223.

11. The term 'foolosopher' comes from Thomas Chaloner's translation of Erasmus's *The Praise of Folly*, ed. Clarence H. Miller (London, New York, Toronto, 1965), p. 10, line 32 (and see note).

12. For the ages of a man's life in early modern England, see Smith, *Shakespeare and Masculinity*, ch. 3.

13. Christopher Marlowe, *Complete Plays and Poems*, ed. E.D. Pendry and J.C. Maxwell, Everyman's Library (London, 1976), p. 405, line 176.

14. For Malvolio's place in the context of Elizabethan servants and service, see Mark Thornton Burnett, *Masters and Servants in English Renaissance Drama and Culture: Authority and Obedience* (Basingstoke and London, 1997), ch. 5.

15. See also 1.5.246–7, where Viola tells Olivia: 'O, such love / Could be but recompens'd, though you were crown'd / The nonpareil of beauty!'

16. It should be mentioned, though, that the theatre-haters were not by any means all of them Puritans. See Arthur F. Kinney, *Markets of Bawdrie: The Dramatic Criticism of Stephen Gosson* (Salzburg, 1974), Introduction.

17. As it does in the plays of John Webster. Both *The White Devil* and *The Duchess of Malfi* can be read in terms of Lodovico's lines in the former: 'Courtly reward, / And punishment! Fortune's a right whore' (1.1.3–4), John Webster, *Three Plays*, ed. David C. Gunby (Harmondsworth, 1972).

18. The story of Apolonius and Silla, from Barnaby Rich's *Rich his Farewell to Military Profession* (1581), is reprinted in *Elizabethan Love Stories*, ed. T.J.B. Spencer (Harmondsworth, 1968), pp. 97–117. See p. 115.

19. This is Ulysses flattering the women of Troy in *Euphues his Censure to Philautus* (1587), *The Life and Complete Works of Robert Greene*, ed. A.B. Grosart, 15 vols (London and Aylesbury, 1881–3), vol. 6, p. 165. In this romance the Trojan women are very far from silent.

20. See Cicero, *De amicitia*, 20–22. For the centrality of *De amicitia* to Renaissance humanist culture see Laurens J. Mills, *One Soul in Bodies Twain:*

Friendship in Tudor Literature and Stuart Drama (Bloomington, 1937); Bruce R. Smith, 'Homosexuality and the Signs of Male Friendship in Elizabethan England', *Queering the Renaissance*, ed. Jonathan Goldberg (Durham and London, 1994), pp. 40–61; and Alan Stewart, *Close Readers: Humanism and Sodomy in Early Modern England* (Princeton, 1997), ch. 4.

21. On sodomy, see Smith, *Shakespeare and Masculinity*, pp. 122–6, and Mario DiGangi, *The Homoerotics of Early Modern Drama* (Cambridge, 1997), introduction.

22. See my Chapter 3, note 33.

23. See Oscar Wilde, 'The Portrait of Mr. W.H.', *The Works of Oscar Wilde*, ed. G.F. Maire (London and Glasgow, 1948), pp. 1089–1112. On the centrality of Shakespeare to Wilde's self-fashioning see Kate Chedgzoy, *Shakespeare's Queer Children: Sexual Politics and Contemporary Culture* (Manchester and New York, 1995), ch. 5.

AFTERWORD: COMEDY FOR A NEW REIGN

1. For an account of *Measure for Measure* in relation to the Shakespearean comic ending see Janet Adelman, 'Bed Tricks: On Marriage as the End of Comedy in *All's Well that Ends Well* and *Measure for Measure*', *Shakespeare's Personality*, ed. Norman N. Holland, Sidney Homan and Bernard J. Paris (Berkeley, Los Angeles and London, 1989), pp. 151–74.

2. For Shakespeare's concern with the union of the kingdoms see *Shakespeare and Scotland*, ed. Willy Maley and Andrew Murphy (Manchester and New York, 2004).

3. Jonathan Goldberg discusses the relationship between Duke Vincentio and James I in *James I and the Politics of Literature: Jonson, Shakespeare, Donne and their Contemporaries* (Baltimore and London, 1983), pp. 230–9. See also *Measure for Measure*, ed. J.W. Lever, The Arden Shakespeare (London and Cambridge, Mass., 1965), pp. xlviii–li.

4. For Stephen Gosson's influential account of the relationship between theatres and brothels see *Markets of Bawdrie: The Dramatic Criticism of Stephen Gosson*, ed. Arthur F. Kinney (Salzburg, 1974), pp. 91–4.

5. James would not have been much shocked by Shakespeare's preoccupation with pimping. The one surviving instance of court comedy from James's reign, the anonymous *Philotus* (after 1584), involves both a talkative procuress ('The Macrell') and a boy disguised as a girl who procures a whore for his/her elderly husband. *Philotus* is reprinted in *The Mercat Anthology of Early Scottish Literature 1375–1707*, ed. R.D.S. Jack and P.A.T. Rozendaal (Edinburgh, 1997), pp. 390–432.

6. For family relations in *Measure for Measure* see Marc Shell, *The End of Kinship:*

Measure for Measure, Incest, and the Ideal of Universal Siblinghood (Stanford, 1988).

7. For 'conversation' in Shakespeare's earlier comedies, see my Chapter 2 above.

8. The story of Philomela is told in Ovid, *Metamorphoses*, Book 6; see Mary M. Innes's translation, Penguin Classics (Harmondsworth, 1955), pp. 146–53.

9. See, for instance, the imprisoned Marina's hope that Governor Lysimachus will behave 'graciously' towards her in a brothel (*Pericles*, 4.6.57); Belarius's assertion that 'grace' manifests itself in a child against all odds (*Cymbeline*, 4.2.24–8); and Hermione's frequent use of the term in adversity, e.g. 'this action I now go on / Is for my better grace' (*The Winter's Tale*, 2.1.121–2).

10. This is presumably the not-so-complimentary implication of Escalus's assessment of the Duke's character: 'Rather rejoicing to see another merry, than merry at anything which professed to make him rejoice' (3.2.229–31). The good magistrate Escalus, by contrast, has a good sense of humour, as he shows in his lenient treatment of Pompey in Act 3, scene 2.

11. Hecuba took revenge on her son's killer by gouging out his eyes with her nails: see Ovid, *Metamorphoses*, trans. Innes, p. 300. Sidney discusses the means of turning this story into a tragedy – as Euripides did – in *An Apology for Poetry*, ed. Geoffrey Shepherd, revised R.W. Maslen (Manchester, 2002), p. 111/31–44.

12. Marc Shell plays on the relationship between the name 'Lucio' and the Latin for light ('lux') in *The End of Kinship*, p. 152ff. For some other Shakespearean names associated with 'light', see my Chapter 1, note 16.

13. The friar-duke acknowledges as much when he tells Lucio, who has just accused him of slandering Vincentio, 'You must, sir, change persons with me, ere you make that my report. You indeed spoke so of him, and much more, much worse' (5.1.333–5).

14. In fact the phrase comes from the New Testament: 'Judge not, that ye be not judged. For with what judgement ye judge, ye shall be judged: and with what measure ye mete, it shall be measured to you again' (Matthew 7:1–3).

15. It is worth noting that the word 'bum' for arse is of much older origin than the word 'bottom', which began to be used in this sense in the eighteenth century (see under both words in the *OED*). Thus Bottom is *A Midsummer Night's Dream* is not named after the arse or ass, despite looking like one.

16. I should add a note of caution. As much as any of Shakespeare's plays, *Measure for Measure* refuses to endorse any single reading, and mine is offered as only one among many. Harriet Hawkins discusses many readings of the play in *Measure for Measure*, Twayne's New Critical Introductions to Shakespeare (Boston, 1987).

BIBLIOGRAPHY

Adams, Joseph Quincy (ed.), *Chief Pre-Shakespearean Dramas* (London, Calcutta and Sydney, n.d.)

Adelman, Janet, 'Bed Tricks: On Marriage as the End of Comedy in *All's Well that Ends Well* and *Measure for Measure*', *Shakespeare's Personality*, ed. Norman N. Holland, Sidney Homan and Bernard J. Paris (Berkeley, Los Angeles and London, 1989), pp. 151–74

Alwes, Derek, *Sons and Authors in Elizabethan England* (Newark, 2004)

Andrews, Richard, 'Shakespeare and Italian Comedy', *Shakespeare and Renaissance Europe*, ed. Andrew Hadfield and Paul Hammond, Arden Critical Companions (London, 2004), pp. 123–49

Axton, Marie (ed.), *Three Tudor Interludes* (Cambridge, 1982)

Bakhtin, Mikhail, *Rabelais and his World*, trans. H. Islowsky (Bloomington, 1984)

Baldwin, T.W., *William Shakspere's Small Latine and Less Greeke*, 2 vols (Urbana, 1944–50)

——, *Shakspere's Five-act Structure* (Urbana, 1947)

Barber, C.L., *Shakespeare's Festive Comedy: A Study of Dramatic Form and its Relation to Social Custom* (Princeton, NJ, 1959)

Barish, Jonas, *The Anti-theatrical Prejudice* (Berkeley, 1981)

Barkan, Leonard, *Nature's Work of Art: The Human Body as Image of the World* (New Haven, 1975)

Barton, Anne, as Anne Righter, *Shakespeare and the Idea of the Play* (Harmondsworth, 1967)

——, *Ben Jonson: Dramatist* (Cambridge, 1984)

Baskervill, Charles Read, *The Elizabethan Jig and Related Song Drama* (Chicago, 1929)

Bate, Jonathan, *Shakespeare and Ovid* (Oxford, 1993)

——, *The Genius of Shakespeare* (London, Basingstoke and Oxford 1998)

Belsey, Catherine, 'Disrupting Sexual Difference: Meaning and Gender in the Comedies', *Alternative Shakespeares*, ed. John Drakakis (London, 1985), pp. 166–90

Berry, Edward, *Shakespeare's Comic Rites* (Cambridge, 1984)

Bevington, David, *et al.* (eds), *English Renaissance Drama: A Norton Anthology* (New York and London, 2002)

Billington, Sandra, *A Social History of the Fool* (Brighton, 1984)

——, *Mock Kings in Medieval Society and Renaissance Drama* (Oxford, 1991)

Boas, George, 'Cycles', *The Dictionary of the History of Ideas: Studies of Selected Pivotal Ideas*, ed. Philip P. Wiener, 5 vols (New York, 1973–4), vol. 1, pp. 621–7

Boose, Lynda E., 'Scolding Brides and Bridling Scolds: Taming the Woman's Unruly Member', *Shakespeare Quarterly* 42 (1991), pp. 179–213

——, 'The 1599 Bishops' Ban, Elizabethan Pornography and the Sexualization of the English Stage', *Enclosure Acts: Sexuality, Property and Culture in Early Modern England*, ed. Richard Burt and John Michael Archer (Ithaca, 1994), pp. 185–200

Borde or Boorde, Andrew, *Andrew Boorde's Introduction and Dyetary*, ed. F.J. Furnivall, Early English Text Society (London, 1870)

Bradbrook, M.C., *The Growth and Structure of Elizabethan Comedy* (Cambridge, 1979)

Briggs, K.M., *The Anatomy of Puck: An Examination of Fairy Belief among Shakespeare's Contemporaries and Successors* (London, 1959)

Bristol, Michael D., *Carnival and Theater: Plebeian Culture and the Structure of Authority in Renaissance England* (New York and London, 1985)

Brown, Pamela Allan, *Better a Shrew than a Sheep: Women, Drama, and the Culture of Jest in Early Modern England* (Ithaca and London, 2003)

Bullough, Geoffrey, *Narrative and Dramatic Sources of Shakespeare*, 8 vols (London and New York, 1957–75)

Callaghan, Dympna (ed.), *A Feminist Companion to Shakespeare* (Oxford, 2000)

Calvino, Italo, *Six Memos for the Next Millenium* (London, 1996)

Campbell, Lily B. (ed.), *The Mirror for Magistrates* (New York, 1960)

Carroll, William C., *The Great Feast of Languages in 'Love's Labour's Lost'* (Princeton, 1976)

——, *The Metamorphoses of Shakespearean Comedy* (Princeton, 1985)

Castiglione, Baldassare, *The Book of the Courtier*, trans. Thomas Hoby, Everyman's Library (London, 1974)

Chambers, E.K., *The Elizabethan Stage*, 4 vols (Oxford, 1923)

Chedgzoy, Kate, *Shakespeare's Queer Children: Sexual Politics and Contemporary Culture* (Manchester and New York, 1995)

Chettle, Henry, *Kind-Heart's Dream* (London, 1592)

Cicero, *De oratore*, trans. E.W. Sutton and H. Rackham, Loeb Classical Library, 2 vols (London and Cambridge, Mass., 1942)

Clare, Janet, *Art Made Tongue-tied by Authority: Elizabethan and Jacobean Dramatic Censorship*, 2nd edn (Manchester, 1999)

Cockburn, J.S., and Thomas A. Green (eds), *Twelve Good Men and True: The Criminal Trial Jury in England, 1200–1800* (Princeton, 1988)

Colie, Rosalie, *The Resources of Kind: Genre Theory in the Renaissance*, ed. Barbara K. Lewalski (Berkeley, 1973)

Collins, Michael J. (ed.), *Shakespeare's Sweet Thunder: Essays on the Early Comedies* (Newark and London, 1997)

Conrad, Peter, *The Everyman History of English Literature* (London and Melbourne, 1985)

Cooper, Helen, *Pastoral: Medieval into Renaissance* (Ipswich, 1977)

Danson, Lawrence, *Shakespeare's Dramatic Genres*, Oxford Shakespeare Topics (Oxford, 2000)

Dekker, Thomas, *The Non-dramatic Works of Thomas Dekker*, ed. A.B. Grosart, 5 vols (n.p., 1885)

DiGangi, Mario, *The Homoerotics of Early Modern Drama* (Cambridge, 1997)

Dillon, Janette, 'Shakespeare and the Traditions of English Stage Comedy', *A Companion to Shakespeare's Works, Volume 3: The Comedies*, ed. Richard Dutton and Jean E. Howard (Oxford, 2003), pp. 1–22

Donaldson, Ian, 'Clockwork Comedy: Time and *The Alchemist*', *Glasgow Review*, Issue One (Spring 1993), pp. 23–38

Donawerth, Jane, *Shakespeare and the Sixteenth-century Study of Language* (Urbana, 1984)

Donne, John, *Selected Prose*, ed. Neil Rhodes (Harmondsworth, 1987)

Doran, Madeline, *Endeavors of Art: A Study of Form in Elizabethan Drama* (Madison, 1954)

Dutton, Richard, *Mastering the Revels: The Regulation and Censorship of English Renaissance Drama* (Basingstoke, 1991)

——, *Licensing, Censorship and Authorship in Early Modern England: Buggeswords* (Basingstoke, 2000)

Edelman, Charles, *Brawl Ridiculous: Swordfighting in Shakespeare's Plays* (New York, 1992)

Edwards, Richard, *The Complete Works of Richard Edwards: Politics, Poetry and Performance in Sixteenth-century England*, ed. Ros King (Manchester, 2001)

Elam, Keir, *Shakespeare's Universe of Discourse: Language-games in the Comedies* (Cambridge, 1984)

Elyot, Sir Thomas, *The Book Named the Governor*, ed. S.E. Lehmberg, Everyman's Library (London and New York, 1962)

Erasmus, Desiderius, *Collected Works of Erasmus: Literary and Educational Writings: 2, De Copia / De Ratione Studii*, ed. Craig R. Thompson (Toronto, Buffalo, London, 1978)

——, *The Praise of Folly*, trans. Thomas Chaloner (1549), ed. Clarence H. Miller, Early English Text Society (London, New York, Toronto, 1965)

Floyd-Wilson, Mary, *English Ethnicity and Race in Early Modern Drama* (Cambridge, 2003)

Forshaw, Cliff, '"Cease Cease to bawle, thou wasp-stung Satyrist": Writers, Printers and the Bishops' Ban of 1599', *EnterText*, vol. 3, no. 1 (Spring

2003), *Renaissance Renegotiations*, ed. William Leahy and Nina Taunton, pp. 101–31

Fraunce, Abraham, *The Third Part of the Countess of Pembroke's Ivychurch, entitled Amyntas' Dale* (London, 1592)

Gascoigne, George, *The Complete Works of George Gascoigne*, ed. John W. Cunliffe, 2 vols. (Cambridge, 1910)

——, *A Hundreth Sundrie Flowres*, ed. G.W. Pigman III (Oxford, 2000)

Gillespie, Stuart, *Shakespeare's Books: A Dictionary of Shakespeare's Sources* (London and New Brunswick, 2001)

Goldberg, Jonathan, *James I and the Politics of Literature: Jonson, Shakespeare, Donne and their Contemporaries* (Baltimore and London, 1983)

——, *Sodometries: Renaissance Texts, Modern Sexualities* (Stanford, 1992)

Gosson, Stephen, *Markets of Bawdrie: The Dramatic Criticism of Stephen Gosson*, ed. Arthur F. Kinney (Salzburg, 1974)

Greenblatt, Stephen, *Renaissance Self-fashioning: From More to Shakespeare* (Chicago and London, 1980)

Greene, Robert, *Life and Works of Robert Greene*, ed. A.B. Grosart, 15 vols (London and Aylesbury, 1881–3)

Guazzo, Stephano, *The Civil Conversation of M. Stephen Guazzo*, trans. George Pettie and Bartholomew Young, ed. Sir Edward Sullivan, 2 vols (London and New York, 1925)

Hadfield, Andrew, *Literature, Politics and National Identity: Reformation to Renaissance* (Cambridge, 1994)

——, *Shakespeare and Renaissance Politics*, Arden Critical Companions (London, 2004)

Hall, Kim F., 'Guess Who's Coming to Dinner? Colonization and Miscegenation in *The Merchant of Venice*', *Renaissance Drama*, new series, vol. 23: *Renaissance Drama in an Age of Colonization*, ed. Mary Beth Rose (Evanston, 1992), pp. 87–111

——, *Things of Darkness: Economies of Race and Gender in Early Modern England* (Ithaca and New York, 1995)

Halliwell, James Orchard (ed.), *Tarlton's Jests, and News out of Purgatory* (London, 1844)

Happé, Peter (ed.), *Tudor Interludes* (Harmondsworth, 1972)

Hardison, O.B., Jr., *et al.* (eds), *Medieval Literary Criticism: Translations and Interpretations* (New York, 1974)

Harrison, William, *The Description of England*, ed. Georges Edelen (Washington, DC and New York, 1994)

Harvey, Paul, *The Oxford Companion to Classical Literature* (Oxford and New York, 1984)

Hawkins, Harriet, *Measure for Measure*, Twayne's New Critical Introductions to Shakespeare (Boston, 1987)

Hazlitt, W. Carew (ed.), *Shakespeare Jest-Books*, 3 vols (London, 1864)

Helgerson, Richard, *The Elizabethan Prodigals* (Berkeley and London, 1976)

Hoeniger, F. David, *Medicine and Shakespeare in the English Renaissance* (Newark, London and Toronto, 1992)

Holderness, Graham, *Shakespeare Recycled: The Making of Historical Drama* (New York, 1992)

Hopkins, Lisa, *The Shakespearean Marriage: Merry Wives and Heavy Husbands* (Basingstoke and London, 1998)

Horace, *Satires, Epistles and Ars Poetica*, trans. H. Rushton Fairclough, Loeb Classical Library (London and Cambridge, Mass., 1966)

Howard, Jean E., *The Stage and Social Struggle in Early Modern England* (London and New York, 1994)

Hunter, G.K., *John Lyly: The Humanist as Courtier* (London, 1962)

Jack, R.D.S., and P.A.T. Rozendaal (eds), *The Mercat Anthology of Early Scottish Literature 1375–1707* (Edinburgh, 1997)

Johnson, Samuel, *Samuel Johnson on Shakespeare*, ed. H.R. Woudhuysen (Harmondsworth, 1989)

Jones, Anne, and Peter Stallybrass, *Renaissance Habits: Clothing and the Materials of Memory* (Cambridge, 2000)

Jonson, Ben, *Three Comedies*, ed. Michael Jamieson (Harmondsworth, 1966)
——, *The Complete Poems*, ed. George Parfitt (Harmondsworth, 1988)

Joubert, Laurent, *Treatise on Laughter* (*Traité du ris*, 1560), trans. Gregory David de Rocher (Alabama, 1980)

Kahn, Coppelia, *Man's Estate: Masculinity and Shakespeare* (Berkeley, 1981)
——, 'The Cuckoo's Note: Male Friendship and Cuckoldry in *The Merchant of Venice*', *Shakespeare's Comedies*, ed. Gary Waller (London and New York, 1991), pp. 128–37

Kastan, David Scott (ed.), *A Companion to Shakespeare* (Oxford, 1989)

Kernan, Alvin, *The Cankered Muse: Satire of the English Renaissance* (New Haven, 1959)

Knowles, Ronald (ed.), *Shakespeare and Carnival: After Bakhtin*, Early Modern Literature in History (Basingstoke and New York, 1998)

Krieger, Elliott, *A Marxist Study of Shakespeare's Plays* (London and Basingstoke, 1979)

Kyd, Thomas, *The Spanish Tragedy*, ed. J.R. Mulryne, New Mermaids (London and New York, 1985)

Lanham, Richard A., *Motives of Eloquence: Literary Rhetoric in the Renaissance* (New Haven and London, 1976)

Laroque, François, *Shakespeare's Festive World: Elizabethan Seasonal Entertainment and the Professional Stage* (Cambridge, 1991)

Leggatt, Alexander, *Shakespeare's Comedy of Love* (London, 1974)
——, (ed.), *The Cambridge Companion to Shakespearean Comedy* (Cambridge, 2002)

Levine, Laura, *Men in Women's Clothing: Anti-theatricality, 1579–1642* (Cambridge and New York, 1994)

Lyly, John, *Complete Works of John Lyly*, ed. R.W. Bond, 3 vols (Oxford, 1902)

——, *Campaspe and Sapho and Phao*, ed. G.K. Hunter and David Bevington (Manchester and New York, 1991)

McCabe, Richard A., 'Elizabethan Satire and the Bishops' Ban of 1599', *Yearbook of English Studies*, 11 (1981), pp. 188–93

McDonald, Russ, *Shakespeare and the Arts of Language* (Oxford, 2001)

McRae, Andrew, *God Speed the Plough: The Representation of Rural England, 1500–1660* (Cambridge, 1996)

Maley, Willy, and Andrew Murphy (eds), *Shakespeare and Scotland* (Manchester and New York, 2004)

Marcus, Leah S., 'Levelling Shakespeare: Local Customs and Local Texts', *Shakespeare Quarterly* 42 (1991), pp. 168–78

Mares, F.H., 'The Origin of the Figure called the Vice', *Huntington Library Quarterly*, vol. 22, no. 1 (1958), pp. 11–29

Marlowe, Christopher, *The Poems*, ed. Millar MacLure, The Revels Plays (Manchester, 1968)

——, *Complete Plays and Poems*, ed. E.D. Pendry and J.C. Maxwell, Everyman's Library (London and Melbourne, 1976)

——, *Complete Plays*, ed. Mark Thornton Burnett, The Everyman Library (London, 1999)

Maslen, R.W., '*Venus and Adonis* and the Death of Orpheus', *The Glasgow Review*, Issue 1 (1993), pp. 67–78

——, *Elizabethan Fictions: Espionage, Counter-espionage and the Duplicity of Fiction in Early Elizabethan Prose Narratives* (Oxford, 1997)

——, 'Myths Exploited: The Metamorphoses of Ovid in Early Elizabethan England', *Shakespeare's Ovid*, ed. A.B. Taylor (Cambridge, 2000), pp. 15–30

——, 'William Baldwin and the Politics of Pseudo-Philosophy in Tudor Prose Fiction', *Studies in Philology*, vol. 97, no. 1 (Winter 2000), pp. 29–60

——, 'The Afterlife of Andrew Borde', *Studies in Philology*, vol. 100, no. 4 (Fall 2003), pp. 463–92

——, 'Lodge's *Glaucus and Scilla* and the Conditions of Catholic Authorship in Elizabethan England', *EnterText*, vol. 3, no. 1 (Spring 2003), *Renaissance Renegotiations*, ed. William Leahy and Nina Taunton, pp. 59–100

A Merry Knack to Know a Knave, ed. G.R. Proudfoot, Malone Society Reprints (Oxford, 1963)

Mills, Laurens J., *One Soul in Bodies Twain: Friendship in Tudor Literature and Stuart Drama* (Bloomington, 1937).

Milton, John, *Complete Shorter Poems*, ed. John Carey, 2nd edn (London and New York, 1997)

Miola, Robert S., *Shakespeare and Classical Comedy: The Influence of Plautus and Terence* (Oxford, 1994)

Montrose, Louis Adrian, '"Shaping Fantasies": Figurations of Gender and Power in Elizabethan Culture', *Representing the Renaissance*, ed. Stephen Greenblatt (Berkeley, Los Angeles, London, 1988)

Munday, Anthony, *et al.*, *Sir Thomas More*, ed. Vittorio Gabrieli and Giorgio Melchiori (Manchester and New York, 1990)

Munro, Ian, 'Shakespeare's Jestbook: Wit, Print, Performance', *English Literary History*, vol. 71, no. 1 (Spring 2004), pp. 89–113

Nashe, Thomas, *The Unfortunate Traveller and Other Works*, ed. J.B. Steane (Harmondsworth, 1985)

Neely, Carol Thomas, 'Lovesickness, Gender, and Subjectivity: *Twelfth Night* and *As You Like It*', *A Feminist Companion to Shakespeare*, ed. Dympna Callaghan (Oxford, 2000), pp. 276–98

Nevo, Ruth, *Comic Transformations in Shakespeare* (London, 1980)

Newcomb, Lori Humphrey, *Reading Popular Romance in Early Modern England* (New York, 2002)

Newman, Karen, *Shakespeare's Rhetoric of Comic Character: Dramatic Convention in Classical and Renaissance Comedy* (New York and London, 1985)

Nicholl, Charles, *The Reckoning: The Murder of Christopher Marlowe* (London and Basingstoke, 1993)

O'Connell, Michael, *The Idolatrous Eye: Iconoclasm and Theater in Early-Modern England* (New York and Oxford, 2000)

Orgel, Stephen, *The Illusion of Power: Political Theater in the Renaissance* (Berkeley and London, 1975)

——, 'Nobody's Perfect: or Why did the English Stage Take Boys for Women?', *South Atlantic Quarterly* 88 (1989), pp. 7–29

Ovid, *The Heroical Epistles of the Learned Poet Publius Ovidius Naso*, trans. George Turberville (London, 1569)

——, *Metamorphoses*, trans. Mary M. Innes (Harmondsworth, 1955)

Painter, William, *The Palace of Pleasure*, ed. Joseph Jacobs, 3 vols (London, 1890)

Parker, Patricia, *Shakespeare from the Margins: Language, Culture, Context* (Chicago and London, 1996)

Partridge, Eric, *Shakespeare's Bawdy: A Literary and Psychological Essay and a Comprehensive Glossary* (London, 1955)

Patterson, Annabel. *Shakespeare and the Popular Voice* (Oxford, 1989)

Peter, John, *Complaint and Satire in Early English Literature* (Oxford, 1956)

Pincombe, Mike, *The Plays of John Lyly: Eros and Eliza* (Manchester, 1996)

Plautus, *Works*, trans. Paul Nixon, Loeb Classical Library, 5 vols. (London and New York, 1928)

Prothero, G.W., *Selected Statutes and Other Constitutional Documents Illustrative of the Reigns of Elizabeth and James I*, 4th edn (Oxford, 1913)

Puttenham, George, *The Art of English Poesy* (1589)

Robin Goodfellow, his Mad Pranks and Merry Jests (London, 1639)

Quintilian, *Institutio oratoria*, trans. H.E. Butler, Loeb Classical Library, 4 vols (London and New York, 1921)

Rhodes, Neil, *Elizabethan Grotesque* (London, Boston and Henley, 1980)

——, *The Power of Eloquence and English Renaissance Literature* (Hemel Hempstead, 1992)

——, *Shakespeare and the Origins of English* (Oxford, 2004)

Richards, Jenny, *Rhetoric and Courtliness in Early Modern Literature* (Cambridge, 2003)

Richmond, Hugh M., 'Shakespeare's Navarre', *Huntington Library Quarterly*, 43 (1978–9), pp. 193–216

Rose, Mary Beth, *The Expense of Spirit: Love and Sexuality in English Renaissance Drama* (Ithaca and London, 1988)

Ryan, Kiernan, *Shakespeare*, 3rd edn (Basingstoke and New York, 2002)

Salingar, Leo, *Shakespeare and the Traditions of Comedy* (Cambridge, 1974)

Salzman, Paul (ed.), *An Anthology of Elizabethan Prose Fiction*, The World's Classics (Oxford, 1987)

Schlauch, Margaret, *Antecedents of the English Novel 1400–1600* (Warsaw and London, 1963)

Scragg, Leah, *The Metamorphosis of Gallathea: A Study in Creative Adaptation* (Washington, DC, 1982)

——, *Shakespeare's Mouldy Tales: Recurrent Plot Motifs in Shakespearian Drama* (London and New York, 1992)

Selden, Raman, *English Verse Satire 1590–1765* (London, 1978)

Shakespeare, William, *The Arden Shakespeare Complete Works*, ed. Richard Proudfoot, Ann Thompson and David Scott Kastan (London, 2001)

——, *The Comedy of Errors*, ed. Charles Whitworth (Oxford, 2002)

——, *Hamlet*, ed. Harold Jenkins, The Arden Shakespeare (London and New York, 1982)

——, *King Henry VI Part 2*, ed. Ronald Knowles, The Arden Shakespeare (Walton-on-Thames, 1999)

——, *Love's Labour's Lost*, ed. H.R. Woudhuysen, The Arden Shakespeare (Walton-on-Thames, 1998)

——, *Measure for Measure*, ed. J.W. Lever, The Arden Shakespeare (London and Cambridge, Mass., 1965)

——, *Much Ado about Nothing*, ed. A.P. Humphreys, The Arden Shakespeare (London and New York, 1981)

——, *The Norton Shakespeare*, ed. Stephen Greenblatt *et al.* (New York and London, 1997)

——, *Romeo and Juliet: Texts and Contexts*, ed. Dympna Callaghan (Boston and New York, 2003)

——, *The Sonnets*, ed. Katherine Duncan-Jones, The Arden Shakespeare (London, 2001)

——, *The Taming of the Shrew*, ed. Barbara Hodgdon, The Arden Shakespeare (London, 2005)

——, *Troilus and Cressida*, ed. Kenneth Palmer, The Arden Shakespeare (London and New York, 1982)

Shapiro, James S., *Shakespeare and the Jews* (New York, 1996)

Shapiro, Michael, *Children of the Revels: The Boy Companies of Shakespeare's Time and their Plays* (New York, 1977)

Shell, Marc, *The End of Kinship: Measure for Measure, Incest, and the Ideal of Universal Siblinghood* (Stanford, 1988)

Shepherd, Simon, *Marlowe and the Politics of Elizabethan Theatre* (Hemel Hempstead, 1986)

Shulman, Jeff, 'At the Crossroads of Myth: The Hermeneutics of Hercules from Ovid to Shakespeare', *English Literary History*, 50 (1983), pp. 83–105

Sidney, Sir Philip, *An Apology for Poetry*, ed. Geoffrey Shepherd, rev. R.W. Maslen (Manchester and New York, 2002)

Slights, Camille Wells, *Shakespeare's Comic Commonwealths* (Toronto, Buffalo and London, 1993)

Smith, Bruce R., *Homosexual Desire in Shakespeare's England* (Chicago, 1991)

——, 'Homosexuality and the Signs of Male Friendship in Elizabethan England', *Queering the Renaissance*, ed. Jonathan Goldberg (Durham and London, 1994), pp. 40–61

——, *Shakespeare and Masculinity*, Oxford Shakespeare Topics (Oxford and New York, 2000)

Smith, Emma (ed.), *Shakespeare's Comedies* (Oxford, 2004)

Smith, G. Gregory (ed.), *Elizabethan Critical Essays*, 2 vols (London, 1904)

Snyder, Susan, *The Comic Matrix of Shakespeare's Tragedies* (Princeton, 1979)

Spencer, T.J.B. (ed.), *Elizabethan Love Stories* (Harmondsworth, 1968)

Stern, Virginia, *Gabriel Harvey: His Life, Marginalia and Library* (Oxford, 1979)

Stewart, Alan, *Close Readers: Humanism and Sodomy in Early Modern England* (Princeton, 1997)

Tennenhouse, Leonard, 'Strategies of State and Political Plays: *A Midsummer Night's Dream, Henry IV, Henry V, Henry VIII*', *Political Shakespeare: Essays in Cultural Materialism*, ed. Jonathan Dollimore and Alan Sinfield, 2nd edn (Manchester, 1994), pp. 109–28

Thorne, Alison, *Vision and Rhetoric in Shakespeare: Looking through Language* (Basingstoke and London, 2000)

Thornton Burnett, Mark, *Masters and Servants in English Renaissance Drama and Culture: Authority and Obedience* (Basingstoke and London, 1997)

Traub, Valerie, *Desire and Anxiety: Circulations of Sexuality in Shakespearean Drama* (London, 1992)

Trevor, Douglas, *The Poetics of Melancholy in Early Modern England* (Cambridge, 2004)

Trousdale, Marion, *Shakespeare and the Rhetoricians* (London, 1982)

Udall, Nicholas, *The Dramatic Writings of Nicholas Udall*, ed. John S. Farmer (Guildford, 1966)

Verdon, Jean, *Rire au Moyen Âge* (Paris, 2001)

Vicary, Thomas, *The Anatomy of the Body of a Man* (1577), ed. F.J. Furnivall and Percy Furnivall, Early English Text Society (London, 1888)

Webster, John, *Three Plays*, ed. David C. Gunby (Harmondsworth, 1972)

Weimann, Robert, *Shakespeare and the Popular Tradition in the Theater: Studies in the Social Dimension of Dramatic Form and Function*, ed. Robert Schwartz (Baltimore and London, 1978), pp. 185–92

Wells, Stanley, Gary Taylor *et al.*, *William Shakespeare: A Textual Companion* (Oxford, 1987)

Welsford, Enid, *The Fool: His Social and Literary History* (London, 1935)

Wilde, Oscar, 'The Portrait of Mr. W.H.', *The Works of Oscar Wilde*, ed. G.F. Maire (London and Glasgow, 1948), pp. 1089–112

Wiles, David, *Shakespeare's Clown: Actor and Text in the Elizabethan Playhouse* (Cambridge, 1987)

Wilson, Thomas, *The Art of Rhetoric* (1560), ed. Thomas J. Derrick (New York and London, 1982)

Wind, Edgar, 'Hercules and Orpheus: Two Mock-heroic Designs by Dürer', *Journal of the Warburg and Courtauld Institutes*, vol. 2, no. 3 (January 1939), pp. 206–18

INDEX